AF304745

THE MEANING
OF HISTORY

ALSO BY HENRY A. KISSINGER

*A World Restored: Metternich, Castlereagh and the
Problems of Peace, 1812–22*

Nuclear Weapons and Foreign Policy

The Necessity for Choice: Prospects of American Foreign Policy

The Troubled Partnership: A Reappraisal of the Atlantic Alliance

American Foreign Policy

White House Years

Years of Upheaval

Diplomacy

Years of Renewal

*Does America Need a Foreign Policy?
Toward a Diplomacy for the 21st Century*

*Ending the Vietnam War: A History of America's Involvement
in and Extrication from the Vietnam War*

Crisis: The Anatomy of Two Major Foreign Policy Crises

On China

World Order

Leadership: Six Studies in World Strategy

COURTESY OF HARVARD UNIVERSITY ARCHIVES

Henry A. Kissinger, Class of
1950 Harvard Yearbook

THE MEANING OF HISTORY

Reflections on
Spengler, Toynbee
and Kant

HENRY A. KISSINGER

BOKFÖRLAGET STOLPE

AXEL AND MARGARET AX:SON JOHNSON FOUNDATION FOR PUBLIC BENEFIT

THE MEANING OF HISTORY
Reflections on Spengler, Toynbee and Kant

Published by Bokförlaget Stolpe, Stockholm, Sweden, 2022, with kind permission of the
Johns Hopkins SAIS Henry A. Kissinger Center for Global Affairs in the United States of America.

Copyright © 1950, 2021 by Henry A. Kissinger
All rights reserved

All rights reserved. No part of this publication may be reproduced, distributed, or transmitted
in any form or by any means, including photocopying, recording, or other electronic or
mechanical methods, without the prior written permission of the publisher, except in the case of
brief quotations embodied in critical reviews and certain other noncommercial uses permitted by
copyright law.

© The author and Bokförlaget Stolpe 2022, in association with
Axel and Margaret Ax:son Johnson Foundation for Public Benefit

This book was first printed in 2021 in a limited edition for the Johns Hopkins SAIS
Henry A. Kissinger Center for Global Affairs in the United States of America.

Design: Patric Leo
Pre-press and print coordinator: Italgraf Media AB, Sweden
Print: Printon, Estonia, via Italgraf Media, 2022
Second edition, first printing
ISBN: 978-91-89425-86-6

BOKFÖRLAGET STOLPE

AXEL AND MARGARET AX:SON JOHNSON
FOUNDATION FOR PUBLIC BENEFIT

To William Y. Elliott and Fritz G. A. Kraemer

TABLE OF CONTENTS

FOREWORD

xiii

A senior thesis is often the first opportunity for a talented university undergraduate to pursue serious, independent scholarly work. While sometimes it can lead to an academic publication, it is unusual for it to have much of an afterlife or wider significance beyond the ivory tower.

And yet there are some rare and notable exceptions to this rule. John F. Kennedy's 1940 book *Why England Slept*, a study of the failures of British appeasement towards Nazi Germany, grew out of his final-year dissertation at Harvard and—supported by Joseph P. Kennedy Sr. and his influential network—sold eighty thousand copies within a year of its release.[1] Completed ten years later in the same institution by a contrasting character, *The Meaning of History: Reflections on Spengler, Toynbee, and Kant* was a strikingly different type of work—more cerebral and philosophical and less obviously policy-relevant—but has arguably, through its author, had more influence on twentieth-century international relations than Kennedy's first published work.

The study is intimidatingly long and weighty in its own right; at almost four hundred typed pages, it wrestles with some of the first-order dilemmas of Western political, philosophical, and moral thought. Its scope ranges from the Enlightenment through to the midpoint of the twentieth century—an era scourged by two world wars and the advent of the nuclear age. Equally important, it provides great insight into the conceptual perspective of its author, Henry Kissinger, who was to become the most influential American scholar-statesman of the post-1945 period.

Kissinger's road to Harvard was not typical, either—particularly when compared with the more classic Kennedy experience. He was born in Fürth, Germany, from which his family escaped the terrors of Nazism in 1938, when he was fifteen, settling in New York City. His studies in accounting at the City College of New York were interrupted when he was drafted into

---

1. John F. Kennedy, *Why England Slept* (New York: Wilfred Funk, 1940).

the U.S. Army in 1943. He saw combat in Europe, including during the Battle of the Bulge. Kissinger also became friends with Fritz Kraemer, a German émigré and intellectual, a mentor who encouraged his broadening intellectual interests. Kissinger stayed in Europe after the war, serving in intelligence in occupied Germany, before enrolling at Harvard. He completed the thesis and his degree in 1950, at the age of twenty-seven, under the tutelage of the American historian William Yandell Elliott.

The Meaning of History explores the thought of three distinct but important thinkers in the canon of Western philosophical and historical thought, in a way that also reflected Kissinger's own transition from the Continental world to the Atlantic. Oswald Spengler (1880–1936) was a German historian and philosopher most famous for his two-volume study *The Decline of the West*. The argument for which he was most famous was that cultures, like people, evolved through a sequence of life phases, from birth to decay until final death. Western civilization, he argued against the backdrop of the end of the First World War and the Spanish flu pandemic which followed, was approaching its twilight, to be subsumed by the cultures of the East. Arnold Toynbee (1889–1975) was a British historian and philosopher who was halfway through what would become a twelve-volume series, *A Study of History*, when Kissinger completed his thesis. This monumental work was the study of almost twenty civilizations, charting each one's rise and fall. For Toynbee, whose work was based on his strong Christian faith, the story of a civilization's emergence and success was that of a people's response to various challenges, led and inspired by creative leaders. Immanuel Kant (1724–1804), a Prussian of the European Enlightenment era, was one of the most important moral and political philosophers to emerge from his time, famed for the concepts of transcendental idealism and perpetual peace.

The focus of Kissinger's study was the dialectic between historical determinism and the exercise of free will, a question he explored by assessing how Spengler, Toynbee, and Kant viewed human purpose and agency over time. For Spengler, history was found in cultures and civilizations, whose shape and form unfolded according to laws not unlike those in biology. There was nothing an individual human could do to fundamentally alter or affect this life cycle. Toynbee allowed for civilizations to emerge, change, and remake themselves based on their responses to various challenges. In other words, civilizations for Toynbee—unlike for Spengler—possessed a purpose and could work towards a higher goal. Yet Kissinger critiqued Toynbee's notion of purpose as being both limited by environmental factors and understood as simply fulfilling a theological end, or God's will. Kant did see a place for individual freedom—not in the external, physical world, but through the inward experience of thought and reflection.

For Kissinger, if existence was the reflection either of natural and physical law or of some kind of spiritual mechanism, there was little point to history, since humans would be unable to alter events as they unfolded over time. His thesis rejects this perspective. While meaning or purpose beyond the scientific could not be proven, the very effort to do so highlighted the act of transcending either physical or religious law. Inward reflection did provide the origins for the freedom of the individual, limited though it was, to act in the world. Unlike Kant, however, Kissinger did not believe this freedom went naturally towards peace or universal values, and he was also closer to Toynbee in embracing the differences amongst cultures and civilizations. In other words, though these opportunities were limited, an individual could act—and could thereby shape history. This basic philosophical premise also fed into *A World Restored*, Kissinger's doctoral study of early-nineteenth-century European diplomacy, which became his first published book.[1]

For those seeking to understand the conceptual outlook of America's most consequential twentieth-century statesman, the thesis offers both great insight and great revelation. Several things in particular stand out. Contemporary analysts might be surprised to see political thought and the philosophy of history, and not international relations theory, as the foundation for his thinking. What is more, Kissinger pushed against some of the popular academic trends of his time. He rejected materialistic and systemic approaches to focus on the inward and the individual. Economics was subordinate to politics, a view he has held consistently ever since. Kissinger wrote at a time when American intellectual life was increasingly dominated by scientific or socio-scientific approaches, including pragmatism, behaviorism, game theory, and logical positivism. These methodologies focused on the collective over the individual, discounted moral considerations, and imported tools used to understand the natural and physical

---

1. Henry A. Kissinger, *A World Restored: Metternich, Castlereagh, and the Problems of Peace, 1812–22* (Boston: Houghton Mifflin, 1957).

world and applied them to politics, policy, and society. Kissinger, by contrast, did not see social and political issues as technical problems amenable to prediction or to be solved according to discoverable, universal laws. This put him at odds with some of his future colleagues who developed the foundations of modern international relations theory, such as Kenneth Waltz and Thomas Schelling, and closer to that of the theologian and philosopher Reinhold Niebuhr and Kissinger's future friend Hans Morgenthau. Kissinger largely rejected a scientific-materialist lens as inadequate to understanding the roles of freedom, value, and meaning in history, and also underplaying the power and force of particular civilizations at particular times.

Nor, less surprisingly, did the thesis indulge the frame of international law and legalism pioneered by Quincy Wright and others. Kissinger does not embrace mystical or magical approaches, nor accept a Whig notion of unending, linear progress in human affairs, or any type of cultural exceptionalism. "The generation of Buchenwald and the Siberian labor camps cannot talk with the same optimism as its fathers." Yet the thesis also rejects the historical determinism and even pessimism popular at the time after the Second World War, such as Karl Popper's notion that history is "merely a chronicle of crime and murder," absent meaning. Thus Kissinger rejected the determinism, universalism, and scientism that increasingly shaped midcentury American intellectual life.

Analysts have also misunderstood Kissinger's views on morality and action. He has often been identified as a realist. Yet the so-called fathers of realism, be they Thucydides, Machiavelli, or Hobbes, play virtually no role in his analysis or worldview and are largely absent from the thesis. Kissinger's worldview is not that of *The Melian Dialogue* or the cruel anarchical world of *Leviathan.* The moral political leader is guided by beliefs, though they go beyond simple individual ethics:

> Though the weight of tradition may preclude an immediate
> modification of institutions, the moral law ever guides his
> quest, a beacon to follow, an aim to attain. The political mor-
> alist knows men, but the moral politician understands man,
> in the dignity of whose personality resides the only possibility
> of conceiving a duty, the sole guide to moral action.

The seeds of Kissinger's future statecraft can be found here. Systemic pressures are powerful, but the leader has a moral responsibility to transcend its constraints. Diplomacy cannot be separated from a nation's purpose and view of the world, perspectives that are not universal. Leaders have a moral obligation to seek order, one that promotes balance while recognizing the fundamental legitimacy of the interlocutor (assuming, of course, that vision of legitimacy is returned).

It is puzzling that *The Meaning of History*, a work that Walter Isaacson says "is still described in awed tones,"[1] has not been published until now. Niall Ferguson argues that the thesis should be read as an "authentically idealist tract" that explains much of Kissinger's frame for understanding the world.[2] Peter Dickson wrote a whole book connecting Kissinger's philosophical insights to his later statecraft, based largely on his reading of *The Meaning of History*.[3] The historian Bruce Kuklick has argued that the thesis was Kissinger's "most intellectually creative and sustained piece of work" and "a key exposition of his concerns."[4] It is especially odd considering that Kissinger's ideas and statecraft are undergoing a resurgence of scholarly and intellectual interest. There have been several biographies in the twenty-first century, including two recent works.[5] There have also been a spate of articles calling for a return to Kissingerian thought and practice in foreign policy.[6] If that is to be done, however, it is important to become

---

1. Walter Isaacson, *Kissinger: A Biography* (New York: Simon & Schuster, 1992), p. 64.

2. Niall Ferguson, *Kissinger*, Vol. 1: *1923–1968: The Idealist* (New York: Penguin Press, 2015), p. 242.

3. Peter W. Dickson, *Kissinger and the Meaning of History* (Cambridge: Cambridge University Press, 1978).

4. Bruce Kuklick, *Blind Oracles: Intellectuals and War from Kennan to Kissinger* (Princeton, N.J.: Princeton University Press, 2006), p. 184.

5. See Barry Gewen, *The Inevitability of Tragedy: Henry Kissinger and His World* (New York: W.W. Norton & Company, 2020), and Thomas A. Schwartz, *Henry Kissinger and American Power: A Political Biography* (New York: Hill and Wang, 2020).

6. For a sample, see John A. Farrell, "How Do You Explain Henry Kissinger?" *New York Times*, April 28, 2020, https://www.nytimes.com/2020/04/28/books/review/barry-gewen-inevitability-of-tragedy-henry-kissinger.html; Jacob Heilbrunn, "The Case for Kissinger," *The National Interest*, June 30, 2020, https://nationalinterest.org/feature/case-kissinger-163805; Michael Hirsh, "Welcome Back to Kissinger's World," *Foreign Policy*, June 7, 2020, https://foreignpolicy.com/2020/06/07/kissinger-review-gewen-realism-liberal-internationalism/; Christopher Meyer, "Where Are the Henry Kissingers When We Need Them?" *Spectator*, May 16, 2020, https://www.spectator.co.uk/article/where-are-the-henry-kissingers-when-we-need-them-; David Pryce-Jones, "Henry Kissinger and the Way of the World," *National Review*, June 18, 2020, https://www.nationalreview.com/magazine/2020/07/06/henry-kissinger-and-the-way-of-the-world/; Treston Wheat, "Kissinger Was Right: Statesmanship in the Digital Age," *Global Security Review*, May 5, 2020, https://globalsecurityreview.com/kissinger-was-right-statesmanship-in-the-digital-age/.

familiar with the thesis, which forms the foundation for Kissinger's extraordinarily influential perspective.

We are very proud to be publishing *The Meaning of History: Reflections on Spengler, Toynbee, and Kant.* It is the combined effort of three institutions: the Centre for Grand Strategy at King's College London, the Henry A. Kissinger Center for Global Affairs at the Johns Hopkins University School of Advanced International Studies, and the Axel and Margaret Ax:son Johnson Foundation for Public Benefit, as part of our program of work on the America and the Future of World Order Project. Mattias Hessérus and Kurt Almqvist played a vital role in conceptualizing and driving the project. We are especially grateful to Chris Crosbie, Andrew Ehrhardt, and Lyndsay Howard for pulling together so many different strands of effort, and to Andrew Wylie and Dr. Henry Kissinger for their willingness to publish this important work.

John Bew and Francis J. Gavin
London and Washington, D.C., November 2020

PREFACE

When Dr. John Bew, professor of history and foreign policy at the War Studies Department of King's College London, suggested that my undergraduate thesis, *The Meaning of History: Reflections on Spengler, Toynbee, and Kant*, might be published, I wondered what would be the value of putting in print a text that had been written seventy years before, and that had all the weaknesses of a student still finding his academic orientation and philosophic principles. But, in any case, I am grateful to Professor Bew, to Professor Francis J. Gavin, director of the Henry A. Kissinger Center for Global Affairs at the Johns Hopkins University School of Advanced International Studies, and to President Kurt Almqvist and Director of Civilization Studies Dr. Mattias Hessérus, of the Axel and Margaret Ax:son Johnson Foundation for Public Benefit, who sponsored the project, and to Lyndsay Howard, distinguished scholar at the Kissinger Center, who presided over the preparation of the manuscript from beginning to end.

Dr. Fritz Gustav Anton Kraemer was the greatest single influence on my formative years. We met in 1944 at Camp Claiborne, Louisiana. We were both privates in the 84th Infantry Division and both refugees from Germany, I by necessity, Kraemer by choice. He was thirty-six years of age when I was nineteen, had two Ph.D. degrees, and had already fought the rise of fascism in both Nazi Germany and Italy. When I first saw Kraemer, he was dressed in a German uniform, wore a monocle, and carried a riding crop to deliver a lecture to our regiment on the moral and political stakes of the war with Nazi Germany. Out of this encounter grew a relationship that changed my life. Over the next decades, Kraemer, a senior civilian adviser at the Pentagon to the U.S. Army Chief of Staff and ultimately several secretaries of defense, shaped my thinking, influenced my choice of college, awakened my interest in political philosophy and history, inspired both my undergraduate and graduate theses, and became an integral and indispensable part of my life. Our roads parted when I became a policy-maker. He thought as a prophet, dealing in absolutes. Policymakers must balance the contingent. I delivered a eulogy at his funeral extolling his importance.

Professor William Yandell Elliott, a distinguished historian and poet, was the next huge influence on me, the first person at Harvard who took a systematic interest in my intellectual evolution. In those days, every student had a professorial tutor. I was assigned to Elliott, who was a commanding personality. When I reported to him, he made it clear that his life would not have been unfulfilled were he not to receive another student advisee that year. Perhaps partly to get rid of me for a while, he instructed, "Why don't you write me a paper about the connection between the political philosophy of Kant and some of his other theoretical views?" I wrote Elliott a paper, and when he read it, he allowed that I had some promise and then encouraged me throughout my undergraduate studies.

Early in my senior year, I listened to a lecture about Hegel by the political theorist Professor Carl Friedrich. Until this lecture, I had never considered, or had the confidence, that a senior honors paper could effectively expound a philosophy of history, which seemed to me an exciting combination of policy and philosophy. I decided then to write a thesis on the topic, intending to educate myself. I had read and thought about Spengler before I wrote the thesis, but not Toynbee, whom I picked because at the time he was the most important historian in that field and one of the most globally discussed scholars. I had studied Kant extensively as a result of my encounter with Professor Elliott but had not yet focused on the applications of Kant's essays on the nature of peace.

What compelled me about Kant was the connection he drew between empirical facts and ethical and metaphysical knowledge. This gave me a theoretical framework for my inquiry. Drawing on Kant's thoughts on the primacy of liberty and the idea of the role of freedom in human life, I began to focus on how to rescue a space for freedom and free choice in politics. This quest is present in all my writings to this day, and its application a requirement for statesmen in any era.

Philosophically as well as politically, one cannot separate the roles of idealism and realism. It is essential to understand the world's real challenges, but one cannot master these challenges except in terms of an overriding purpose that is, in essence, philosophical. Pure realists insistent on never-ending stability will stagnate sooner or later, because the essence of historical life is that new problems will present themselves constantly, now perhaps even more than before.

The connection between the philosophical, ethical, and metaphysical underpinnings of the thesis and my later diplomacy has not operated in a straight line, though it has had a deep influence. Intense review, as an undergraduate, of the philosophy of history produced the habitual practice I employed in later years of distilling the basic philosophy of my counterpart in a negotiation and decoding the depths of its historical antecedents.

My hope is that the revival of this work will help fuel the aspirations of current and future generations of young scholars and leaders to acquire a fuller perspective in the study of history and philosophy. These disciplines of knowledge are necessary to illuminating the realities that shape our world and to enhancing human capacity to exercise individual choice and freedom in order to produce peace and prosperity.

Henry A. Kissinger
Kent, Connecticut, November 2020

THE MEANING
OF HISTORY

INTRODUCTORY NOTE

An introduction to an undergraduate honor thesis may seem presumptuous, but I believe that its inordinate length and unorthodox method require an explanation. As a general reason, the length is due to the fact that I did not realize the implications of the subject when I started to work on the thesis. As it grew, I have made several efforts to cut it down, such as omitting the chapters I had written on Hegel and Schweitzer. Since this still did not succeed in reducing this thesis to a more manageable size, I have pointed out, at the end of this introductory note, those portions which I believe to be the nucleus of my analysis and which may be considered my honor thesis.

The methodology results from my dissatisfaction with the critical treatments of Spengler and, to a lesser degree, of Toynbee. I had the impression that merely analytical criticism of Spengler falsifies the real essence of his philosophy. Just as in the case of Nietzsche, part of Spengler's impact resides in the poetic imaginativeness of his descriptions. I have therefore made a conscious effort in my expository passages to capture as much as possible of Spengler's style. This has entailed rather lengthy quotations and, in one or two places, close reliance on the text. To present Spengler's philosophy as fairly as possible, I have kept such clauses as "Spengler argues," "according to Spengler," *et cetera*, to a minimum. The expository passages are to be understood as containing Spengler's arguments. My comments are concentrated in discussions at the end of each section. My basic analysis is to be found in my "Conclusions" on the chapter "History as Intuition."

I have followed essentially the same methodology with Toynbee. Here, too, purely analytical criticism falsifies the stately empirical approach. I have discussed each of Toynbee's main headings at sufficient length to indicate his method, though, except for a very few instances, I have omitted all his illustrations. Again, all my comments are contained in an introductory paragraph and in a concluding section to each heading. Again, my fundamental criticisms are to be found under the title "Conclusions" at the end of the chapter "History as an Empirical Science."

In each case the expository passages are preceded by a discussion of the author's metaphysical assumptions, to explain their structuring effect on the subsequent philosophy.

Since many excellent treatments of Kant's philosophy exist, my discussion of his philosophy is orthodox. My last chapter is intended to explain the general position from which I approached the philosophy of history. Needless to say, this is a still tentative viewpoint.

The Appendix was written after listening to a seminar paper by a logical positivist, in order to clarify my own thought on the meaning of "meaning," and also to indicate what criteria of validity logic offers to philosophy. It is based on a course with Professor Henry Sheffer and also personal consultations. The philosophical interpretation of the logical systems is my own.

Though this analysis was written as a unit, the reader may, if he wishes, consider only the following sections as my honor thesis:

The Argument (Introduction and Summary)

Spengler (History as Intuition)
    Metaphysics
    Politics, Economics, the Machine
    Conclusions

Toynbee
    Metaphysics
    The Nature and Genesis of Civilizations
    Schism in the Soul
    Conclusions

Kant (Entire Chapter)

The Sense of Responsibility

CHAPTER I

THE ARGUMENT:

INTRODUCTION AND SUMMARY

The Problem

In the life of every person there comes a point when he realizes that, out of all the seemingly limitless possibilities of his youth, he has in fact become one actuality. No longer is life a broad plain with forests and mountains beckoning all around, but it becomes apparent that one's journey across the meadows has indeed followed a regular path, that one can no longer go this way or that, but that the direction is set, the limits defined.

Each step, once taken so thoughtlessly, now becomes fraught with tremendous portent, each advance to be made appears unalterable. Looking back across the path, we are struck by the inexorability of the road, how every step both limited and served as a condition for the next, and, viewing the plain, we feel with a certainty approaching knowledge that many roads were possible, that many incidents shaped our wandering, that we are here because it was we who journeyed, and we could be in a different spot had we wished. And we know, further, that whatever road we had chosen, we could not have remained stationary. We were unable to avoid in any manner our being now in fact somewhere and in some position. We have come up against the problem of Necessity and Freedom, of the irrevocability of our actions, of the directedness of our life.

What is the meaning of necessity, and where does it arise? Necessity is an attribute of the past. Events viewed in retrospect appear inevitable, the fact of occurrence testifies to irrevocability. Causality expresses the pattern which the mind imposes on a sequence of events in order to make their appearance comprehensible.[1] It is formulated as a law, which reveals a trend of recurrence and an assertion of comparability. Law ever fights against the unique, against the personal experience, the inward bliss. Necessity recognizes only quantitative differences, and conceives of sur-

---

1. This follows Kant's analysis of the categories. See *post.*

vival as its sole test of historical fitness. Necessity discovers the typical in man, the inexorable in events, the inevitable in existence. Its doctrine is the philosophy of eternal recurrence, of which the Devil tells Ivan Karamazov, "But our present earth may have been repeated a billion times. Why, it's become extinct, been frozen; cracked, broken to bits, disintegrated into its elements, again 'the water above the firmament,' then again a comet, again a sun, again from the sun it becomes earth—and the same sequence may have been repeated endlessly and exactly the same to every detail ..."

Yet every event is not only an effect but also an inward experience. As an effect it is ruled by necessity, as an experience it reveals the unique in the personality. The desire to reconcile an experience of freedom with a determined environment is the lament of poetry and the dilemma of philosophy. Rationalism attempted to solve this problem by considering its purposes as the objective pattern of occurrences and equating Freedom with Necessity. The British skeptics, particularly Hume, submitted these notions to rigorous criticism and denied necessity as well as purposiveness. They argued that perception involves the impact of empirical entities on a wax-like mind, whose sensations of pleasure are largely passive, whose concept of necessity describes a constant conjunction, and to which freedom is meaningless.[1] The limits of thought cannot be established by thought, however. Hume's skepticism caused him to abandon philosophy while still a young man, and Descartes was forced to invoke God as a guarantor of external reality with the aid of the very faculty the accuracy of which he had seriously questioned.[2]

Kant realized that only an inward experience can transcend the inexorability of completed action. He "abolish[ed] knowledge to make room for belief." He affirmed that the reality that is subject to the laws of causality is given by sensuous experience and exhausted in the phenomenal world. But beyond that, man has a transcendental experience of freedom which elevates him above the realm of necessity into a higher world order that conditions all appearances. Freedom is an inward state, an attitude that accompanies all action. This disproves Hume's assertion that nothing can be definitely known, since one can always imagine the opposite of any thought. Our experience of freedom testifies to a fact of existence

---

1. See *post* Ch. "History and Man's Experience of Morality."
2. See *post* for full discussion, Ch. "History and Man's Experience of Morality."

which no thought process can deny and for the demonstration of which Descartes' *cogito ergo sum* was not really necessary.[1] Whatever conception one may form about the inevitability of actions, their accomplishment occurred with an inward conviction of choice. Freedom is the causality that motivates man. "To conceive a man having no freedom is impossible except as a man deprived of life," says Tolstoy.

What is the solution to the paradox of irrevocable action accomplished with the conviction of choice? How can we reconcile the experience of freedom with our knowledge that our intentions so frequently issue forth into totally incommensurate consequences? What is the meaning of a causality that accomplishes itself under the mode of freedom?

The philosophy of history has addressed itself to these problems. It testifies to humanity's yearning to understand the fatedness of life, to a mystic drive for an absolute, to an attempt to give meaning to the basic questions of existence. For this reason the philosophy of history is indissolubly connected with metaphysics;[2] is indeed metaphysics of a very high order. The next section will examine whether history can in fact give an answer to these problems.

Is There a Meaning to History?

History, according to Popper,[3] has no meaning. It is the chronicle of international crime and mass murder and takes no account of the tears and suffering of mankind. It is up to us, however, he states at a later point,[4] to give meaning to history by assisting the open society to triumph in its eternal struggle with the closed society.

Aside from the inner contradiction of this argument—for if history has no meaning, the eternal conflict between freedom and rationality against

---

1. See *post* Ch. "History and Man's Experience of Morality."
2. For this reason I have avoided the usual classification of philosophies of history into cyclical and progress theories. It seems to me that a classification in terms of metaphysical assumptions presents wider possibilities. Moreover, the philosophers discussed do not lend themselves well to such a classification. Toynbee combines the cyclical and the progress concepts. Spengler is a cyclical philosopher in Vico's tradition. Kant has a theory of progress, achieved by conflict, which in its implications is very similar to Toynbee's. (See *post* Ch. "History and Man's Experience of Morality.")
3. Popper, *The Open Society and Its Enemies*, Vol. 2, p. 256.
4. Popper, *op. cit.*, Vol. 2, p. 264.

mysticism, historicism, and tyranny cannot be its motif—the passage illustrates the difficulty, and confusion, inherent in the word *meaning*. It implies:

1. History has no meaning.
2. History has a meaning, but that meaning is unacceptable to Popper.
3. History has no meaning, but if freedom and rationality triumph, it will suddenly acquire content.

These implications contain the dilemma of the problem of the meaning of history. Is history an open book, a set of theorems that contains in itself all the aspirations of mankind, as well as the key to the world's purpose? Or does history reveal a series of meaningless incidents, a challenge for our normative concepts, only through conformity to which it can obtain significance? Is meaning, in short, an attribute of reality or a metaphysical construction attendant on our recognition of significance?[1]

The logical positivists accept the former alternative. Meaning results from verifying statements with empirical facts. The researches of anthropologists have, however, dispelled the hope that the meaning of assertions could be given a firmer basis by making the physical world their criterion. It has been demonstrated that each culture, and to a certain extent each individual, constructs his own image of "reality," and that "facts" are in no manner as absolute and unshakeable as assumed. The history of modern physics, moreover, has been a continuous process of dissolving external reality and laying bare such mysterious and incompatible prime data as energy that works under the aspect of mass, as light that is demonstrably a wave, but equally certainly contains all its physical properties in an elemental particle, the photon.

Moreover, on this theory, as classical logic has well realized, not only all value judgments, but all quality judgments, are meaningless. The difference between affirming an object's worth or its color is a difference in achieving a consensus, but not of empirical verifiability.

Traditional logic, at any rate, was better aware of this problem. In its concepts, each proposition had as its subject ultimate reality.[2] A judgment,

---

1. For full discussion of the concept of "meaning" see *post* Appendix, "The Concepts of Meaning."
2. Joseph, *An Introduction to Logic*, p. 166.

of which the proposition constitutes the expression in words, is the act of distinguishing a particular element, the predicate, in the being of a subject that could not be thought of unless it contained some other than the predicated character. The distinguishing characteristic of a judgment is its truth or falsity. However, and this is the cardinal point, only true judgments matter, for unless a man says what he does not really think, he is affirming the truth of his assertion. All propositions, therefore, besides affirming or denying the predicate of a subject, imply existence. Reality is thus implied by, not requisite for, judgments.

The existential import theory of propositions presented too many difficulties, however. Though logicians could always argue that statements about square circles did not imply existence, since they involved mutually exclusive terms, or contrast logical constructions which only have a mode of being with real existence,[1] the reconciliation of definitional reality and all possible judgments proved impossible.

Sentential logic[2] abandoned the concept of the existential import of propositions. Its logical primitive is a sentence, which exhibits but a grouping together of symbols that in their general characteristics represent but empirical entities. Only by being brought into relation with other physical objects and facts do these sentences acquire meaning. Since a determination of truth and falsity obviously does not precede every statement, sentential logic was forced to invoke another predicate of propositions, truth-weight. This, however, is a purely psychological relation.

But even this theory stumbled on the problem of just what constituted a fact and on the difficulty of reconciling truth-value and weight. Russell, in his later writings, and Professor Sheffer[3] have achieved a formulation which attempts to give the greatest possibility of determining the essence of meaning. Statements become replies to pure hypotheses which, moreover, have to be endorsed by the proper criterion. The statement "Scott is the author of *Waverley*" is the affirmative answer, empirically endorsed, to the questions:

---

1. Russell, *Principles of Mathematics*, p. 449.
2. Based on Reichenbach, *Experience and Prediction.*
3. Professor Sheffer has not published his theory. (See Preface.)

1. Did at least one man write *Waverley?*
2. Did only one man write *Waverley?*
3. Was this man Scott?

The range of meaningful propositions is, however, not exhausted by the empirical realm. Proper criteria can be obtained for value theorems or aesthetic judgments. This theory recognizes the variability of metaphysical assumptions as a condition of meaning. Meaning becomes the function of three factors: the logical, expressed in the most precise formulation of the hypothesis; the psychological, inherent in the act of judging; the philosophical, expressed in the endorsement.[1] Universality depends on the consensus which this ascription of meaning enjoys and not, in the first instance, on its empirical verifiability.

Thus, meaning represents the emanation of a metaphysical context. Just as every man in a certain sense creates his pictures of the world, just as the scientist can find in nature only what he puts in it in the formulation of his hypothesis, just as every question determines at least the range of answers, so history does not exhibit the same portent to everybody but yields only the meanings inherent in the nature of our query. Therefore, too, the philosophy of history is inseparable from metaphysics, and involves a deep awareness of the mysteries and possibilities not only of nature but of human nature. In the reactions of the various thinkers to the problems of human necessity and human freedom, in their capacity to experience depths inaccessible to reason alone, lies the answer to the meaning of history. Therefore, Popper's statement that history presents merely a chronicle of crime and murder, with no awareness of the heartbreak of humanity, reveals his normative concepts but does not represent a necessary attribute of events. That other levels of meaning exist is shown by Dostoevsky and Schweitzer, Homer and Shakespeare, to whom history was a deeply felt experience of transcendental import.[2]

Who is right, then? Is history the self-realization of the spirit of freedom, as Hegel held? Or does it represent the growth and decline of organic cultures, their essence a mystery, their moving force longing, and their mani-

---

1. The endorsement, in turn, is composed of a metaphysical (the criterion) and an epistemological (the assertion, not the judgment of truth and falsity) element. See *post* Appendix, "The Concepts of Meaning."
2. See, on this point, Alfred Weber, *Farewell to European History.*

festation power, as Spengler argued? Is there a deeper purpose in all this emergence and decay of civilizations, a realization of salvation by faith, as Toynbee implies? Does history amount to no more than eternal recurrence, the stage for the man who surpasses himself of Nietzsche, or does it reveal the drama of a divine plan, gradually unfolding and culminating in universal peace, as Kant asserts?[1]

If meaning is the metaphysical context that ascribes significance, does this preclude differentiae by which to judge validity? These criteria exist, but they are not as obvious as the logical positivists assumed.

Though the questions delimit the range of answers, we can require the answers to be relevant to the problem. Though each culture, and perhaps each individual, interprets his data in an intensely personal way, we can insist that the data be adhered to. We can analyze internal consistency.[2] On another level we can judge the adequacy of the thinker's philosophical assumptions by their scope, by their grasp of the totality of life, instead of just its appearances.[3] Newton sitting under the apple tree might have correctly concluded that apples fall when ripe. It is not a question of right or wrong, therefore, but of depth and shallowness. It does not suffice to show logically deduced theorems as an absolute test of validity. There must also exist a relation to the pervasiveness of an inward experience which transcends phenomenal reality. For though man is a thinking being, it does not follow that his being exhausts itself in thinking. The ultimate mysteries of life are perhaps not approachable by dissection, but may require the poet's view who grasps the unity of life, which is greater than any, however painstaking, analysis of its manifestations.

The philosophy of history exhibits, therefore, in its metaphysical assumptions, an attitude towards the basic problems of existence. They reveal whether life is approached with reverence and humility or with the assertive tool of a reason that admits no reality outside itself. The resolution of the dilemma of historical events serving as the condition for a transcendental experience or reality exhausting itself in phenomenal appearances discloses the ethical predispositions of a personality, not a property of historical data.[4]

---

1. Kant did not ascribe the self-realization of peace to a divine plan, but to a natural unfolding. The implication, just as in Spinoza, is, however, of a divine order in the Cosmos.
2. See *post* Appendix, "The Concepts of Meaning."
3. This, however, involves utilization of another set of assumptions. See *post* Appendix, "The Concepts of Meaning."
4. See *post* Ch. "The Sense of Responsibility."

Birth is the beginning of death, life the process of mortality. Everything existing is modified by time; history exhibits the unfolding of growth, fulfillment, and outward decay. Man strives for knowledge and, having attained it, cannot bear it. All of literature contains an expression of this dilemma and of mankind's lament at the shortness of their lot. Hamlet becomes paralyzed by knowledge; Achilles purchases it at the price of his death. Thus is the appearance of life but not necessarily its meaning.

The magic attitude towards life seeks to escape the transitoriness of its existence by conjuring its data. It attempts to find in history the necessary realization of its purposive concepts, to be classified as attributes of events. But purpose represents the emanation of a metaphysical context, not a necessary deduction from phenomena. No ethical value can be ascribed to the mere survival which history exhibits. For this reason the magic attitude develops a philosophy of eternal recurrence, as a condition for its cognition. Death becomes the result of fulfillment, life exhibits merely mortality, history represents a machine continually reproducing new manifestations of power. Values are, at best, a mode of causality. The mystery of life is limited by classifiable data; it exhausts itself in the riddle of the first cause. The fact of occurrence reveals the only criterion of inward fitness.[1]

The prayerful attitude, on the other hand, experiences life as a vision of reconciliation as one views a vast plain from a mountaintop when the haze obscures the countryside and everything merges in a total impression of peace and harmony. The inevitability exhibited by retrospection attains a deeper meaning through a transcendental experience. The recognition of necessity becomes the condition for the attainment of inward liberation. Resignation as to the purposes of the universe serves as the first step towards ethical activity,[2] and the realization ensues that the meaning of history is not confined to its mere manifestations and that no causal analysis can absolve man from giving his own content to his own existence.

The philosophies of Spengler, Toynbee, and Kant contain expressions of these attitudes in the quest for the apprehension of the meaning of history.

Spengler asserted that progress was not a category of meaning for history. Life contains the problem of motion, which results from the irrevoca-

---

1. See discussion of Ch. "Toynbee."
2. See *post* Ch. "The Sense of Responsibility." See also Schweitzer, *The Philosophy of Civilization.*

bility of our actions and prevents us, in the eternal flux of things, to ever observe that which is in the act of observing itself, to ever causally determine the inner connectedness of events. This directedness of life is the source of the dual qualities of world longing and world dread that arise from our consciousness of mortality and our loneliness in a world in which we can never grasp the total inner meaning of others. The riddle of time opens up for man, not to be classified as a category of reason, as Kant attempted. Space is a conception, but time represents a denotation for something inconceivable. It expresses itself in the eternal becoming that is the essence of man and that attains pure being—pure space—only at the moment of his death. Causality applies to the stiff forms of being; Destiny, fate, dominate becoming. Destiny answers the question of when, Causality of how. All of life is permeated by an inner destiny that can never be defined; history discloses a majestic unfolding that one can only intuitively perceive, never causally classify. Existence constitutes a mystic relationship to the extended, especially accessible to the artist and the great statesman, the mystery and the essence of which each culture perceives in a different fashion.

And what does Spengler see with this intuitive vision? "A boundless mass of human Being, flowing in a stream without banks; upstream, a dark past wherein our time-sense loses all powers of definition and restless or uneasy fancy conjures up geological periods to hide away an eternally unsolvable riddle; downstream, a future even so dark and timeless"[1]—such is Spengler's view of human history. Over this surface there suddenly emerge the forms of the great cultures, organic beings with their own inner necessity and their deep logic of becoming. They go through all the stages of organic life, youth, maturity, decline, and old age. Their youth is a period of infinite yearning in which every action is an augury of things to come and in which art, philosophy, and politics unconsciously embody the cosmic best. In the gradual maturity of growth the mystery of life is dissipated, its problems answered, the questions thought through, the great form lost. Irrevocably, over the bodies of a humanity that can no longer but accept, Caesarism approaches, embodying itself in all the traditional trappings of life. Humanity flows into cities and, amidst bread and circuses, amidst a repetition of cataclysmic wars, the civilization petrifies and dies.

---

1. Spengler, *The Decline of the West*, Vol. I, p. 105.

Therewith disappears not only its outward power, but also its inner meaning, of which each culture constructs its own life symbol. Thus the Greek gods died with the classical soul and so the Western world has started on its slow but certain decline.

Spengler grasped the essential mystery of life that Kant found in the experience of freedom. He realized that every event represents not only an effect, but also an inward experience, the key to results incommensurable with our intentions. He affirmed that there are certain ultimate goals, which no hypothesis can prove, and no sophistry ever deny, expressed in such words as *hope, love, beauty, luck,* and *fear.* These are the symbols that are veiled in mystery, and no definition can get in touch with what we feel when we utter these words. He knew that intuitive perception (the German *erfühlen*) contains the key to some mysteries, just as Causality reveals the solution to others.

Yet what does Spengler experience in history? An endless unfolding of a cosmic beat that expresses itself in the sole alternatives of subject and object, a vast succession of catastrophic upheavals of which power is not only the manifestation but the exclusive aim; a stimulus of blood that not only pulses through veins but must be shed and will be shed. He feels, in short, only what history also demonstrates phenomenally: he has not experienced the mysteries and thereby derived a level of transcendence; he has solved them and will see in that solution history's only meaning.[1]

"… Everything is determined," the Devil tells Ivan Karamazov,[2] "and humanity is settled for ever. But as, owing to man's inveterate stupidity, this cannot come about for at least a thousand years, every one who recognizes the truth even now may legitimately order his life as he pleases, on the new principles. In that sense, 'all things are lawful' for him. What's more, even if this period never comes to pass, since there is anyway no God and no immortality, the new man may well become the man-god …"

This discloses the true implications of Spengler's position, the dilemma of which is expressed in this striking phrase: "In the one world, the historical, the Roman caused the Galilean to be crucified—that was his Destiny. In the other world [of Causality and Morality], Rome was cast for perdition

---

1. This analysis holds true only if one interprets Spengler's philosophy as embodying norms of activity. Though this is the usual analysis, it is by no means a necessary one. See *post* Ch. "Spengler," Ch. "The Sense of Responsibility."

2. Dostoevsky, *The Brothers Karamazov*, p. 789.

and the Cross became the pledge of Redemption—that was the 'will of God.'"[1] But the Cross on the hills of Jerusalem has long disappeared, the temple is in ruins, and the Roman legions are not even a memory. Yet on roadsides all over the world, in the souls of whole civilizations, the Cross still stands. Is that all that is implied by Destiny, then, this death and that Cross? Spengler had a vision of the world-as-experience, but his conclusions do not fill its vastness. His poetic imagination became fascinated by the mere analysis of power phenomena. His approach through intuitive perception reveals no more than the empirical analysis of Toynbee.[2] The narrow confinement of meaning to the specific souls of each culture seems arbitrary. There is meaning not only in the aspirations and symbols long dead, but in those that have been continued as the matrix for other civilizations. Though Spengler would reply that no culture ever understands another in just its original connotation, he has failed to do justice to the impact the adoption of any alien form must of necessity exert on its user.[3] The continuity of certain aspects of ethical, aesthetic, and political problemation is as significant as its cyclical fluctuation and should have been especially accessible to a vision of History as Inward Experience. Though Spengler's insights are challenging and his predictions perhaps correct, they do not exhaust the meaning of history.

Toynbee probed for this deeper meaning but looked for empirical verification into history instead of into himself. Accepting almost completely Spengler's methodology of comparing civilizations in their political occurrences, as well as in their aesthetic and theological manifestations, he attempted to solve one problem to which Spengler never addressed himself: What causes the emergence, out of formless humanity, of the genus culture?

Toynbee finds the answer in the doctrine of Challenge-and-Response. Life presents a series of problems, each a challenge to undergo an ordeal. The initial successful reaction constitutes the civilization's birth. Its growth is not determined by an organic necessity but accomplishes itself through the response to successive challenges. Each solution does not lead to an equilibrium but creates an overbalance, which in turn becomes a new challenge. Progress ceases when societies fail to react to new stimuli.

---

1. Spengler, *op. cit.*, Vol. II, p. 116.
2. For interdependence of two philosophers, see *post* Ch. "Toynbee."
3. See *post* Ch. "Spengler."

A civilization grows through the leadership of a creative minority which directs the majority, by mimesis, a social drill, in the absence of direct inspiration. Yet in every civilization, mimesis eventually breaks down and the creative minority becomes a dominant minority, substituting force for charm. The progressive differentiation of a civilization into a dominant minority and an internal proletariat, which is in, but not of, a given society, with creativity and meaning stunted, diverts energies into otherworldly pursuits, culminating in a transcendental knowledge of the unity of mankind through a universal church. By this act of faith the internal proletariat rescues the values of the collapsing society, which it embodies in the new civilization erected by the victorious external proletariat on the ruins of the old. The decay of civilizations has as its outward manifestations a universal state, in which the internal schism occurs, a Period of Contending States, and a final apocalyptic emergence of a higher religion as the embodiment of the meaning of history.

Toynbee's theory of Challenge-and-Response is very similar to Hegel's dialectic. It consequently does not represent a negation of determinism but a description of its operation. The analysis of response almost exclusively in terms of challenges leads to a mere refinement of the environment theory. Since Toynbee attempts to verify theological assumptions by an empirical method, success becomes the only criterion of moral fitness. Survival reveals God's sanction to the elect. History's purpose is identical with man's aspirations.

The unsatisfactoriness of Toynbee's philosophy derives from this method. Though his conclusions give an intimation of transcendental experience,[1] they are not supported by his data. The attempt to find a causal realization of a divine purpose in the manifestations of political power results in such inconsistencies as the assertion that the miracles of Christianity will save the West, despite the collapse of every other civilization, and despite the fact that in Toynbee's scheme universal churches appear as concomitants of disintegration.

An inward experience cannot be proved by empirical data, however. A philosophy of history without a profound metaphysics will forever juxtapose surface data and can never satisfy the totality of man's desire for meaning.

---

1. In the concept of Transfiguration.

Spengler had a vision but did not press its implications. Yet his intuition of History as Inward Experience has pointed the way to the solution of the enigma posed by the experience of freedom and the knowledge of necessity. Kant realized that the phenomenal world is explored in vain for a proof of those ideas, "the possibility of which no human intelligence will ever fathom, but the truth of which no sophistry will ever wrest from the conviction of even the commonest man."[1] An analysis of historical phenomena reveals but the inevitability inherent in completed action. Freedom, on the other hand, testifies to an act of self-transcendence which overcomes the inexorability of events by infusing them with its spirituality. The ultimate meaning of history—as of life—we can find only within ourselves.

What is the content of this transcendental experience? This is not easy to express. When Socrates in *The Republic* is asked to explain the "Idea of the Good," he replies that it cannot be defined. Man can attain its vision only by analogy, by studying those objects which contain some portion of the ultimate reality, such as beauty, astronomy, mathematics. Reflection may then lead to a sudden illumination which will reveal the transcendental condition of all knowledge.

Dostoevsky has been called "the great criminal."[2] Yet Dostoevsky's insight into the depths, his very ability to do so without flinching, rested on a saintly recognition of this transcendence, on an apprehension of the unity of mankind, expressed in the concept of love as the mystical bond of the universe.

"If you love everything," says Father Zosima,[3] "you will perceive the divine mystery of things," and "What grows lives and is alive only through the feeling of its contact with other mysterious worlds. If that feeling grows weak or is destroyed in you, the heavenly growth will die away in you."

And *The Idiot* expresses the longing for a final culmination of all destinies: "What does it matter that it is an abnormal intensity, if the result, if the minute of sensation, remembered and analysed afterwards in health, turns out to be the acme of harmony and beauty, and gives a feeling, unknown and undivined till then, of completeness, of proportion, of reconciliation, and of ecstatic devotional merging in the highest synthesis of life?"[4]

---

1. Kant, *Critique of Practical Reason*, in *Kant's Critique of Practical Reason and Other Works*, p. 231.
2. Thomas Mann, Introduction to *Short Novels of Dostoevsky*.
3. Dostoevsky, *The Brothers Karamazov*, p. 383.
4. Dostoevsky, *The Idiot*, p. 214.

There exist two levels of historical analysis, then: the empirical, which classifies historical data by its phenomenal appearance and will perforce discover a cyclical pattern, and the ethical, which views history as a key to action. The doctrine of immanent necessity represents the outsider's view of history, the conception of a person who has not experienced the accomplishment of the event. No representation of inevitability can, however, absolve the individual from giving his own meaning to his own existence. Necessity describes the past, but freedom rules the future. Purposes reveal a task to be achieved, an expression of a soul, not an attribute of historical events. The ethical basis of conduct depends on the transcendental experience implied by Plato, Kant, or Dostoevsky.

Does this mean that mysticism contains the only key to history, with reason but an obstacle to the ultimate determination of the meaning of life? Kant has already answered the question. Morality derives from a mystic relationship to the Infinite,[1] a personal experience which elevates man above the realm of necessity. This transcendental experience, however, enables reason to give rules of general applicability. The categorical imperative is not a law in the ordinary sense but a guide to an action postulated by the experience of freedom.[2] Kant's philosophy of history is an emanation of this transcendence, a corollary to demonstrate the kingdom of ends, where each man is both subject and legislator, the highest concept achieved by the Western mind of the dignity of the individual.[3]

What is the relationship then of morality to a philosophy of history? The magic attitude can find no such relation and must have recourse in the "man-god," and a deterministic psychology. Viewing the succession of growth and decay, the wars, the destruction of values, one is tempted to agree with Hegel:[4] "Only by consoling ourselves that it would not be otherwise can we accept these enormities." Life does seem just a process of dying, power does seem the criterion of values, Thrasymachus' question does appear unanswerable.

Yet out of this unfolding of seeming inevitability, there appears to emerge

---

1. Kant does not really say this. But his postulations of God, freedom, and immortality imply it. For the categorical imperative can only serve as a necessity of thought to a certain attitude. See *post* Ch. "History and Man's Experience of Morality."

2. Indissolubly connected with a concept of limits; see *post* Ch. "The Sense of Responsibility."

3. Only in "On Eternal Peace," not in the "Idea for a Universal History"; see *post.*

4. Hegel, *The Philosophy of History*, p. 35.

a feeling of humility, a recognition by man of his limits. "Know thyself" was the motto of the Oracle of Delphi. This was not meant psychoanalytically but implied: "Know that you are a man and not a god." From the acceptance of limits derives the feeling of reverence which sees history not merely as an ordeal, or mankind as a tool but as a deep fulfillment. This feeling of humility, this acknowledgment that one is man and not God, has as its full implication the concept of tolerance, the very basis for the dignity of the moral personality of the individual.[1]

And yet a last dilemma emerges. Even though our contemplation of history may yield as its deepest meaning a feeling of limits as the basis of the ultimate moral personality of man, we are still faced with the fact that no civilization has yet been permanent, no longing completely fulfilled, no answer ever gone unchallenged. It is a difficult question and one must not reply dogmatically.

It is not easy to define what degree of permanence, what hope of apocalyptic fulfillment, a value or an attitude requires. Perhaps the experience of living offers a clue. We know we must die and yet live with a sense of eternity. We can never prove that our action, even a second ago, was really freely willed and yet entertain no doubt of our freedom as each new situation arises. Despite the limits of our life, we know that our actions are irrevocable and that even inactivity posits an absolute relation. We can live this dilemma only by a measure of acceptance and, despite the knowledge of the transitoriness of our lot, with a mode of permanence.

This acceptance is not a kismetic resignation but an active recognition of limits, which enables man to face and transcend the majesty of the flow of history and the directness of life.[2] This is the profounder meaning of Goethe's poem that Spengler chose as the theme of his philosophy:

---

1. See *post* Ch. "The Sense of Responsibility."
2. For full development see *post* Ch. "The Sense of Responsibility."

In the Endless, self-repeating
   flows for evermore the same.
Myriad arches, springing, meeting,
   hold at rest the mighty frame.
Streams from all things love of living,
   grandest star and humblest clod.
All the straining, all the striving
   is eternal peace in God.[1]

---

1. Wenn im Unendlichen dasselbe
Sich wiederholend ewig fließt,
Das tausendfältige Gewölbe
Sich kräftig ineinander schließt;
Strömt Lebenslust aus allen Dingen,
Dem kleinsten wie dem größten Stern,
Und alles Drängen, alles Ringen
Ist ewige Ruh in Gott, dem Herrn.
   Goethe, "Sprüche," quoted in Spengler, *op. cit.*, Vol. I, p. viii.

CHAPTER II

HISTORY AS INTUITION:

SPENGLER

Introduction

Spengler denied that history worked towards purposes ascertainable by rational analysis. Progress is a causality imposed by the intellect, man's reaction to the dual qualities of world longing and world fear that are the result of his relation as a microcosm towards a macrocosm, his knowledge of limits, and the certainty of death.

History, on the other hand, contains the problem of motion, the enigma of the ever unique experience, the dilemma that forces man not only to observe the movement in a scene, but at the same time to participate in that movement. This impossibility of ever observing that which is in the process of observing itself leads to the inner experience of a destiny idea, which is lived with absolute certainty by every man of the early culture and the beat of which is ever decreasing in the late megalopolitan. Destiny represents eternal becoming, the intuitive answer to the question of when, the source and resolution of all of man's hope, the ultimate realization of inevitability.

Causality governs the become, with space as its representation. Becoming and being, Space and Time, Wisdom and Intellect, Freedom and Necessity constitute the true polarities of life, giving rise to man's interpretation of existence either under the aspect of the world-as-history or the world-as-nature.

The ordering of history into ancient, medieval, and modern, the Darwinian theory of evolution, and the concept of infinite human progress become equally meaningless. Instead, there emerge the shapes of the great cultures, as the carriers of all of the meaning of humanity. Each is a product of the soil in which it grew, awakening in a moment when the fear of death and the longing for life synthesized into a picture of the world from which emerges the Grand Myth, the symbol of all the problems and all the potentialities inherent in the culture. The inward representation of this image is the culture's soul. Each culture has a determinate life span before returning to the biological ages that spawned it in the shape of civilization, a state of absolute finishedness with the problems answered, the style lost. Philosophy of history to Spengler is not a question of industriously adding epochs to epochs, nor of the mere scientific collection of data. Data provides but the raw material, the condition for the higher experience, the physiognomic tact, which illuminates the meaning of the symbols and explains the stages of development. The morphology of history is Spengler's task, one eminently fit for a Faustian (Western) thinker.[1] Cultures are compared in terms of their inner meaning. Their contemporary epochs reveal functions of identical stages in development.

Becoming and become, Destiny and Causality, emerge as man's problems at every stage and permeate all his creations: art, the state, religion, economics, and natural science. And at the end of the road, while Caesarism rules in the megalopolis and man's dilemmas are thought through to steel-bright sharpness, occurs a moment of realization that, after all, the analysis had not led to its goal, that man holds in his hand nothing but the early myth in another shape. At this point the Second Religiousness comes over mankind and ideation in the grand style ceases in all fields of activities. The civilization petrifies, the period of fellah existence, as objects to a destiny that is no longer experienced, commences.

Since Destiny is the representation of the will-to-live, dependent on the self-assurance of its exponent, an analysis of the elements of political success ensues, not in a normative framework of purposive realization but as an answer to the pragmatic problem of prevailing.

Professor von Beckerath[2] rejects Spengler's philosophy as a metaphysical creation, not in the first instance based on empirically verified observations. This misses the essence[3] of an inductive method. Not the existence, but the adequacy of metaphysical concepts, not their exclusive foundation in particular observations, but their applicability to the pervasiveness of experience, must be the subject of analysis.[4]

We must further decide how far Spengler is a follower of Hegel's, despite

---

1. See *post.*
2. *Schmollers Jahrbuch für Gesetzgebung,* Vol. 47, p. 33.
3. See Appendix, "The Concepts of Meaning."
4. See *ante* Introduction, *post* Appendix, "The Concepts of Meaning."

his attacks on the ascription of rational purposes to history, and what was his relation to Darwin, the object of his ridicule and yet the chronicler in the biological world of Spengler's political realm.

And so the last question emerges: Is it possible to describe the mere components of political success without imparting into the evaluation of its elements normative concepts? Is it possible to utilize necessity as a guide to conduct, not merely as the description of completed action? The solution to these problems cannot be found in phenomena but only in a personality, expressed philosophically by its metaphysical assumptions.

Metaphysics

"Regard[1] the flowers at eventide as, one after the other, they close in the setting sun. Strange is the feeling that then presses in upon you—a feeling of enigmatic fear in the presence of this blind dreamlike earth-bound existence. The dumb forest, the silent meadows, this bush, that twig, do not stir themselves, it is the wind that plays with them. Only the little gnat is free—he dances still in the evening light, he moves whither he will ...

"Servitude and freedom—this is in last and deepest analysis the differentia by which we distinguish vegetable and animal existence. Yet only the plant is wholly and entirely what it is; in the being of the animal there is something dual. A vegetable is only a vegetable; an animal is a vegetable and something more besides. A herd that huddles together trembling in the presence of danger, a child that clings weeping to its mother, a man desperately striving to force his way into his God—all these are seeking to return out of the life of freedom into the vegetal servitude from which they were emancipated into individuality and loneliness."

So begins Volume II of Spengler's *Decline of the West*, and therein is to be found the essence of his metaphysical doctrine. Everything existing contains something cosmic, the periodicity of the seasons, the rhythm of birth, life, and decay. But animals do not merely exist. They represent a unit that has separated itself from the All, and can define its position in a world-around that is felt by it as environment. They are a microcosm in a macrocosm.

The cosmic has rhythm, tact, the grand harmony that binds together

---

1. Spengler, *The Decline of the West*, Vol. II, p. 3.

lovers or crowds in moments of absolute wordless understanding, the pulse that unites a sequence of generations into a meaningful whole. This is Destiny, the symbol of the blood, of sex, of duration. This answers the question of when and whither, and represents the only method of approaching the problem of time. It is felt by the great artist in his moment of contemplation, it is embodied by the statesman in action and is lived by the man of the springtime culture. It constitutes the essence of tragedy, the problem of "too late," when a moment of the present is irrevocably consigned to the past.

The microcosm contains tension and polarity, the loneliness of the individual in a world of strange significances, in which the total inner meaning of others remains an eternal riddle. Rhythm and tension, longing and fear, characterize the relationship of the microcosm to the macrocosm. Organisms contain consciousness (*Dasein*-being). Animals represent waking-being (waking-consciousness, *Wachsein*). Only in sleep everything existing reverts to mere being.

For man, waking-being is confined to the realm of the eye. The sounds of the night, the odor of flowers all stimulate a "whither" in the world of light. Of the world of scent, man knows little, of the nature of the butterfly, whose crystalline eyes focus a picture of myriad possibilities, nothing. Thus night has always been felt as akin to death, and the idea of an invisible God constitutes the highest manifestation of human transcendence.

This has made the depth experience the most significant concept in man's life. The awareness of the I depends on the recognition of the Thou, of the existence of the other in the environment. Just as the notion of Destiny is tied up with the rhythm of becoming and the felt pulse of the organic, so waking-consciousness comes to the full awareness of space, extended only through the experience of death. At that moment, man first realizes his immense loneliness in the universe, the episodic nature of his existence. The animal lives in a pure present and dies without knowledge of the fact, but for man life is a short span between birth and death.

The enigma of Time first appears, the realization of limits, of the transitoriness of existence. Therefore, the first manifestation of higher thought occurs as a meditation upon death.

Man rebels at the thought of the episodic nature of life, at its mystery and his loneliness in the universe. The enigmatic, which ever threatens the existence of primitive man, begins to be mastered by the act of naming objects, which serves as a limitation and an assertion of supremacy. The wish to transcend mortality develops into the process of conjuring the world, achieved under the aspect of cult by the religious soul and under that of technique in an age the numina of which are expressed in theory.

In primitive societies the enigmatic is conquered by religion, which requires forms, the knowledge of which is restricted and whose rites must be exact. As a function of the soul's depth experience, religion contains the grand myth of each culture, the actualization of its prime symbol, expressed in the upward-striving forceful God of the Gothic, the Spirit of God hovering in the cave world of the Magian soul, and the statuesque body of the Apollinian.[1]

The reactions, which originally were total, tend to become permeated by an understanding of significances. Understanding separated from sensation is called thought. Profane Causality appears, supplanting the holy Causality of religion, in order to withdraw from the world of becoming the data which it then dissects. Yet natural science is neither new nor self-contained, but a consequence of the religious world-picture that preceded it, all its theories merely an analysis—and even a rebuttal presupposes an object—of the lived metaphysics of the culture's youth. No matter how far natural science advances, at its edge, in the inexplicable residue, ever hovers God as everything beyond the possibility of causal analysis.

The insolvable dilemma of time emerges: each act is unique, yet science must postulate on endless comparability of phenomena. The world reveals a process of eternal becoming, but Causality can operate only on the become. The realm of becoming knows only singularly occurring facts, the world of pure being operates with eternal truths. The conflict of rhythm against tension, Destiny against Causality, permeates existence and history.

Two pictures of the world are possible: the world-as-history, in which the become is ordered with reference to the becoming, or the world-as-nature, in which the opposite occurs. The world-as-history represents a dynamic process of growth, with the will-to-live the only criterion of success, the only source of motivation. In this world of facts, only subjects and objects exist. To live for abstractions involves suffering a destiny instead of being one. Its chroniclers are those individuals whose physiognomic tact enables

---

1. For explanation of term see *post* "The Souls of the Culture."

them to apprehend the totality of events in a poetic unity, with a clear realization of the insufficiency of a causal analysis. Its representatives are the great statesmen who embody the meaning of the occurrences, the men of blood who feel the cosmic beat and actualize it. "I feel myself driven towards an end that I do not know," Napoleon stated at the beginning of the Russian campaign. "As soon as I shall have reached it, as soon as I shall become unnecessary, an atom will suffice to shatter me. Till then, not all the forces of mankind can do anything against me."[1]

Yet the world-as-nature, too, has its triumphs. Its linkages represent man's attempt at attaining mastery over his destiny. It can achieve in its highest form liberation and freedom from the world-born fear which is the lot of waking-consciousness, the ego's loneliness in the face of impassable boundaries. It is ever the task of religion to fight against the powers of the blood, to withdraw from the world into ascetism, to realize the necessity of tension, and in the end, finally, to love it. Morality "is a conscious and planned causality of conduct,"[2] of eternal validity and by definition applicable even if man did not exist.[3] The saint must realize, however, that his victories are not of this world. If he wants temporal success, the logic of events forces him to use political weapons. The meeting of Pilate and Christ[4] constitutes Spengler's poetic representation of this dilemma. The Roman asked, "What is truth?" And in that question expressed the self-confidence of the state, the pride of eminent fitness, the entire meaning of history. And the answer, not indeed spoken but implicit in the actions of the prisoner, was: "What is actuality?"

This contains the final differentia between the two form-worlds, between becoming and being, Destiny and Causality, history and nature. Becoming with waking-consciousness as its subject, or a waking-being that attempts to dominate Destiny, are the essence of the antinomy, the real alternatives of life. The politician despises the thinker and dreamer—and rightly. For the believer, all worldly ambition is sham and deception—he, too, is right. "A ruler who wishes to improve religion in the direction of political, practical purposes is a fool. A sociologist-preacher

---

1. Spengler, *op. cit.*, Vol. I, p. 144.
2. Spengler, *op. cit.*, Vol. II, p. 272.
3. See Kant's definition of the categorical imperative as applied to all rational beings, not only to man.
4. Spengler, *op. cit.*, Vol. II, p. 216.

who tries to bring truth, righteousness, peace, and forgiveness into the world of actuality is a fool also. No faith yet has altered the world, and no fact can ever rebut a faith[1] ... Let a man be either a hero or a saint. In between lies, not wisdom, but banality."[2]

Spengler resolved the dilemma of our experience of freedom and our knowledge of necessity into a postulate of alternatives. The opposition of becoming and being, the tension between Destiny and Causality, constitutes the metaphysical basis of Spengler's philosophy of history. The actualization of the immanent pulse achieves its highest form as long as its direction is taken for granted. Waking-consciousness achieves a gradual dominance only by reducing the lived experience of the cosmic beat. Finally man is adrift in a world whose purpose is no longer his own. The culture turns into a civilization, petrifies, and dies.

The imaginativeness of this philosophy cannot hide its inner complexities, however. The opposition of becoming and being, Destiny and Causality, Necessity and Freedom, seems to reduce existence to a mere vegetating. But necessity explains only past actions. Its actualization in conduct requires a waking-consciousness, which moreover operates with the inner conviction of choice. If the cultures are distinguished by their struggle for the actualization of an idea,[3] then the specificity of history resides in an element of purposiveness, not in an inexorable destiny. The world-as-history and the world-as-nature are, after all, merely metaphysical abstractions for the apprehension of events, not objective modes of real occurrences.[4]

Spengler implies that the man of fact lives a destiny and thereby achieves his triumphs. But, again, this does not seem to prove the dominance of becoming over being, of history over waking-consciousness. The recognition of the immanence depends on waking-consciousness. Instinct is no guide to political conduct. Effective leadership is always forced—whatever its motives—to represent itself as the carrier of ideas, embodying purposes. All truly great achievements in history resulted from the actualization of principles, not from the clever evaluation of political conditions.[5]

---

1. Spengler, *op. cit.*, Vol. II, p. 216.
2. Spengler, *op. cit.*, Vol. II, p. 274.
3. Spengler, *op. cit.*, Vol. I, p. 54.
4. See *post* Ch. "History and Man's Experience of Morality" for full discussion.
5. One may, of course, define all actuality as necessary, and then all events become

Only plants are pure pragmatists. The Causality which motivates man is an experience of freedom, not derived from the physical world but from a personal, mystic relationship to the Infinite.[1]

Conversely the man of truths, the saint, represents not merely waking-consciousness. "To constrain one's blood, one must have blood," says Spengler[2] and thereby refutes himself. What gives the majesty to Christ's thought and the driving force to Mohammed is not their logical consistency but their pertinency to the very basis of human longing. Why was Hus burned and why did Luther split the church? What is the real meaning of the triumph of Christianity? Because the time was ripe, Spengler would answer. Because at the time, the coming of the Messiah, the end of the world, the longing for the brotherhood of man had obliterated the classical world-feeling and thus each man expressed in conversion his own religiousness. Yet does this not mean that self-contained being is no more possible than all-pervasive becoming? Christ may have been like a child in a strange, remote world. Perhaps the sentry under the Cross heard His anguished cry that God had forsaken Him.[3] Yet it was not, as Spengler asserts, the sentry who represented the facts of history but the man on the Cross.

It might be maintained, of course, that if Christ had never existed, something like His beliefs would have triumphed in the form of the mystery cults. It is in the "something," however, wherein lies the difference between Necessity and Freedom, between a tendency and the creative act. No activity, no society is without its motivations that are given in common experience and understood without affirmation. But equally common experience will not suffice to predict individual behavior. Every event is not only an effect but an inner experience. Yet the inner experience is not separated from the effect. Destiny may condition Causality, but equally the truths of waking-consciousness became the "facts" of history.

And so we find that there is no real opposition between being and waking-being, only two connected modes of human existence, the organic and the purposive,[4] nothing but our original question in a different form: "What is this necessity that accomplishes itself under the mode of freedom?"

---

functions of an inexorability. See *post* "Conclusions."
1. See *post* Ch. "The Sense of Responsibility."
2. Spengler, *op. cit.*, Vol. II, p. 273.
3. Spengler, *op. cit.*, Vol. II, p. 215.
4. W. Y. Elliott, *The Pragmatic Revolt in Politics.*

Spengler saw in his metaphysical antinomy the key to the growth and decay of cultures, the essence of their soul-image, the basis of politics. Historical development constitutes an organic process, its distinguishing characteristic the gradual assertion of the power of waking-consciousness. The demarcation which distinguishes the relative predominance of the two possible world-views is that between culture and civilization, the former an expression of the eternal rhythm, the latter a manifestation of a continuously decreasing cosmic beat.

Spengler envisioned existence as a biological process which attains meaning only with the emergence of the cultures. Primitive humanity was engaged in a constant struggle for mere survival. The marginal nature of life left no room for profound ideation, only for a transitory religiosity dependent on its supposed power of conjuring the lurking, enigmatic dangers.

Suddenly, at approximately 3000 B.C., there emerged the forms of the great cultures, organic beings with their own inner conception of Destiny. They brought about so fundamental a change that Spengler postulates a transformation in the human constitution. Henceforth man constructs his world-image, his depth experience, no longer with reference to himself alone, but as part of an experienced whole. The degree of interrelationship of this experience and its lived significance characterizes common membership in a culture.

Each culture constitutes an organic being with growth, maturity, old age, and death. They awaken in a moment of infinite longing, when the fear of death, the end of the world, the dark mystery of the universe oppress everybody's heart. Such was the time when at the birth of Christ, the Magian soul attained life, when the world was full of tales of a Messiah and the classical soul was dissipating itself in Neo-Platonism and the Oriental mystery cults. Such was the moment when in the years 900–1000, the end of the world seemed near, and out of the confused groping of the Merovingian and Carolingian period (Charlemagne as a "ray from Baghdad") the upward-striving soul of the Western (Faustian)[1] culture emerged. At these moments, in the higher minds of the young culture, the environment suddenly coalesces into a meaningful picture. All the problems and

---

1. See *post.*

possibilities of the future history are already immanent in the formations of those early years, in the construction of its Grand Myth.

Each culture begins with a great renunciation, the refusal to take over the symbols of the preceding civilization, the selection of its own appropriate representations. Even if outward manifestations of other cultures are adopted, the very selectivity and the content ascribed will be unique, solitary, and essentially incommunicable to outsiders. The myth of each culture contains its image of the world, the essence of its longing, the possibility of its nature knowledge, the basis of its religion. All of the later history reveals a process of actualizing this idea and a fight against the forces that tend to dissolve it from within (waking-consciousness) and the material dangers of the environment. Since the birth occurs in a moment of oppressive tension, all early manifestations of human endeavor are in their essence religious. Natural science emerges only as a concomitant of the gradual self-assertion of waking-consciousness. Spengler considers both manifestations of the same phenomena. "World-knowing for the man of the higher Cultures [is] a need, seen as a duty, of expressing his own essence."[1]

The culture grows in a landscape and remains tied to it for the remainder of its existence. In the biological period that precedes the historical era, a peasantry develops that is close to the soil, and feels the rhythm of the cosmic beat. Out of the anonymous countryside develops at the beginning of each culture a feudal order whose essence is expressed in a customary ethic of which the frame of reference is not good and evil but good and bad, and whose stigma attaches to vulgarity, not sin.[2] This aristocracy represents the world of facts and of the meaning of what is about to happen. The peasantry is history, the aristocracy makes history.

A priesthood, too, appears, born out of the world fear of the early period, the mediator between man and the other that is felt as enigmatic. The style and influence of that priesthood depends on the symbol of the culture and its depth experience. The Faustian man, a lonely ego in a world of infinite extent, whose God as the manifestation of omnipotent force is all-pervasive, buffeted on all sides by the terrible fear of the Devil, requires a powerful priesthood and the possibility of understanding forgiveness. The Apollinian soul, in all essentials almost the exact opposite of the Faustian, with its feeling for pure presence, against the background of

1. Spengler, *op. cit.*, Vol. I, p. 99.
2. See *post* "The Faustian Soul."

a Golden Age, its passionate denial of infinity, of necessity felt the existence of a strong priesthood as a danger, and none developed. The Magian cave world, in which the Divine Pneuma hovers uneasily over man, who might ever fall to the forces of evil and whose salvation consists in the consensus of the believers, produces a type of nation that is a church.

The existence of the springtime culture represents a lived metaphysics, each of its manifestations a tentative groping towards the knowledge it will have during its noon. But soon the harmony of the countryside begins to be disturbed by the emergence of towns. Initially merely marketplaces—though primitive peasantry ever regards even technical mastery of nature with mixed awe and terror (for example, blacksmiths)—they develop into places from which the countryside is henceforth felt as environs.[1] This is the age when Scholasticism appears, a presumption for the permanence of the world.

The growth of the city involves the emancipation of the intellect. The liberated waking-consciousness begins the process of dominating the organic factor, until with the complete destruction of the great focus, a shapeless Caesarism rules all problemation.[2] Formerly, knowledge was faith supported, but with the growing assurance of its powers it becomes faith controverted. The countryside fights a losing battle against the city, which represents the focus of events—in the political field against democracy, in the spiritual against nationalism, in the economic against money.[3] The spirit of the city is critical and practical. Life, which used to be lived out of the self-evidence of its meaning, develops into a calculation of utilitarian purposes. The great tradition itself becomes questionable.

Spengler finds the same tendencies in the religious field. The political requirements of a growing culture had involved faith in the affairs of the world of facts. The ascetic spirit, which sees the purpose of religion in the negation of the life of this world, in the restraining of the blood, which opposes the timeless love of God to the love of the sexes, rouses itself to a final effort. Reformation stands at the end, not at the beginning, of a religious development. But where the early religion originated from the countryside, expressed the optimism of infinite longing, and represented

---

1. Spengler, *op. cit.*, Vol. II, p. 91.
2. Note similarity of this concept to Plato's disintegration of the Republic, which begins with an assertion of a questioning selfishness.
3. Spengler, *op. cit.*, Vol. II, p. 97.

the pulse of eternal becoming, the Reformation is the product of the city, cold, brilliant, austere. The bliss of the young culture, the peace typified by the smiling Mary, is irrevocably lost. Religious fervor rises once more, but it expresses now the hard intelligence, the "pedantic ecstasy," of the Neo-Pythagoreans, Islam, and the Puritans.[1] It holds on to its creation, a product of the deep inwardness of the city, with a sort of terror lest it prove unreal and is therefore impatient, pitiless, unforgiving.[2] The lived metaphysic of the early period has in the independent been replaced by a common devotion to a concept,[3] a set of abstract and critical judgments on the faith that is no longer experienced. Life becomes a comprehended mechanics out of which all Puritans develop predestination as a technical guarantee for the triumph of the elect. Another fifty years and rational criticism alone remains supreme.

This leads to the age of the megalopolis, the world-as-city, the acme of a temporarily triumphant waking-consciousness. The countryside has long reverted to its biological state. It gazes on the strange creation of human art with uncomprehending hatred. Such is the feeling of Dostoevsky towards St. Petersburg, which he felt "one day might vanish with the morning mist."[4] All the thought and decisions of life are concentrated in the cosmopolis. The spirit of the city is coldly practical. Philosophy frees itself from its dependence on religion and submits the whole universe, including religion, to epistemological criticism. "In the one period [of growth] life reveals itself, the other [city-period] has life as its object."[5] It is symbolized by the deep spirituality of Pascal against the shallow utilitarianism of Mill. Life is no longer lived as something self-evident but becomes a problem of maximum happiness. Each culture develops at this stage its own mode of spiritual extinction.

The Apollinian soul, its ideal pure body, with the opposition of Ent and Non-Ent, its tragedy of the senseless incident buffeting man by the blind threads of Tyche, with the hero's only possibility consisting of the grand gesture, develops Stoicism, a purging of the soul of whatever is alien to it, so that it emerges in its pure statuesque bodiliness.

---

1. Spengler, *op. cit.*, Vol. II, p. 301.
2. Spengler, *op. cit.*, Vol. II, p. 301.
3. Spengler, *op. cit.*, Vol. II, p. 302.
4. Spengler, *op. cit.*, Vol. II, p. 193.
5. Spengler, *op. cit.*, Vol. I, p. 365.

The Western will-to-power, its expression ever a commanding imperative, completes the materialization of its soul, by the mechanistic solution of Socialism.[1]

Philosophy in the great style is finished. No great thinkers developed in the classical period after the Stoics, and Western thought has been stated in its final form by Kant. All the nineteenth century accomplished was the mechanization of his concepts in the spirit of a utilitarian will-to-life. Formerly profound thinking was associated with mathematics; now it becomes sociopolitical. The metaphysics of the Baroque develops into the critique of society of Hegel, Schopenhauer, and Nietzsche. Dimly man yearns for a return to nature. It is not the landscape of the early Gothic, however, but the conceptual definition of Rousseau, the natural relation of Marx. Kant had a vision of the world as appearance or phenomena, but to Schopenhauer it is merely a brain phenomenon with utilitarian connotations.[2] The change from the tragic view to the plebeian, from the felt intuition of Goethe, from the inward necessity of Shakespeare, to the frog perspective[3] of Marx is complete. "Poets of our great cities build … but they do not sing. Shapes are called into being, not to be, but to prove something."[4] The Darwinian theory of evolution, which imports the Manchester School theories into the world of Destiny and replaces the inward harmony of the Gothic with the mechanistic conception of aims, called progress, is the necessary product of that period. But every deeper thinker of the nineteenth century is Socialistic, defined by Spengler as the imposition of one's views on behalf of all with attention "directed to that welfare of mankind that Goethe and Kant never spent a thought upon."[5] Francis of Assisi and the saints of the culture's youth could think of renouncing; the Socialist conceives only of distributing temporal possessions.

Art, too, has become formless. The early religious self-assurance, the great style which represented a rhythm of self-implementation, is becoming ever less well defined, the self-consciousness ever greater. To Michelangelo, Leonardo, Rembrandt, Bach, and Beethoven, the great style was an aid, the schools of art produced a high average. It liberated the artist from

---

1. Spengler, *op. cit.*, Vol. I, p. 341.
2. Spengler, *op. cit.*, Vol. I, p. 393.
3. Spengler, *op. cit.*, Vol. I, p. 368.
4. Spengler, *op. cit.*, Vol. I, p. 156.
5. Spengler, *op. cit.*, Vol. I, p. 370.

struggling with form, enabling him to pour the essence of his soul into the creation. But with Wagner and Pergamos, the style is felt as a hindrance. Everything becomes huge, ever more esoteric and abstract in the Western, ever more ornate and hovering in the Apollinian culture. Finally the great style is lost and instead of ideas there are continually new art problems coaxed out of an inwardly meaningless creativeness. Instead of a school, the only criterion is taste.

Natural science had begun by dissecting the religious world-picture, both a product of man's astonishment at the motion of his universe, both an attempt to dominate the inexorability of fate. The intellect ever thinks that it has mastered truths of eternal applicability, but it cannot rest until every question has been answered and no riddle remains. Yet since nature is what man constructs for himself out of his depth experience, that which we are observing lives with us in the process of observation.[1] Moreover, every scientific result is the consequence of a method, and the method presupposes a belief in its conclusiveness. "Descartes meant to doubt everything, but certainly not the value of this doubting."[2] No Western thinker would question the efficacy of empirical observation, just as no Magian scientist needs to invoke the aid of a miracle to explain phenomena not amenable to causal analysis. Thus, there came into existence the Western science of dynamics, with an assertive mastery over nature, and the Magian alchemy, which tends to wheedle its results from a substance, which in the final analysis represents only a different mode of the immanently divine.

But after a period of easy optimism when both critical philosophy and scientific research reign supreme, the old enigmas reappear. That which had brought natural science to a maximum of inner fulfillment suddenly operates as a solvent.[3] Each culture discovers that the ultimate questions are unanswerable causally; the problem of motion remains unresolved. Force as the source or the cause of motion represents the Western dilemma, the perfect form of substance, the causality of its movement the classical. The hypotheses grow progressively more abstract and inclusive; the various fields of knowledge converge ever closer. In a moment of painful clarity it becomes apparent that amidst all the abstruseness, the ever sharper definition of conceptual quantities, which moreover, like the concept of force,

---

1. Spengler, *op. cit.*, Vol. I, p. 388.
2. Spengler, *op. cit.*, Vol. II, p. 12.
3. Spengler, *op. cit.*, Vol. I, p. 417.

determine the structure of the experiment *a priori*, there emerges nothing but the myths of springtime in modern form.[1] Then, in the grey light of the beginning civilization, man realizes that the tension created by his waking-consciousness has become too great, that the quest for knowledge is without end, and his tired soul plunges into the peace of the Second Religiousness.

Yet where the early religion was the good symbolism of an emerging soul, the citizen of the megalopolis, with the cosmic beat in him ever decreasing, clings desperately to his cults, his theosophy, his religious fads. In the springtime, reason was felt as a support of faith; in the maturity, faith was conceived as subject to critical analysis, and an enlightened waking-consciousness sought to find its own position towards life (*Weltanschauung*), but now faith alone is the criterion. The flight from reason prevails, the belief that there is some mystic constitution of actuality as to which formal proofs are barren.[2]

As the culture turns itself into a civilization and the masses of the world-city seek to find release from the polarities in their soul in *panem et circenses*, in Negro dances and sports, Caesarism[3] emerges in the political organization, replacing democracy, which has become an empty shell, and ending the dictatorship of money, which is by now the real master of political life.[4] It represents the eventual triumph of the blood, of being, over the strained waking-consciousness of the megalopolis. Pure power, the coursing rhythm of ever-becoming, reassert themselves and despite traditional trappings, even because of them, a formless force permeates all aspects of political life.

Nothing, according to Spengler, can save the dying civilization. The sterility of all late man ensues, a metaphysical turn towards death.[5] The tragic symbolism which in Shakespeare could lift an incident into a destiny has in Ibsen become the problemation of social events. Woman, whom the man of the springtime culture conceives as the mother of his children, constitutes for the cosmopolitan a companion for life, an object for the blending of dispositions. No attempt, however frantic, can arrest the

---

1. Spengler, *op. cit.*, Vol. I, p. 425.
2. Spengler, *op. cit.*, Vol. II, p. 310.
3. See *post* "Politics, Economics, the Machine."
4. See *post* "Politics, Economics, the Machine."
5. Spengler, *op. cit.*, Vol. II, p. 105.

decline in population. Neither the marriage laws of Augustus, nor the wholesale adoptions, nor the incessant implantation of barbarians, availed to chock this process in the Hellenic world.[1]

"When reasons have to be put forward at all in a question of life, life itself has become questionable."[2] The animal element, the strained waking-consciousness, has eaten up the plant side, and the drive into the future, which binds together a sequence of generations into a purposeful organism, is at an end. The population returns to a fellah-type state such as the Egyptians at the time of the Romans, and the Chinese and Indians today. Here all growth has ceased and the biological sequence of generations, with millennia for the time span, re-emerges. Waking-consciousness has succeeded in stiffening the becoming, in petrifying the great symbolism. As in the living culture the estate and race are in antithesis as the impersonal and the personal, so in the fellah state the opposition is between the mass and the caste, as the formal against the formless. The intellectuality, subtlety, and dignity of this form-world may be considerable, as attested by the heights from which an Indian Brahmin looks down on a Westerner. But history has ceased for the civilization. It has become an object for cultures and peoples who will to be a destiny, and the Period of Contending States has left it physically and morally exhausted.[3]

"High history also lays itself down weary to sleep. Man becomes a plant again, adhering to the soil, dumb and enduring. The timeless village and the 'eternal' peasant reappear, begetting children and burying seed in Mother Earth—a busy, not inadequate swarm, over which the tempest of soldier-emperors passingly blows. In the midst of the land lie the old world-cities, empty receptacles of an extinguished soul, in which a history-less mankind slowly nests itself. Men live from hand to mouth, with petty thrifts and petty fortunes, and endure. Masses are trampled on in the conflicts of the conquerors who contend for the power and the spoil of this world, but the survivors fill up the gaps with a primitive fertility and suffer on. And while in high places there is the eternal alternance of victory and defeat, those in the depths pray, pray with that mighty piety of the Second Religiousness that has overcome all doubts forever. There, in the souls, world peace, the peace of God, the bliss of grey-haired monks and hermits,

---

1. Spengler, *op. cit.*, Vol. II, p. 106.
2. Spengler, *op. cit.*, Vol. II, p. 104.
3. Spengler, *op. cit.*, Vol. II, p. 108.

is become actual—and there alone. It has awakened that depth in the endurance of suffering which the historical man in the thousand years of his development has never known. Only with the end of grand History does holy, still being reappear. It is a drama noble in its aimlessness, noble and aimless as the course of the stars, the rotation of the earth, and alternance of land and sea, of ice and virgin forest upon its face. We may marvel at it or we may lament it—but it is there."[1]

Spengler rejected the theory that history revealed the causal working out of rational plans. He substituted a morphology of history, the world-as-experience, evoked by images of compelling power and great inward beauty. Cultures are organisms, their life span, extent, and death implicit in the very problems of their youth. The soul of each culture, a function of its depth of experience, constructs an image of the world which binds it to the soil in which it grew, sets the limits for the possibilities of its natural science and religion, and determines the problems that must be answered. Gradually, the tension created by the dominance of waking-being becomes too great, the form is lost, the culture transforms itself into a civilization. Slowly, it stiffens and dies, returning to the biological ages that spawned it, its inner meaning fulfilled, no longer the master but the object of Destiny.

Yet the brilliance of this picture and its in many ways psychological depth cannot overcome the difficulties inherent in the underlying metaphysical assumptions, which frequently fail to meet our twin tests of consistency and relevancy.[2] They fall short of the former because Spengler never makes clear what exactly he means by Destiny or the experience of Time. In the biological ages which precede the culture, and in the fellah state that follows, waking-consciousness is at a minimum. Does this enduring mankind represent the essence of the Destiny-experience? The life of the culture constitutes a process of actualizing the possible,[3] all its manifestations profound symbols of its view of the world. Yet the soul of the culture, its depth experience, is given symbolic expression by making consciousness. It appears that everything which gives deeper meaning to the culture and lifts it above the level of primitive societies results from an aware purposiveness, not a purely organic destiny. "The Culture had bound up all its forces in strict form. Now they were released, and 'Nature'—that is, the

---

1. Spengler, *op. cit.*, Vol. II, p. 435.
2. See *post* Appendix, "The Concepts of Meaning."
3. Spengler's definition of the soul, Vol. I, p. 54.

cosmic—broke forth"[1] seems an admission that the creative aspect of growth reveals the construction of waking-consciousness.

Each culture not only goes through similar phases of youth, maturity, age, and decline, but its political and artistic embodiment at each stage is identical.[2] This, too, is difficult to accept. If each soul constitutes a counter-concept to the world and its life span represents the gradual realization of its immanence, one would expect the historical development to differ according to the vision of its environment and the idea attempted to be actualized. Though everything organic has its periods of youth, growth, and decay, these phenomena do not embody themselves in identical form. "Western history was willed and Indian history happened"[3] means nothing if we postulate the necessity of a political development that has the same political organization at each stage.[4]

As a matter of fact, Spengler is hard put to find uniformity, even between the classical and Western cultures, resulting in the definition of the Athenian polis as the classical equivalent of dynastic feeling. But granting Spengler's thesis of identical political institutionalization, two conclusions seem inescapable. To begin with, reality as an emanation of the ego may not present totally different aspects to each culture, but contain a modicum of continuity of problemation. In this sense, significance attaches not only to the newly adopted symbols, not only to the "Great Renunciation," but also to the taking over of symbols and institutions and their recurrence at similar stages of development.

Furthermore, Spengler's empirical data[5] is confined almost exclusively to the Apollinian, Magian, and Faustian cultures, with contemporary periods in other cultures frequently merely postulated. The very possibility of making an analysis of the "soul" of a culture implies a degree of inner correlation. The divergences between the cultures may merely hide an underlying unity, expressing itself in a continuity of problemation. These problems emerge more clearly in Spengler's elaboration of the souls of the culture.

---

1. Spengler, *op. cit.*, Vol. II, p. 419.
2. Or morphologous, as Spengler calls functional interrelationship.
3. Spengler, *op. cit.*, Vol. I, p. 125.
4. Spengler, *op. cit.*, Vol. II, p. 296.
5. On test of relevancy, see *post* Appendix, "The Concepts of Meaning."

THE APOLLINIAN SOUL-IMAGE[1]

Spengler—in obvious reliance on Kant—calls his philosophy a Copernican revolution freeing the study of history from theoretical misconceptions that had prevented the full realization of its implications. Just as Copernicus liberated natural science by treating the earth as accidental instead of normative, so Spengler conceived his morphology as an analysis of functional rather than temporal interrelationships.[2] History represents the self-realization of the souls of cultures, their differences consequences of varying world-views. "Contemporary" means identical stages of an organic development.

Yet what is the soul? Spengler finds his answer in the belief of every philosopher or scientist in the existence of something subject to rational analysis.[3] "The question of whether the forms of thought are ever approachable by thought," which to the layman might appear dubious, is nevertheless held as an article of faith by every psychologist. The barrenness of technical psychology results from the impossibility of conceptually dissecting the inwardly certain, of importing definitional notions into the world of becoming. No system can offer analytical criteria for such realities as jealousy, regret, or artistic intention.[4]

Spengler's metaphysical antinomies reappear. Causality can serve for the apprehension of phenomena only insofar as nature is conceived as eternally possible. The soul, however, is not a phenomenon, but an image derived from the primary and continuing experience of life and death. Every free-moving being must understand the world around it as a condition for survival. The knowledge of the macrocosm as a technical and empirical mastery is the world-as-nature. But beyond the environment, man divines the presence of a "something other" in both himself and others, which by virtue of its physiognomically impressive powers evokes the desire to know and is anxiously pondered. Thus the notion of the soul arises, as an image of everything in man which can never be causally

---

1. In order to maintain the unity of Spengler's development, I have placed all my comments *post* at the end of the section "The Magian Soul."
2. Spengler, *op. cit.*, Vol. I, p. 94.
3. Spengler, *op. cit.*, Vol. II, p. 311.
4. Spengler, *op. cit.*, Vol. I, p. 299.

known, as a counterworld to nature, as a mode of visualizing what will always be inaccessible by the light-world of the eye.

The soul's representation reflects Spengler's metaphysical scheme. Its image is a myth pondered religiously by the spirituality that still sees God in nature and analyzed conceptually as soon as nature comes to be observed critically. Just as Time constitutes a counter-concept to Space, so the notion of a soul is the inverse of the picture of the world. "Every psychology is a counter-physics."[1] This prevents an exact science of the soul, of universal applicability, since such an analysis is a function of the depth experience of its culture. The Apollinian constructed its inner world as a group of excellent parts. The Western thinker conceives his image as forces of thinking, feeling, willing. The Magian psychologist views his soul as an airy substance (*nephesh*, *ruach*) in conjunction with a bodily substance, both deriving reality only from an infusion of the Divine Pneuma.

Spengler defines the image of the soul as the possible and the world as the actual.[2] Thus life is the process of actualizing the possible, the history of each culture constituting a ripening and deepening of its soul-picture. This accounts for the profound symbolism of all manifestations of activity of cultures, and the complete lack of inner meaning of every creation of both the primitive and fellah state.

Since the waking-consciousness arrives at self-knowledge through the experience and fear of death, the rites of burial and the disposal of the bodies serve as profound indications of the depth experience of the different cultures. Because all art is an expression of world longing and all natural science an analysis of the religious world-picture, the grand symbolism of the culture includes all their manifestations, with the proviso that the maturity and decline will see a diminution of the cosmic beat, its emanations ever more uncertain and inconclusive until the inevitable approach of the fellah state at the end of the civilization.

The classical or Apollinian soul conceived of existence as exhausting itself in a pure present against the background of the Golden Age. Its passionate denial of infinity came to expression at its inception in the great refusal to take over the form-world and architectural style of the Minoan world. Suddenly, about 1100 B.C., with the emergence of the Mycenaean

---

1. Spengler, *op. cit.*, Vol. I, p. 301.
2. Spengler, *op. cit.*, Vol. I, p. 54.

culture, great architecture ceased. The barrow for the burial of the dead is supplanted by the burning of the corpses. Wood replaces stone as building material despite an abundance of quarries in Hellas. Existence consists of a denial of infinity, an emphasis on pure being. Thucydides states in his *History of the Peloponnesian War* that before the year 400, his time, not much of importance had happened in Greece.

Life in the Apollinian world constituted a spiritual static. The Greek word for personality is *persona*,[1] which does not express the concept of character but describes the public mien, the "gesture" of its carrier. The ideal of the classical was Cosmos, the perfectly defined, absolute Ent, in opposition to which space was felt not as a challenge, but as Non-Ent, Chaos, the not-yet-formed. The self-asserting ego of Western culture, or its forceful, all-pervasive God, would have been equally alien to the Apollinian world-feeling. Man as a body achieves reality through his relation to other bodies, with the gods as the upper limit and the slave as the lower. This explains Aristotle's statement that only a fool or a god could live alone and makes the idea of an Athenian Robinson Crusoe unthinkable.[2] The gods were merely perfectly formed bodies of more than average powers, though equally subject with other bodies to the blind working of Tyche. Zeus in the *Iliad* holds up the scale not to determine, but to learn Hector's fate.

The Platonic conception of the soul, as a sum of excellent parts, with reason in the Olympian commanding position, emerges as the classical image just as its yearning for concreteness constructed a scientific theory of static mechanics. The problem of the relation between the knower and the known Plato resolved as a matter of course into a passage of knowledge to the recipient. His captives in the cave were really captives, objects of the light from the common sun, not—as in Kant egos—imposing their forms on the world, not suns themselves irradiating the universe.[3]

The Attic drama was a drama of the moment. Its heroes represent Euclidean bodies, stuck in a position they did not choose, assailed by the blind forces of fate, the jealousy of the gods, the sudden total negation of being, as the most terrible of experiences. What happens to Hamlet is the consequence of a meaningful inner development, but Oedipus is the victim of circumstances that could happen to anyone. The grand gesture,

1. Spengler, *op. cit.*, Vol. I, p. 316.
2. Spengler, *op. cit.*, Vol. I, p. 316.
3. Spengler, *op. cit.*, Vol. I, p. 311.

which defines a being to other bodies, represents the only possible course of action of the *soma* that is being gratuitously destroyed. Spiritual characterization was prevented by the wearing of masks, and the padding of figures made movement almost impossible.[1]

Classical architecture was ever forced to fight against the assertiveness of pure being, which it threatened by the implication of permanence inherent in building. This gave rise to the classical temple, of extreme poverty of form, since the recognition of many styles would have been an admission of a type of infinity. Its columns of uneven spacing, its accentuation of beam and load, its flat roof all served as a denial of space and an affirmation of the exclusive validity of the present. Apollinian art became a production of great feebleness of characterization, but also of timeless evenness.[2]

Since natural science is the outward expression of the soul-image, the causal description of the religious view, a static mechanics resulted. The human tendency to reduce its nature-picture to the minimal forms capable of intellectual manipulation issued in an atomic theory, of small, perfectly elastic bodies, of unpredictable motion operating through shock and countershock. Motion became not a spatial force but an attribute of bodies.[3] Thus the greatest creation of the classical scientific mind was Euclidean geometry, the measurement and circumscription of concrete representations.

This, too, applied to classical political life. The feudal kingdoms of the Homeric period ever contracted their horizon until the poleis were reached, a pure point of being, where the Greek, a body among other bodies, could view his world from the Acropolis. This conception of a political organization as a self-contained city-state, which made everything beyond the horizon strange and potentially hostile, led to the struggle to sheer extinction which ever characterized the politics of Hellas. The only issue of these campaigns could be the razing of the city and the extermination or enslavement of the hostile populations. The ideal of each polis was *autarkeia*, complete economic independence, a minimum of intercourse with other city-states, a state of blissful present being, the utopia of Plato, Aristotle, and all Greek statesmen. The anti-historical instinct expressed itself in the complete spoilage of natural resources. The prudent long-term policies of

---

1. Spengler, *op. cit.*, Vol. I, p. 325.
2. Spengler, *op. cit.*, Vol. I, p. 316.
3. Spengler, *op. cit.*, Vol. I, p. 385.

Western cultures were completely unknown. Surpluses, when achieved, were distributed among the population.[1]

Even Rome was merely a polis become immense. It dotted the Mediterranean with dependencies in polis-form, its focus of attention ever the embodiment in a point of regional existence. Thus Rome knew Alexandria, but not Egypt. Even after citizenship was granted to all Italians, the center and meaning of events remained Rome. The idea of transferring the vote from Rome to the residence of the citizen never occurred to any Roman statesman.

Spengler's conception of the classical soul reveals its essence as a negation of Time, just as its history was episodic, of a great mass of detail but no inner relation.[2] It clung to the coast of the Mediterranean in clusters of tightly organized city-states, with no serious attempt to explore the hinterland. To settle far from the coast would have meant to lose touch with home. The immigration into the U.S., the lonely pioneering in the West, the explorations of a Columbus or Marco Polo, all were beyond the possibilities of classical mankind.[3]

So the Apollinian culture grew in the process of actualizing its life-symbol of pure bodily presence, and so it died without knowing it through its lack of historical perspective.

THE FAUSTIAN SOUL

Spengler dates the history of the Western culture from the years 900–1000. At that time, the fear of the end of the world, the confused yearning of the Merovingian and Carolingian period, the dark groping of the migrations suddenly coalesced and the Western soul appeared, its essence a striving into the Infinite, a passionate drive to overcome all limit, to lose itself in the quest for the eternal. Its representative for Spengler is the Faustian man, an integer of force, will, and action-at-a-distance, a lonely ego in an endless void, feeling time as an expression of directedness, projecting his determination into all his activities. In almost every respect this emerging culture represents the polar opposite of the Apollinian. The Greek gods dwell on Olympus, "but Valhalla is nowhere. Lost in the limitless, it appears with its inharmonious gods and heroes the supreme symbol of solitude."[4]

---

1. Spengler, *op. cit.*, Vol. II, p. 407.
2. No inner relation to the classical mind.
3. Spengler, *op. cit.*, Vol. I, p. 336.
4. Spengler, *op. cit.*, Vol. I, p. 186.

The Faustian culture, too, made its great refusal. It, too, was faced with the symbols of a civilization inwardly disconnected and ever remote. Though the West took over the Magian religion of Christianity, it remodeled those concepts to fit the dynamic yearning in its soul and replaced the theology of the substantiality of God and His modes, by its passionate assertion of the Father God, Force itself, constant activity, not capable of embodiment in a shape comprehensible by the human mind.[1] Yet the whole longing of the young soul, its feeling of Care, the determination to prevail extending in time both into the past and into the future over many generations, coalesced in its specific creation, the Mother Mary. Her crowning in heaven was one of the earliest motifs of Faustian art. She became the light-figure in blue, the smiling dispenser of grace, finally culminating in the festival among the English Benedictines of the Immaculate Conception, which completed Her disembodiment.

Yet this world of purity, bliss, and happiness involved at the same time the counter-creation of the early Gothic—the realm of the Devil, who throughout Mary's world of infinite understanding was lurking in the background, ever ready to tempt, to lead astray, to destroy the soul. Only the late condition of his culture prevents Western man—according to Spengler—from understanding the terrible fear that then hung over humanity, of stumbling into the abyss. There were witches' sabbaths and black magic, night feasts on mountaintops and charm-formulas.[2] A pitiless, constant war had to be waged against the prince from Hell and his fallen angels. Wretches confessed to witchcraft, sincerely imagining it to be true, and inquisitors with tears in their eyes sentenced them to the pyre, for it was Hell, not death, that humanity feared.[3]

This explains the sense of guilt that permeates all Gothic longing. The cathedrals rose ever more pleadingly towards heaven, the vaulting turned into hands folded in prayer, and little help came to man through the stained-glass windows into the semi-darkness of the naves.[4] Man was a lonely ego, lost in the Infinite, with the powers of darkness all around. "For Magian man the world-cavern had been close and the heaven impending, but for Gothic [Faustian] man heaven was infinitely far." There arose the ever finer

---

1. Spengler, *op. cit.*, Vol. II, p. 288.
2. Spengler, *op. cit.*, Vol. II, p. 279.
3. Spengler, *op. cit.*, Vol. II, p. 290.
4. Spengler, *op. cit.*, Vol. I, p. 290.

differentiation of notions, the desire to lose selfness, the universal cry for the grace that unbinds the will.[1]

To be able to will freely is the highest desire of Faustian transcendence. The sacraments elevated into dogma by the Lateran Council of 1215 mean in their deepest significance the unbinding of the will. The transformation of the meaning of the altar sacrament into an assertion of free being results—the conception of the one who sacrificed himself to insure for his own freedom to will.[2]

The sacrament of Contrition represents the noblest manifestation of the Faustian world longing. Baptism one receives by virtue of one's humanity; contrition is the recognition of the uniqueness of the personality, which alone determines the value of the act. Each man can search only his own conscience. The release and bliss given by this sacrament constitutes one of the profoundest creations of all religious effort, a release from the dark clouds of unresolved doubts that ever remain in the big crisis of life. The insecurity resulting from the decline of this sacrament caused the Mary world of light to fade out. Only the world of the Devil remained.[3] "The concept of the priesthood of all believers is one to which a few strong souls can win through, but only as the part of priesthood that involves duties, not powers, for no man ever confesses to himself with the inward certainty of absolution."[4] So the Faustian yearning for release from its longing, for an expression of its conviction that *"tout comprendre c'est tout pardonner,"* to overcome the inner warfare within its soul, calls on its contemporaries instead of the Infinite as judges and priests. Thus is born the autobiographical art of Rembrandt's self-portraits, of Bach's and, above all, Beethoven's music, each a confession of a tortured soul seeking release. But in this tension, too, the concern with the ego causes a loss of the felt unity of the universe, a symptom of the beginning of the "late" stage of the culture.

Thus arises the Faustian feeling that evaluates the act with reference to the doer not the deed, the psychology that sees forces of willing, feeling, and thinking striving for dominance in a dynamic cosmology.

Faustian art, too, is an embodiment of this yearning for infinity. Though

---

1. Spengler, *op. cit.*, Vol. II, p. 292.
2. Spengler, *op. cit.*, Vol. II, p. 293.
3. Spengler, *op. cit.*, Vol. II, p. 294.
4. Spengler, *op. cit.*, Vol. II, p. 295.

its early manifestation was architectural, stone, with its affirmation of the body, could never serve as the final expression of the Western soul. Michelangelo passionately fought with its limitations, each of his creations a battle frozen in stone. But only the advent of perspective painting began to give release. One stands before a Greek fresco, but one sinks into a Rembrandt painting. The depth experience of the Western culture, which experiences everything as mere centers of gravity in a spatial dynamics, is expressed in the Western perspective, which directs the position of the spectator and pulls him into its space treatment.[1] But the true Western art, which represents the eternal straining of its restless soul, is that of contrapuntal music. This completes the disembodiment of space, expressed in the upsoaring drive, filled the cathedrals in Bach, and burst beyond into space in Mozart, Haydn, and Beethoven. But with Wagner, size is no longer the inward representation of greatness but the dissimulation of its absence,[2] and just as Pergamos, it heralds the end of the great tradition.

Faustian natural science represents a mere mirror of these tendencies. What is felt as God in religious experience becomes the concept of all-pervasive force in physics. Where the Apollinian world-feeling consists of a passionate assertion of the bodiliness of its objects, the Western soul tends towards a denial of all substantiality. Space itself is felt as a force, expressed by Newton as gravity and stated by atomic physics in the form of quanta of energy.[3] Natural science becomes ever more esoteric and abstract, dissolving in its hypothesis all sense experience of phenomenal reality. The infinite space of the universe postulated by astronomy, the endless geological periods are not empirical observations, but a resolve of the soul, that considers the recognition of limits a denial of its existence. It is the spirit that motivated the invention of gunpowder—action-at-a-distance—and discovered independently by the Chinese, whose destiny idea is comparable to the Western, at a contemporary stage of development.

This is the mentality that produces dynasties as the objects of reverence, the embodiment of its feeling of Care, in the political world.[4] Cabinet diplomacy, the determination to master space, the travels of Spanish and Portuguese explorers, the pioneers of the American West, the drive for

---

1. Spengler, *op. cit.*, Vol. I, p. 241 and p. 330.
2. Spengler, *op. cit.*, Vol. I, p. 291.
3. Spengler, *op. cit.*, Vol. I, p. 385.
4. See *post* "Politics, Economics, the Machine."

records of any sort all are emanations of the Faustian will-to-infinity. The immense practicability of the West, that views the whole world as a working hypothesis, and its great symbol, the machine, as a *perpetuum mobile*, represents the assertion of mastery over nature, which appears in metaphysical shape in the Kantian forms *a priori*.

The Faustian will-to-power expresses the inner need of a culture that recognizes toleration only as the non-interference with a field of activity, which ever attempts to impose its views on behalf of mankind. This accounts for the loneliness of Faustian man, of which Lear on the heath, buffeted by man and nature, and Hamlet are the tragic exponents. Where the lament of the hero expresses the essence of the Apollinian dramatic intention, the inner distance of Shakespearean heroes is unbridgeable.

The ethics of the great deed, which in Gothic times was felt as an inner experience in one's fight towards God, is transformed by the plebeian morale of the late culture into a right to work. This is Socialism, which seeks to impose its views on behalf of all and which will soon press its concepts to the ultimate Faustian conclusion—the duty to work.[1] The ethical force of the West contains always the imperative, ever the "Thou shalt."

This, then, is Spengler's representation of the Faustian soul: a boundless drive towards infinity, a will-to-power, a longing of a lonely ego in a boundless space that has lost its bliss with the Reformation, and its God with the Enlightenment. In the years of autumn and approaching decline, its major efforts will lie in the technical field before the advent of mysticism and Caesarism will stifle all intellectual activity. But just because Western man represents a transcendent view of history, he is eminently fit to write its morphology. The classical could not encompass such a view. Its tragedy was the senseless incident. But the culture of Shakespeare, who lifts the incident into a token of destiny, can view manifestations as symbols and can judge them not by their truth, but by their ever-changing trueness, their aptness in the flux of eternal becoming, in which it will be the fate of his culture, too, to die.

PSEUDOMORPHOSIS
"In a rock-stratum are embedded crystals of a mineral. Clefts and cracks occur, water filters in, and the crystals are gradually washed out so that in

---

1. Spengler, *op. cit.*, Vol. I, p. 372. Written in 1918.

due course only their hollow mold remains. Then come volcanic outbursts which explode the mountain; molten masses pour in, stiffen, and crystallize out in their turn. But these are not free to do so in their own special forms. They must fill up the spaces that they find available. Thus there arise distorted forms, crystals whose inner structure contradicts their external shape, stones of one kind presenting the appearance of stones of another kind. The mineralogists call this phenomenon *Pseudomorphosis.*"[1]

Historical pseudomorphosis Spengler defines as the process in which an alien culture hangs so heavily over the birthplace of a young culture that the latter cannot attain its own inner development. Its spirituality is forced into strange forms, which are infused with new meaning, but at the same time serve to stifle the inner drive of the culture's youth. Such cultures can only look on the strange form with all-consuming hatred, spending their latent creativity in half-hearted efforts, ever ready to burst through the fetters in a violent orgy.

Such—for Spengler—was the case of Petrine Russia, which accepted a dynastic form of government in imitation of a culture from which it was inwardly remote. Only the formless power of the early Romanovs could have succeeded in guiding this young soul, which felt the large cities as effervescent illusions and which remained a peasantry longing for the soil no matter how large the cosmopolis. Thus there developed no aristocracy that embodied a destiny, only a senseless aping of alien practices. The intelligentsia grew up as an adjunct to the court, ever bent on discovering problems that were not felt against the background of a peasantry that mixed a hatred for the alien form that was stifling the culture with a disgust with its own overgrowth.[2] Dostoevsky, the peasant, and Tolstoy, the man of Western society, represent this opposition. "The one could never in his soul get away from the land; the other, in spite of his desperate efforts, could never get near it."[3] Tolstoy is the spokesman of Petrinism—even in his denial. His rejection of society is intellectual, his hatred of property based on economics. The very inability to shake off the West leads to his hatred of all existing forms and he therefore becomes the true precursor of Bolshevism. For Bolshevism is merely the rebellion of the lowest stratum of the Petrine society, which has ever talked about Christ but in its heart meant

---

1. Spengler, *op. cit.*, Vol. II, p. 189.
2. Spengler, *op. cit.*, Vol. II, p. 194.
3. Spengler, *op. cit.*, Vol. II, p. 194.

Marx. It represents the final debasing of the metaphysical by the social and becomes thereby a new form of the pseudomorphosis.[1]

Dostoevsky is the true enemy of this upheaval, representing in his soul the future of Russia. All agitation about social reform, all technical schemes for world betterment remain equally meaningless to him. Just as Christ, he would have felt no difference between working for one's own material benefit or the mere social betterment of others. For how can Communism aid the agony of the soul?[2] Thus Dostoevsky embodies the destiny of Russia, the victim now of the last stages of its pseudomorphosis, the forms of which are ever filled with the deep spirituality of the boundless plain and which will be swept away just as its predecessor, without hatred, by the inner logic of the actualizing of the Russian soul.[3]

So it was with the Magian soul which grew up in the forms of the classical after Actium. All the mystic longing of that East, where strange tales of a Messiah were current, which felt the existence of an immanent God, a Yahweh, Ahuramazda, or Marduk-Baal, with the certainty of an apocalyptic fulfillment, had to realize itself in the West in the forms of the classical cult. The Apollinian gods were deities of places, bodies of the sensuously near. Each locality possessed its divinity, to which homage was due. This explains the altar to the unknown gods, which Paul, as a child of the pseudomorphosis, misunderstood in a monotheistic sense. This was designed for gods not known by name whom the foreign sailors at the great seaports worshipped.[4] Thus classical toleration could extend to all sects that made no claim to exclusive validity, and any transgression of these limits resulted in the intermittent persecution of the Stoa in Athens and the Christians in Rome.

This explains, too, the change of world-feeling implied by the universal law of reason of the Stoa and the mystery cults typified by the cult of Mithras. Formerly the god was conceived as adhering to the place of worship, but now a community of any two believers constituted a church. The Spirit of God hovering in the above, ever ready to descend into his elect, is the universal production of this age. Only the incomparable symbolism of

---

1. Spengler, *op. cit.*, Vol. II, p. 195.
2. Spengler, *op. cit.*, Vol. II, p. 217.
3. Attention is drawn to the description by Bedell Smith of Christmas Mass in Moscow.
B. Smith, *My Three Years in Moscow.*
4. Spengler, *op. cit.*, Vol. I, p. 404.

the person of Christ, representing the very essence of the opposition between fact and truth, Time and Space, History and Causality, distinguishes Neo-Platonism, Mithraism, and Christianity. A Magian nation is a consensus of believers. When Constantine recognized Christianity as the official religion, he did not acknowledge a cult but established a new community. But long before, the spirit of the East had permeated Roman institutions, symbolized by the transfer of the capital to Byzantium and the Divus cult, which made the Roman emperors the first caliphs.

Yet the spirit of the West was that of a civilization, cold, and highly conceptualized. The direction of Christianity under the guidance of Paul, who preached in the cities, remained ever aloof from the apocalyptic feeling of the countryside in the East. The attempt of conceptually defining the Logos idea led to the violent secession of the Monophysites and Nestorians. And when Islam appeared, it was greeted as liberator by the spirit which recognized its own inner essence and spread with the rapidity of a soul that was robbed of its youth and feels its time is limited.

THE MAGIAN SOUL

Spengler's symbol for the Magian world-image is a cavern, filled with dim light. In the uneasy tensions of waking-consciousness, the opposition of becoming and being, that the classical conceived as beam and load, and the Faustian felt as force and mass, consists for the Magian of an unsure swaying of substantial realities. Up and down, heaven and earth are substances that contend with one another in a Cosmos revealing the divine. Death is not the end of life but a death substance that struggles with a life substance for the mastery of man.[1] Out of this basic yearning, with man the theater of battles between the powers of darkness and evil, emerges the concept of God the Divine Mediator, who transforms this state from torment into bliss.[2]

Man consists of a soul and body, both different modes of the same substance, deriving their reality and participating in the light only through the infusion of the Divine Pneuma, which serves as the condition for the heroic deeds of a Samson, the holy wrath of Elijah, the enlightenment of Solomon. This infusion of the divine into the bodies of the faithful binds the community of believers into a consensus and makes it at one with the enigmatic

---

1. Spengler, *op. cit.*, Vol. II, p. 237.
2. Spengler, *op. cit.*, Vol. II, p. 236.

power above. Thus man as body and soul belongs to himself alone. But at the same time he contains something else, something higher, an emanation of God, which precludes error but also makes totally meaningless a self-asserting ego. Will and thought are not prime phenomena, but already manifestations of the divine in man.[1]

God is immanent in every manifestation of phenomenal appearance, the one Cause immediately underlying all visible workings. Magian science concerns itself with apprehending the substance which appears in only different modes in actuality, with purging it of its "foreign" element, with alchemy.

Time, too, is cavernlike. The thrusting outward into infinity of the Faustian soul develops into the divine plan for salvation, into the essence of which any inquiry constitutes profanation. The Magian soul first identified the story of the world with the history of man, into inexorable stages of world beginning, world development, and a world catastrophe, which contains the sanction of the moral history of humanity.[2] The operation of the autocratic will precludes not only individual causes and effects, not only obviates the concept of the miraculous, but also denies any necessary relation between sin and punishment, any claim to reward for virtue. Man's reality consists of his participation in the Divine Pneuma, which after its infusion allows only will-less resignation (Islam = resignation) into the mysterious working out of God's plan. Magian man received "Grace ... but does not acquire it."[3] Job is the Magian Faust.

Three emanations of the divine occur: God, the Word of God, the Spirit of God. The consensus of the faithful, imbued with the Spirit of God, is beyond the possibility of deception. "My people," said Mohammed, "can never agree in error."[4] This explains the early church council, which the West, in its re-evaluation of all things Magian, transformed into a political concept for the limitation of a dynamic papacy. The God-as-Word represents the substantial infusion of the divine into the sacred texts. This form of revelation is the rule in the Magian religion. The only change that an unalterable Koran permits is commentary, leading to the development of an exegesis with mystical undermeanings, the Halaka, of which the

---

1. Spengler, *op. cit.*, Vol. II, p. 235.
2. Spengler, *op. cit.*, Vol. II, p. 240.
3. Spengler, *op. cit.*, Vol. II, p. 241.
4. Spengler, *op. cit.*, Vol. II, p. 243.

Gospels in early Christianity and the Talmud of Judaism are examples.[1]

It follows that a separation of church and state is impossible in the Magian culture. The consensus is itself a church, its law in the sacred book the only idea of nationality open to the believers. But also the development of a strong priesthood is precluded. Man stands in direct relation to the divine insofar as he participates in the *pneuma*, and beyond that nothing avails. The true priest of the Magian culture is the hermit, the true bliss of its religion ecstasy when the soul is at one with God and the dark forces of materiality are defeated.

Yet until the coming of Islam, this Magian world had to live under the forms of the classical, which it gradually infused with its own spirituality. The pillars of the temple moved inside the mosque, a cupola replaced the flat roof, giving the impression of space, but a space enclosed in the cave. Into it a window in the roof let the dim light that, reflected from the gold-ground walls, created an atmosphere of fairy-land unreality, the scene for the operation of an omnipotent, ever present God. Such was Saint Sophia and the Pantheon in Rome.[2] This, too, is the world of Spinoza, whose *causa sui* represents the immanent Deity and to whom inner certainty was the only criterion of knowledge, the geometric method representing merely a manifestation of Western pseudomorphosis. It is the world that Christ knew and that Faustian religion can scarcely comprehend. It petrified around 800 and since the Crusades has persisted in the fellah state of unchanging dogmatism and creative impotence.

Spengler's metaphors on the forms of the soul are deeply suggestive, and yet they rest on an intuition striving for absolutes, ever expressing itself in the crassest possible manner. His evocation of the souls of the cultures is of a persuasiveness that makes abstract criticism appear dogmatic. Still, one must ask whether he was not describing tendencies, instead of unchangeable relations. Achilles is hardly a body, placed in a position he did not choose, nor does the *Iliad* assume constancy of personality. Indeed, the very essence of its tragedy consists of the efforts of a man to master fate—to exact conditions from this world—and of the final acceptance of his humanity, his recognition of limits. Polybius, moreover, wrote a philoso-phy of history that compares favorably with many creations of the "histor-

---

1. Spengler, *op. cit.*, Vol. II, p. 245.
2. Spengler, *op. cit.*, Vol. II, p. 229.

ical" Faustian culture, and the scheme of which is very similar to Spengler's concepts of gradual, inevitable degeneration. Spinoza may be a product of the Magian soul, but Friedrich[1] has characterized him with equal persuasiveness as a product of the Calvinist concept of predestination, his *conatus* God's sanction to the "elect."[2] The idea of a consensus represents perhaps an emanation of the Magian soul, but not exclusively so. The history of the law of nature in Western philosophy demonstrates the pervasiveness of his concept; Rousseau's general will reveals its theoretical application to politics.

Thus the eloquence of the soul-image is nevertheless unable to hide the fact that alternative explanations of equal conviction are possible. This does not disprove Spengler's concepts, but it does cast doubt on the inexorability of a development which constitutes a function of these soul-images.

Spengler considers the interrelationship of cultures, except for pseudomorphosis, of only incidental importance. It was an accident that the Spaniards landed in Mexico, but inward necessity that the Maya Empire collapsed, since it already had reached the fellah stage. The adoption of Christianity by the West represents but an incident, a symbol, which was then necessarily infused with the specific Gothic religiosity. Yet such a strict separation seems untenable. It can hardly be maintained that this outpouring of spirituality was not itself influenced by the forms which it used. The superimposition of a ripe dogma, of the universality of law on an essentially primitive community, undoubtedly permeated the later history of what was so significantly called "Holy Roman Empire, German by nation." Spengler himself has shown[3] how the forms of language determine the structure of cognition, the meaninglessness of the equation $S = gt^2$ unless expressed in words. How much more strongly must the transfer of a high legal tradition, a profound philosophy, have affected a nascent culture?

Similarly, the dynamic stage of each culture seems to involve a radiation of its influence, in art, religion, and political form, over neighboring societies, as Eduard Meyer and Toynbee show. Conversely, the border regions are never free from foreign influence, particularly during the periods of decline. The British influence on India has proved of significance regard-

---

1. Friedrich, *Inevitable Peace*, p. 145 *et seq.*
2. For my brief analysis, see *post* Ch. "History and Man's Experience of Morality."
3. Spengler, *op. cit.*, Vol. II, p. 113.

less of the adaptation which parliamentary government may eventually receive. The infusion of new meaning into established forms cannot be equivalent to original creation.

To be sure, at times, Spengler recognizes this. He speaks of the effect of Christianity on a soul already predisposed to reverence. He regrets the shackles put by classical mathematics on Western science until Descartes. He expresses gratification about the fortuitous circumstances that freed Western painting through the loss of almost all the classical fresco art. But what does *fortuitous* mean in such a context? Is it not a recognition of the interrelationship of cultures, an admission of a continuation of certain forms which, moreover, in turn condition their user? Spengler fails to explain just what factor underlies any continuity of ideation or how the selection of symbols is accomplished.

Politics, Economics, the Machine

The metaphysical opposition between becoming and being, the assertion of the ultimate supremacy of Time over Space, form the basis of Spengler's political theory. Just as the development of the culture constitutes an organic growth characterized by the gradual dominance of a waking-consciousness doomed to self-destruction, so politics exhibits an eternal conflict between blood and concept, tradition and dogma. The ageing of the culture is accompanied by the decline of that sureness of political form which signifies a mature organism. Mere interest replaces the earlier subordination to an all-embracing idea, money supplants tradition as the motive force. At each stage, however, the race aspect of life triumphs over its causal representation, first in the victory of economics over abstract political systems and finally in the emergence of the naked power of Caesarism.

Spengler considers politics as the essence of life, manifested in a will for survival, its criterion self-assurance, which allows only the choice between victory and ruin, not between war and peace. He distinguishes two aspects in the destiny side of life, the preserving and the mastering. They are symbolized by the separation of the sexes. The woman is history and represents the life of the race; the man makes history. The woman accepts only with difficulty that other history which takes her sons from her, and the man ever experiences a conflict of duties between the public and the private manifestations of destiny, the sword and the spindle of being,[1] the state or the family emanation of directional Time.

Property, too, as a trait of race, belonging to history and reduced to a concept only with the advent of the cosmopolis, exhibits this duality. It is expressed in the twin attributes of possession: having as power and having as booty. From the feeling of power stems conquest, politics, and law; from that of booty derives trade, spoil, and money. This explains the superiority of money over dogma in the constitutional struggle of the early civilization, but the emergence of money as the dominant form in turn heralds a decline of political vitality.

Spengler argues that all success in history, war, and "in that continuation of war by intellectual means that we call politics"[2] has been the product of unities that found themselves "in form." A being is in form in the same sense as the term is used in sports. When athletes are in form, the ease of their performance hides the difficulty of their acts. A style that has become second nature signifies an art period "in form." A political unit is in condition when its tradition breeds a high average, enabling it to dispense with the great men, whose incidental appearance frequently does more harm than good by the void their death leaves in the flow of events.[3]

The components of a culture attain "form" as a people, which grows to inward greatness only against other peoples. A people is in form as a "state," representing history at rest. Since it belongs to Time, a mere description of constitutional provisions cannot explain the state's essence, the real expressions of which are those conventions and practices of which the constitution is all the more silent for their being taken for granted.

World history for Spengler is state history and not class history. Political leadership belongs always to a small minority possessing the instinct of statesmanship and representing the nation in the struggle of existence.[4] The more naturally the internal arrangements of the state have developed, the surer they adapt themselves to crisis situations. The inner constitution

---

1. Spengler, *op. cit.*, Vol. II, p. 327.
2. Spengler, *op. cit.*, Vol. II, p. 330.
3. Spengler, *op. cit.*, Vol. II, p. 444. See also T. S. Eliot, *Notes Towards the Definition of Culture.*
4. Spengler, *op. cit.*, Vol. II, p. 369.

of a nation must always aim at readiness for the outer fight. This involves the management of internal opposition by the ruling stratum in such a fashion that the energies of the nation do not exhaust themselves in party conflicts and treason not be thought of as a last resort.[1] Foreign policy is the ultimate criterion of domestic fitness.

The private and the public aspects of the destiny idea are symbolized in each culture by a peasantry, which is history, and a society, which makes it and comes to consciousness of itself only against the background of a peasantry. A society organizes itself as estates, of which only two have symbolic significance. Nobility and priesthood constitute Spengler's symbols for the antinomy of becoming and being, Destiny and Causality, Time and Space.[2] The nobility represents the cosmic, the eternal flow of events, the exclusive validity of the deed. Its educational ideal is training (*Zucht*), acquired only by living in an environment, and a customary ethics which bases itself on its self-evident existence, not on its truth.[3]

The priesthood serves as the mediator to the enigmatic and constitutes the symbol of the eternally possible. Its education consists of shaping (*Bildung*), dependent on studies, and a moral of eternal validity. A ripe nobility exhibits finished living, the highly developed priesthood that dignity of bearing which denies mere actuality as unessential. The priesthood is "excluded from history by celibacy and from time by its *character indelebilis*."[4]

The early political organization of feudalism bases itself on the estates, its hierarchy of orders viewing the kind merely as a *primus inter pares*. The ruler possesses subjects only insofar as they owe allegiance to a vassal of his. Private law serves as the bond of union; a customary ethics stresses honor and loyalty. The two sides of property are here united. The Norman conquests, though consequences of a dynamic world-feeling, the outpouring of a soul that felt the Infinite as challenge, were nevertheless managed with prudent calculation typified by the Domesday Book of England and the financial arrangements of Frederick II.

Politics, as in every manifestation of existence, in Spengler's scheme exhibits the gradual dominance of waking-consciousness. The idea emerges that life is not merely to be lived but involves a task as well. The

---

1. Spengler, *op. cit.*, Vol. II, p. 367.
2. For an analysis of this inconsistency see *post* "Conclusions," the outpouring of a soul.
3. Spengler, *op. cit.*, Vol. II, p. 341.
4. Spengler, *op. cit.*, Vol. II, p. 352.

writ that should run through the whole realm expresses the claim of the state, the care of which extends to all and in which the estates represent merely functional parts. This evokes a violent resistance by the old feudal orders, subdued only with the aid of the nascent Third Estate in the First Tyrannis, the time of the Abbasids, or the Fronde. After this victory, the affinity between Estate and State, implicit in the ability of a nobility to live an idea, develops into the dynastic state, which exhibits a purity of form that constitutes the maturity of the culture.[1] Feudal unity is overcome by national, and the fact of rulership elevated into the symbol of sovereignty.[2] The Faustian feeling of Care finds its profound symbol in the dynasty which actualizes the unity of a sequence of generations. It produces cabinet diplomacy of strict rules and masterly conception, the very embodiment of action-at-a-distance, of a will-to-power asserting itself in a planned manipulation of force-relations.

The development of the nation-state is a symptom of the emerging dominance of the cities. The city spirit is practical, valuing objects by their utility, incapable of living a tradition. The unity of the Third Estate results from its opposition to the political dominance of the nobility. The age of conceptual controversy about liberty begins. Freedom for the emancipated understanding of the city is always freedom "from" something, the ever finer subtilizing of what should be an inner experience. In the Baroque, the First Tyrannis political controversy was the manifestation of the pulse of breeding, but the Third Estate constitutes merely a community of waking-consciousness in the educated, whose numina are systems elaborated with an eye to their inner consistency, without regard to their pertinency.

But "the effect of a truth is always quite different from its tendency."[3] Abstract money appears divorced from the value of the land. Its concern with freedom is merely as a tool for achieving political dominance. It does not ask public opinion but attempts to form it. Its interest is not the franchise but electioneering, not the party membership but the party machine. The power and booty outlook separate in the nobility, as do cult and learning in the priesthood. The history of all "late cultures" exhibits a ceaseless struggle of money against law, of intellect against tradition. But money belongs to the world of facts, and intellect to the realm of truths, with the

---

1. For discussion of this inconsistency see "Conclusions."
2. Spengler, *op. cit.*, Vol. II, p. 378.
3. Spengler, *op. cit.*, Vol. II, p. 401.

inevitable consequences. "Intellect rejects, money directs" characterizes the last phase of each culture.[1] The tragic irony of this period resides in the fact that the theorists of freedom are in the final analysis only assisting money to be effective. At the end of this development stands Napoleonism.

Spengler finds in England the laboratory in which both sides of Third Estate politics, the ideal and the real, graduated. Here the Fronde triumphed and so the bourgeoisie could grow up in the strong forms of the First Estate, which disarmed it with its inner superiority[2] and never allowed training to be substituted for breeding in the development of its tradition. Basing its actions on the self-evidence of England's greatness,[3] it substituted the absolutism of class-delegation for the absolutism of the state, which in Britain never attained the symbolism of an inward idea. Its place was taken by "society," as the symbol of the nation being "in form" under the class regime, a word which in the French rationalists became the vehicle for the expression of their hatred of authority. In England, however, authority was well defined. It resided in the Parliament, which, as a creation of the Baroque, embodied the cosmic flow of the culture's maturity and therefore had music in it.[4] The genealogical principle was represented by the upper stratum of society, which divided itself, according to the relative predominance of the power or the booty outlook, into a "respectable" and a "fashionable" party. Though the state's care for all was replaced by a frank assertion of class-interest, the organization of the major parties was such that they represented all effective members of society.[5] The parliamentary style represented the British equivalent of cabinet diplomacy.

On the other hand, there never occurred any confusion of the intellectual concepts and practical politics. "The successful utilization of the bourgeois catchwords in politics presupposes the shrewd eye of a ruling class for the intellectual constitution of the stratum which intends to attain power, but will not be capable of wielding it when attained."[6] Consequently, in England the generation of "free" opinion was most highly developed by the press, and political campaigns as well as Parliament were systematically managed.

1. Spengler, *op. cit.*, Vol. II, p. 402.
2. Spengler, *op. cit.*, Vol. II, p. 444.
3. Spengler, *op. cit.*, Vol. II, p. 392.
4. Spengler, *op. cit.*, Vol. II, p. 403.
5. Spengler, *op. cit.*, Vol. II, p. 392.
6. Spengler, *op. cit.*, Vol. II, p. 403.

It was different on the Continent. There the two sides of liberalism—freedom from the restrictions of soil-bound life; freedom of the intellect for all criticism and of money for any business activity—operated as solvent of all form. There the distrust of authority felt by the Third Estate was so great that it was ready to assure its freedom by means of a dictatorship.[1] This represents the panic felt by any multitude that no longer feels itself "in condition." The waking-consciousness of which has so dominated the Destiny aspect that it is ready to salvage its inner cohesiveness by submission to an authority that would never be tolerated, if legitimate.[2] This is the essence of the second Tyrannis, of Alexander, of Napoleon. The self-evident basis for new creativeness has disappeared, and naked power becomes the criterion for success.

Out of the depths of the megalopolis emerges at this stage, in Rome, in Paris, a formless mass that expresses itself no longer as mere opposition to traditional values, but is the very embodiment of nihilistic power—to which various languages attach equally contemptuous labels: *canaille, Pöbel, mob.* Its influence is out of proportion to its numbers, since it is always present, forcing its way into the forefront of events, overshadowing all political activity by its threat. The bourgeoisie henceforth risks its inner cohesiveness at any moment, because of its smaller effective numbers, the absence of a positive guiding idea, and the inferiority of its determination.[3] The fear of the masses causes a turn by the Third Estate at the beginning of each civilization to a constitutional monarchy, of which the most extreme form is the Republic. Here in the estate-state, the British model could be copied to advantage.

Two inner contradictions ever harassed the nineteenth-century parliamentary state, however: the genealogical principle, of such strength that it saw in the state an embodiment of a dynasty that no longer existed, and the cold intellect that only recognized the perfect form of government. This again symbolized the opposition of Time and Space, becoming and being. While in England the parties were "distinguished by their possession of different but well-tested modes of government," on the Continent the criterion was "according to the direction in which they respectively desired to alter the constitution—namely, towards tradition or theory." In this contest

<hr>

1. Spengler, *op. cit.*, Vol. II, p. 404.
2. Spengler, *op. cit.*, Vol. II, p. 405.
3. Spengler, *op. cit.*, Vol. II, p. 400.

it was forgotten that foreign policy is the ultimate standard of inward fitness.[1] The domestic and diplomatic service developed in opposite directions, and the real victor of the dilemma was abstract money.

This involves the reason for the decay of democracy. The Third Estate attains political effectiveness as a party, to which one adheres because of agreement with its conceptual program, but to which one does not inwardly belong. Only the bourgeoisie is "in form" as a party. The aristocracy, though as a defensive action it may thus constitute itself and its values, does not count, and therefore merely adopts liberal methods as a mode of survival. The Marxists, also forced into bourgeois forms, exhibit a continual conflict between their will, which is of necessity outside constitutionalism and is defined by Spengler as civil war,[2] and its appearance. But the growth of party entails the eventual degeneration into interest groups, the reason for the cohesiveness of the bourgeoisie having disappeared with the elimination of the political eminence of the First Estate. For democracy to work as intended by its theorists requires the almost total absence of interested leadership. Yet a tendency that has once embodied itself in political form not only motivates parties but becomes their tool. "In the beginning the [parties] come into existence for the sake of the program. Then they are held on to defensively by their incumbents for the sake of power and booty … Lastly the program vanishes from memory, and the organization works for its own sake."[3] This Spengler calls Caesarism, the dominance of formless power.

Thus the rights of the people and the influence of the people must be sharply differentiated, according to Spengler. Indeed, the influence of the electorate varies inversely with the degree of universality of the franchise. The people's fundamental right of choosing its own representatives is in practice denied, for every fully developed organization recruits itself.[4] The effective control of politics reverts to the party leadership, the limit of its capabilities determined by the availability of money. For money emerges as the dominating force in the final stages of democracy. Elections require funds, and public opinion must be made amenable by campaigns. In this phase, free formation of public opinion is impossible. The press becomes an independent force manipulating minds by the constant repetition of

1. Spengler, *op. cit.*, Vol. II, p. 414.
2. Spengler, *op. cit.*, Vol. II, p. 461.
3. Spengler, *op. cit.*, Vol. II, p. 452.
4. Spengler, *op. cit.*, Vol. II, p. 456.

party slogans, suppressing hostile or financially ineffective criticism by its conspiracy of silence and forestalling the possible adverse effects of occasional books by reviewing them.[1]

This is magnified by the particular dynamism of Faustian man, who already in Scholasticism achieved a willed unity that allowed no hostile criticism. This state it ever strives for. The dictatorship of the party machines supports itself on the press. Election campaigns become civil wars fought with the ballot. "To preserve the form, even when it contradicts the advantage"[2] forms the theoretical basis of democracy, but this is exactly what the non-estate finds itself incapable of doing. Gradually the feeling grows that the Constitution contains no effective guarantees and the rights that the grandparents died for cease to be meaningful to the descendants. People become tired of the gleaming concepts and turn to the release afforded by the Second Religiousness. The political form-world has been thought to completion, and destiny begins to reassert itself over dogmatic causality. The West has produced no political theorist with an ability to reach the soul since Marx. Democracy then represents not a summit of achievement but an inevitable stage on the road from Napoleonism to that of Caesarism, which for the last time concentrates in itself all that remains of blood, of dynastic feeling, of the idea of the state.

The period of Caesarism is preceded by an age of gigantic conflict, the "Period of Contending States,"[3] lasting from Alexander to Caesar in the classical and beginning with Napoleon in the West. This epoch exhibits in the crassest shape the opposition between the great form and the great individual. The loss of the felt relation to the cosmic beat opens opportunities for private individuals who will have power at any price and who, as embodiments of force, can shape the destiny of a culture. The great tradition, which made genius dispensable, there is replaced by great fact-men, whose accidental appearance can elevate an era into an epoch and whose death can cause the total collapse of all their enterprise.[4] To be sure, the transition period from the culture to the civilization also had its phenomena of pure force—Napoleon or Alexander. But there was always the strong tradition of the Baroque at its back, and the pulse of being had not

---

1. Spengler, *op. cit.*, Vol. II, p. 461.
2. Spengler, *op. cit.*, Vol. II, p. 416.
3. Spengler, *op. cit.*, Vol. II, p. 418.
4. Spengler, *op. cit.*, Vol. II, p. 418.

yet completely died out. The culture had bound up all forces in a strict form. But with the appearance of Napoleonism, they were released—and in time nature broke forth.[1] Cabinet diplomacy had been conducted within definite rules. The wars of the eighteenth century consisted of the maneuvers of small armies under well-understood conditions. But the era preceding Caesarism replaces the absolute state with a battling society of states. This is the dawn of the great individual, beginning in the classical with Hannibal and in the West with the First World War.

Wars become ever more violent and uncompromising. Until the beginning of civilization the technique of war had always been subsidiary to the development of craftsmanship.[2] But now the requirements of continuous war or potential war require the subservience of all mechanical means to instruments of destruction and largely condition technical progress by its assumed fitness for military operations. Universal military service and mass charges dominate battles that would to contemporaries of Frederick the Great have appeared madness.

The ruthlessness of the peace conditions matches the expenditure of force. Starting with Napoleon the conventions of eighteenth-century warfare began to be violated. Only the physical restrictions tend to limit the exploitation of military successes.[3] The Treaty of Versailles deliberately avoided final conditions of peace, enabling the victors to modify their demands with the changing situation.[4]

Imperialism is the inevitable product of civilization, an outward thrust to hide the inner void. After the formlessness of the early conflicts, the most self-assured power emerges as the dominating force. The vacuum created by the collapse of all inner meaning has such strength that it does not matter whether a people wills to assume this role. It is seized and pushed into it. Rome did not conquer its empire; it condensed itself into that form, and despite Scipio's awareness of the dangers, Rome could not escape its destiny. So it will be with the West. The power centers will become ever fewer, the tensions ever greater, the wars more violent. The great foci of power will decide the fate of continents until Caesarism in its political form will supervene and life gradually slip back into biological periods.

---

1. Spengler, *op. cit.*, Vol. II, p. 418.
2. Spengler, *op. cit.*, Vol. II, p. 420.
3. Spengler, *op. cit.*, Vol. II, p. 422.
4. Spengler, *op. cit.*, Vol. II, p. 422.

In the souls of the people arises at this stage a great desire for peace. Every civilization knows the cry for reconciliation and universal understanding. But the logic of the age of Caesarism will not allow it. "The Hague Conference of 1907 was a prelude to the World War; the Washington Conference of 1921 will have been that of others."[1] A civilization does not permit a people to choose its mode of life, judging it by its fitness for the struggle. In this task, whatever remains of old traditions, representing the organic factors, such as the U.S. Constitution, acquires tremendous force and can bring about historical results of great magnitude.[2]

Money at the beginning of this period permeated public life. Economics, the activity which belongs to the spindle side of being, its mere preserving aspects, is the primary mode of thought in the young cosmopolis. Ethics becomes social engineering. "Property is theft" represents the ultra-materialistic conception of thought: "What shall it profit a man if he shall gain the whole world and lose his own soul."[3] But money is merely a form of thought, ordering all activity with reference to itself. Like all problems of the culture, it will reach a state of absolute inner finishedness, no matter how powerful its present manifestations. The dynamic economics of the Faustian culture, symbolized by double-entry bookkeeping, a pure spatial analysis of an economic condition, and in which the true values are production and work, not, as mistakenly[4] assumed, gold,[5] has reached the limit of its inner possibilities. Just as at the time of Diocletian, thinking in terms of money will gradually cease and the force of law, the power aspect of becoming, triumph over the mere acquisitive side.[6]

This, Spengler believes, may be the fate, too, of that prime symbol of the West, the machine. No other culture has constructed its relationship to the macrocosm in such masterful fashion, or achieved such a thoroughgoing revision of its environment. The working hypothesis ever exhibits the Faustian attitude towards the universe. Work and deed are the great ethical concepts of this culture, Kant's categorical imperative a command of activity. But technical knowledge will be of no avail to a soul that has lost its

---

1. Spengler, *op. cit.*, Vol. II, p. 430.
2. Spengler, *op. cit.*, Vol. II, p. 430.
3. Spengler, *op. cit.*, Vol. II, p. 344.
4. Written in 1918.
5. Spengler, *op. cit.*, Vol. II, p. 493.
6. Spengler, *op. cit.*, Vol. II, p. 196.

meaning. If the best young minds of the future will no longer see life's purpose in practical pursuit and withdraw into mysticism, if the succeeding generations become obsessed with the Satanism of their creations, then nothing can stop the decay of this prime symbol, a creation of the intellect and not of pure labor, as Marx supposed.[1]

This will be the stage of pure Caesarism, the formless force, which, whatever its outward trappings, will depend on the personal power of its possessor. The huge citizen militia is replaced by the chief's followings, private armies whose destinies depend on their leaders as in the time of Caesar, Pompey, and Octavian. The real focus of events becomes the megalopolis, in which wars of infinite bloodiness because of their private nature herald the beginning of the final contest for power. The victorious Caesarism will then constitute the last attempt by the powers of the blood, doomed to petrification because the fire in the soul of the civilization has long died out. Its outward manifestations are mere appearance. People's rights take the place of the scepter and crown in constitutional monarchy. They are carefully paraded for the multitudes to hide their total lack of real meaning. With power without tradition as its last manifestation, with waking-consciousness defeated by itself, the civilization turns itself into a fellah state where time is meaningless, and history at an end:

"And so the drama of a high culture—that wondrous world of deities, arts, thoughts, battles, cities—closes with the return of the pristine facts of the blood eternal that is one and the same as the ever-circling cosmic flow. The bright imaginative waking-being submerges itself into the silent service of being, as the Chinese and Roman empires tell us. Time triumphs over Space, and it is Time whose inexorable movement embeds the ephemeral incident of the culture, on this planet, in the incident of man—a form wherein the incident life flows on for a time, while behind it all the streaming horizons of geological and stellar histories pile up in the light-world of our eyes.

"For us, however, whom a Destiny has placed in this culture and at this moment of its development–the moment when money is celebrating its last victories, and the Caesarism that is to succeed approaches with quiet, firm step–our direction, willed and obligatory at once, is set for us within narrow limits, and on any other terms life is not worth the living. We have not

---

1. Spengler, *op. cit.*, Vol. II, p. 344.

the freedom to reach to this or to that, but the freedom to do the necessary
or to do nothing. And a task that historic necessity has set will be accomplished with the individual or against him."[1]

Spengler's metaphysical dilemma permeates his political theory, which
contains many similarities with the Platonic conception of degeneration as
the consequence of a loss of tradition and the dominance of selfishness. The
estates represent the quintessence of creativity embodying breed and training and thereby become the foci of world history. Yet just how is this creativity accomplished? The nobility symbolizes pure becoming, and the
priesthood typifies waking-consciousness. Since the essence of the former
is comprised in living a destiny and that of the latter in confining itself to the
world as eternally possible, expressed by a withdrawal from history, it is
difficult to see what constitutes Spengler's criterion for ascribing equal
symbolic significance to their appearance as estates. If the nobility does
nothing but live a destiny, it cannot be creative. If the priesthood represents
mere waking-consciousness, it does not possess any characteristic symbolism. Again, if religion is a construction of waking-consciousness, one should
expect its early manifestations to be hesitant, unsure of themselves, attaining ever greater mastery of form with the emancipation of the waking-
consciousness in the development of the culture. In fact, exactly the opposite is true in Spengler's scheme. The period of greatest religious creative
force occurs at the beginning of the culture, and Caesarism finds religion,
just as all other problemation, devoid of any symbolic significance.

The nobility as the prime estate appears unable by itself to achieve that
inner purposiveness which Spengler considers the outstanding characteristic of the state. Indeed, the state comes into existence only over its opposition.
If the symbolism of the state finds its expression in an idea which transcends
mere becoming, it seems evident that this idea is a function of waking-
consciousness, not of an immanent Destiny. Moreover, as Spengler points
out, the Magian cultures articulate themselves almost exclusively through
the symbolism of a priesthood, with the nobility playing a subsidiary role.

The conclusion appears again, despite many striking insights, that the
strict separation of becoming and being into a postulate of alternatives has
no standing in reality. Both are merely tendencies, the relative predominance of which characterizes modes of world experience.

---

1. Spengler, *op. cit.*, Vol. II, p. 507.

Purposiveness without an organic framework is meaningless.[1] Pure existence describes an animal state. All creativity requires waking-consciousness, but effective leadership will take into account the unconscious factors of motivation. It must be admitted that in many respects Spengler acknowledges this. In the chapter on mathematics,[2] he explicitly affirms the interrelationship. The confrontation of Pilate and Christ, of profound and compelling beauty, contains a poetic implication not only of the opposition but also the connection of these aspects of life. But ever the temptation to shock and the approach to history as a machine perpetually reproducing new manifestations of power, which man is impotent to influence, gains the upper hand and leads to the elaboration of the opposition between Time and Space, Destiny and Causality, the world-as-history and the world-as-nature.

"Luther was the creation, not of intellectual necessity but of destiny."[3] It would be better to say that destiny embodies itself in intellectual necessity. Political conduct reveals not just an inexorable immanence but a process of becoming consciously evaluated. Luther was consequently more than the creation of historical necessity, but the shaper of a tendency, the inspiration of a dimly felt longing. Life reveals not merely activity, but purposeful activity. Politics is not a simple problem of living the organic immanence, but of recognizing the possibilities of the situation. This recognition, however, constitutes the emanation of a normative framework. Necessity can only serve as a foil for the transcendental experience of freedom,[4] not as a guide to action.

Conclusions

Spengler's philosophy of history reveals all the implications of his metaphysical assumptions. The forms of the great cultures emerge out of the stream of nameless humanity, their whole life an effort to actualize their immanence. The directedness of existence, the experience of destiny, soon come into conflict with waking-consciousness, however. Stifled by a

1. See *post* Ch. "The Sense of Responsibility."
2. Spengler, *op. cit.*, Vol. I, p. 54.
3. Spengler, *op. cit.*, Vol. II, p. 295.
4. See *post* Ch. "History and Man's Experience of Morality," Ch. "The Sense of Responsibility," for full development of this idea.

rationalism that recognizes no mysteries, ideation in the great style ceases. In religion, in politics, in art, formlessness rules a humanity which can find refuge from the tensions in its soul only in mystery cults, in *panem et circenses*, and in silent resignation to political Caesarism. As the cosmic beat gradually decreases, the culture turns itself into a civilization amidst a series of cataclysmic wars. Finally, with waking-consciousness defeated by itself, the powers of the blood reassert themselves, life reverts to the fellah state of creative impotence, the civilization petrifies and dies.

Despite the poetic imaginativeness of this philosophy and its many startlingly accurate predictions, our analysis has revealed serious difficulties. The opposition between waking-consciousness and becoming, between Time and Space, History and Causality, expresses, but does not resolve, the dilemma of the experience of freedom in a determined environment. Spengler believes that history reveals an inexorable destiny, its triumphs the consequence of an almost unconscious participation in the process of becoming. But much of his data disproves these contentions. If each culture constructs its own image of the world and spends its existence in an attempt to actualize it, then the biological sequence of generations attains symbolism only through an inward experience. But since experiences are unique and necessity can govern only the general, we find that the specificity of each culture is a function of freedom, not a blindly working organic immanence. Destiny requires waking-consciousness to actualize its possibilities.

On the other hand, if the life of each culture represents an effort to actualize its prime symbol, one would expect the historical development of the culture to vary as much as its symbolism. Spengler, however, has postulated an identical political institutionalization at comparable stages of existence. This leads to the conclusion that the cultures may not be represented as self-contained organisms, as Spengler suggests. The very possibility of making an analysis of another culture's soul indicates, moreover, a degree of inner relationship, compounded by the fact that Spengler seriously examines only the Faustian, Apollinian, and Magian cultures.[1]

Spengler's denial of the interrelationship of cultures and their inability to ever understand each other's symbols is thus refuted by his approach. If the symbols of another culture must always remain inwardly remote, it is difficult to see what governs the continuation of any ideation. If, however,

---

1. For more complete analysis see *ante* discussion at end of previous section.

most cultures begin by taking over foreign symbols, then it can hardly be asserted that these forms did not condition their users. Though Christianity may have been adapted to fit the needs of the Faustian soul, the whole history of the West was permeated by the particular spirituality of this well-organized institution, with its heritage of the Greco-Roman tradition. The infusion of new meaning into old forms involves a different process than spontaneous creativity.

Spengler's political theory contains similar inconsistencies. It proved impossible to reconcile the metaphysical postulate of alternative modes of behavior with a political symbolism expressed in estates. The nobility as the representative of an inexorable destiny appears to have no scope for creativity, and the priesthood, as the exponent of pure waking-consciousness, lacks symbolism.[1] Spengler's difficulty derives from the resolution of tendencies whose relative predominance characterizes modes of world experience into incompatible alternatives. He forgot that the world-as-history and the world-as-nature are merely symbolic representations of possible apprehensions of reality, not objective attributes of existence. History and Causality represent types of analysis concerned respectively with noumenal and phenomenal occurrences.[2] This does not prove their opposition, however. It merely indicates levels of meaning for events which can be understood only as a unity, as Destiny purposively evaluated, as history consciously lived.

Purely analytical criticism of Spengler will, however, never discover the profounder levels of his philosophy.[3] These reside in his evocation of those elements of life that will ever be the subject of an inner experience, in his intuition of a mystic relationship to the Infinite that expresses personality. Spengler's vision encompassed an approach to history which—whatever our opinion of his conclusions—transcended the mere causal analysis of

---

1. These arguments are presented at considerably greater length at the ends of the respective chapters.

2. See *post* Ch. "History and Man's Experience of Morality" for complete analysis.

3. In any philosophical discussion one must sharply distinguish the philosophical assumptions from their argument. A refutation of the latter may merely mean that the metaphysical postulates are capable of stronger supporting formulation. Logic can aid in evaluating internal consistency and relevance but is no test for the metaphysical assumptions, which can be analyzed only by utilizing another set of assumptions, not an objective standard of validity. It is possible, therefore, to offer different explanations for all of Spengler's symbols of soul-images without refuting the concept of the soul of a creature. (See Appendix, "The Concepts of Meaning.")

data and the shallow dogmatism of many progress theories. No discussion of internal structure can invalidate the force of Spengler's description of Christ's journey to Jerusalem or the dramatic quality of the exposition of the dilemma in Michelangelo's soul. After all has been said, the conviction remains that Spengler has found a poetry in life which rises above the barren systematization of its manifestations.

To be sure, such an approach presents dangers. The latent anti-intellectualism may well lead to a cult of sheer power, of which recent history has seen many examples. But the fact that certain arguments, if pressed to an extremity, involve unacceptable consequences does not necessarily disprove their validity. It indicates rather that in the ultimate problems of life, man must find the sanction for his conduct within himself, not in technical solutions. Every event is not merely an effect but also an experience. As an effect it is subject to causal determination; as an experience it contains the meaning of freedom and the essence of personality. This accounts for the unsatisfactoriness of ethical systems such as Northrop's, who conceives values as approachable by mere methodology. It was not, after all, Spinoza's geometrical method that led to his ethical concepts, but his inner attitude which *a priori* directed the method.

It was Spengler's merit that he understood this, as well as the underlying unity of all manifestations of human endeavor, though his poetic imagination caused him to overvalue the realm of necessity and underestimate the purposive element.[1] Perhaps the most serious criticism to be made against Spengler consists of his uneasy swaying between the world-as-experience, which is the only approach to an apprehension of purposiveness, and his vision of it as mere repetition of power phenomena. He constantly stresses the uniqueness of experience and yet finds in history no more than the generality of phenomena. The totality of man's longing cannot, however, achieve a sanction through a mere cataloguing of appearances, but must attain meaning through the specific in man's experiences. Spengler attempts to resolve these difficulties by his emphasis on the historical

---

1. Dante has illustrated, in perhaps the only way possible, the interdependence of reason and inner experience, causality and grace. On the climb to the top of Mount Purgatory, he has absorbed the essence of human wisdom. Henceforth only an inner experience can conduct him. When Beatrice appears, he turns for guidance to Virgil, but reason is here powerless. Just as Plato's Idea of the Good, just as Kant's experience of freedom, the final attainment of human transcendence is a matter of inner illumination, not technical manipulation. See *post* for full development of this idea: Ch. "The Sense of Responsibility."

rather than the moral aspects of existence.[1] He is ever concerned with an evaluation of the elements of success, which really represents a manifestation of a will-to-system from a pragmatic rather than an ethical point of view. This emphasis on success leads to that strict separation of History and Causality, of which the person of Christ constitutes not a proof but a contradiction. But no truth is without its historical tendency, and every effective conduct implies some normative element.

What else is the meaning of Canossa, where not even dire political necessity availed to turn away a supplicant supported by dogma, but who was reduced to that position, at least in part, by the very strength of the moral sanction of the church?

On the other hand, Spengler's attempted pragmatism makes the charge of pessimism largely inapplicable. Pessimism in the ethical sense implies the existence of standards.[2] Spengler, however, makes no more claim to embodying moral principles in his analysis of politics than Machiavelli. On the contrary, again like Machiavelli, one can easily detect a preference for the lived metaphysics of an earlier time, when longing and life embodied itself in more virile forms. Spengler conceives himself in the role of a physician, who, by informing a patient of the incurability of cancer, does not advocate it as a way of life.

To be sure, an acceptance of his conclusions and the recognition of the transitoriness of existence may well lead to a kismetic resignation or a complex unconcern with anything except material conditions of success. But this is only one tendency implicit in Spengler. Its acceptance constitutes the revelation of a personality rather than an invalidation of Spengler's position. No necessary connection exists between permanence of existence and moral conduct in the historical realm, any more than in private life. Ethics cannot be derived from a purposiveness of the universe revealed in phenomenal appearances. That certainty of action is not given to man. On the other hand, the recognition of limits, that one is man and

---

1. See footnote Spengler, *op. cit.,* Vol. II, p. 216. "The method of the present work is historical. It therefore recognizes the anti-historical as well as the historical as a *fact.* The religious method, on the contrary, necessarily looks upon itself as the *true* and the opposite as *false.* The difference is quite insuperable."

2. The problem might be raised whether pessimism is not the condition for ethical progress. Certainly the assumption that this is the best of all possible worlds does not lend itself to an attitude of purposive morality.

not God, may in nations, as in individuals, serve as the basis for ethical criteria and the concept of the moral personality of man.[1]

Spengler states at one point that the West is composed of Kantians who do not know how Kantian they are. It is certain that he, too, has followed Kant's position to its ultimate conclusion. All phenomenal appearance requires for its cognition not only forms imposed by the human mind, but those very forms are functions of particular cultures. They do not exhaust themselves in establishing patterns of phenomenal knowledge, but include all manifestations of human activity, including those noumena specifically excepted by Kant: our knowledge of God, freedom, immortality, and morality.

If Kant conditioned all subsequent metaphysics, it is certain that Hegel is immanent in most of the philosophy of history, no matter how passionate the denial. His concept of history as the manifestation of the idea in Time and nature as the representation of the spirit in Space[2] was adopted by Spengler with but minor modifications. The destiny that is our experience of history differs neither in its inward necessity nor in anything more essential than formulation from the self-realization of the Spirit. For Hegel's rationality was not, after all, Kant's pure reason but had as its ultimate criterion actuality.

Darwin, too, be he ever so derided, is implicit in much of Spengler. The theory of evolution may well be no more than a working hypothesis, particularly adapted to the mentality of nineteenth-century England and logically replaceable by a catastrophe concept. Nevertheless, its primary test of physical survival is repeated by Spengler as the criterion of fitness in his world-as-history.[3]

Scholarly criticism of Spengler has been sporadic and frequently beside the point. Sabine's brief summary is a tirade and not an analysis.[4]

---

1. See *post* Ch. "History and Man's Experience of Morality," Ch. "The Sense of Responsibility," for full development.

2. Hegel, *The Philosophy of History*, p. 72.

3. Spengler's striking counterpart is Vico's philosophy of history, which, however, is never mentioned in *The Decline of the West*. Vico, too, saw in history a cyclical recurrence of civilizations, their growth exhibiting discrete phases of activity. The occult wisdom of the early stage bases itself on a religious experience. But as the mystery of life disappears, reason becomes dominant. The philosophical wisdom of the culture's maturity expresses the claims of a rationality fully conscious of its power. No stage of development can be maintained, however. The necessary realization of a culture's immanence follows an inevitable pattern. Vico is thus the modern precursor of a systematic cyclical theory of history.

4. Sabine, *A History of Political Theory*, p. 705.

V. S. Yarros confines himself to characterizing Spengler as the apostle of the new pessimism, citing in opposition the "progress" achieved in social legislation and political liberty by Western man.[1] The article suffers from having been written on the eve of the most demoniac outburst of the "progressive" West.

The most profound analysis is probably that of Eduard Meyer,[2] who, though accepting many of Spengler's conclusions, opposes to the concept of the organic culture of definite extents and fixed duration that of overlapping culture circles, whose capability of absorbing alien influences as well as their possibility of different development is manifold and whose decline is a result, not a cause, of excessive involvement in imperialistic ventures.[3] Thus a purposive element of choice is imported into Spengler's development, its fatedness the result, at least in part, of human volition.[4]

Is Spengler a determinist? This question is not as absurd as might appear from a cursory reading of his philosophy. Determinism is, after all, a flexible concept. Freedom can never mean unlimited choice, nor determinism plantlike dependence. Any manifestation of the problems of Necessity and Freedom constitutes a question of the relative weight of tendencies rather than a crass assertion of incompatibles. Spengler took this into account, though his enthusiasm leads to a formulation that seems to negate his theoretical awareness. Incident and Destiny are the differentiae which represent the opposition. The historical direction which is fixed and unalterable, inescapable as a death, constitutes Destiny. Its embodiment in actuality, however, depends on Incident.[5] It was an incident that Columbus discovered America as the agent of the Spanish rather than the French throne and that thereby the style of politics of the next centuries was set by Madrid instead of Paris. But it was a destiny that the late period of the West should accomplish itself through absolutism to a revolution. That this revolution occurred in France was an incident, but it was a destiny that Napoleonism should accompany the turn of the culture into a civilization. There are personal incidents when a great man such as Napoleon concentrates the whole meaning of an epoch in himself and thereby accomplishes in a few

---

1. *Open Court*, Vol. 47: 253, June 8, 1933.

2. Schroeter, *Der Streit um Spengler*, presents primarily an analysis of conflicting points of view.

3. Meyer, *Oswald Spengler's Untergang des Abendlandes*.

4. Though, of course, it can be argued that this volition is itself a function of destiny.

5. Spengler, *op. cit.*, Vol. I, p. 139 *et seq.*

years what, under the impersonal incident of an epoch, it took the classical decades to achieve.[1] The inner logic of events is fixed, the general tendencies of the development determined, but its incidental appearance is the result of the self-assurance and the work of people who can live a destiny rather than suffer for it.[2]

This leads to the dilemma inherent in all philosophy of history that stresses the organic aspect as a postulate of action: the connection between the necessary and the possible. It is a problem which Kant, too, considered and failed to solve completely. In order to establish the validity of his categorical imperative as a foundation of eternal peace, Kant was forced to demonstrate the possibility of its application. But his proof of feasibility became a dictum of necessity and seems to negate the moral basis of the categorical imperative.[3]

Similarly, Spengler concluded by posing the alternatives of doing the necessary or doing nothing. Yet this is the description of a psychological state rather than a guide to action. Just as the pleasure principle in psychology, it ascribes a definitional motivation to past action but is totally useless as a standard for the prediction of future events.[4] Man may ever desire to do the necessary or pleasurable, if in varying fields of activity, and though the emphasis may be on either the moral or material aspect of life. However, not the postulate of necessity but the content ascribed to it constitutes the real criterion for motivated activity. Spengler's only standard for a

---

1. Spengler, *op. cit.*, Vol. I, p. 149.

2. This refutes the argument that Spengler's later work *The Hour of Decision* represents a logical inconsistency. He merely describes in that book the possible lines of actions open to the Western culture in its present stage of development.

3. See *post* Ch. "History and Man's Experience of Morality."

4. The difficulty of the pleasure principle derives from the hedonistic implications of the word in everyday language. For what is really meant by the pleasure principle? The psychologist counters arguments that most persons are incapable of striking a rational balance between various possible sources of satisfaction with an assertion of the unconscious factor of motivation. Since it is a fact that many persons commit acts which are actually painful, the psychologist finds refuge in a balance of greater and lesser pain. But what he is really saying is that every action must have a preponderance of motives for its performance, and he is thus describing motivated activity—if not merely activity—not pleasure. Of course, a scientist has a perfect right to adopt any definition suitable (see Appendix) provided that he stays within the conventional meaning of his terms. Moreover the equating of pleasure and motive is really no help at all, for it merely shifts the main problem from a definition of motive to a definition of pleasure. It is never clear whether actions result from pleasure or whether pleasure is that from which actions result, and in the final analysis both conceptions must be used. The same argument holds for the "necessary concept."

necessary action is its success. Apart from the fact that this represents no aid whatever in the really crucial personal or political decisions—for what makes them problematical is the existence of difficult alternatives—he offers no standard for what he means by success. Christ died on the Cross, and His mission to Jerusalem was a miserable momentary failure. Was his action therefore historically unnecessary? Hus was burned in Constance, and Luther split the church. Whose action embodied necessity? Was Luther possible without Hus? Someday, Protestant Christianity may disappear from the face of the earth. Will that reduce Luther to a meaningless incident? Moreover, since history is itself a function of the soul-image of a culture and its awareness a result of its symbolism, it appears that Destiny and Incident, necessary and accidental, are merely transitory manifestations of a particular depth experience and not applicable as a guide to activity.

Two misconceptions seem to be involved in the problem of necessity as a sanction of conduct: a confusion of the doer and the action, and of the intent with the tendency. No activity can in retrospect be proved to have resulted from free will—the fact of action indicating a preponderance of factors on one side. In this view all actions are determined. On the other hand, only deeds embodying the logic of history are necessary. How can one reconcile this dilemma?

The intent and the tendency of historical figures are radically different, as Spengler frequently points out. Of what use then is a rule to do the necessary? Wherein lies the mystery of results totally incommensurable with intention and yet dependent for their appearance on such willed activity?

The greater the interval between the event and the analysis, the more determined does the act appear, as Tolstoy already emphasized.[1] With the passage of time, all the manifold possibilities that accompanied performance are forgotten and only the action remains, a testimony to its irrevocability. Man, despite Hume, can never imagine anything totally out of his frame of reference, and the detailed historical development that might have ensued if, for example Richelieu had not interfered in the Thirty Years' War is beyond the scope of even the most poetic historian.

Undoubtedly, the frustrated soul of a suddenly traditionless Germany in the 1920s cried out for something to hold on to. But none of Hitler's lieutenants, as evidence abundantly shows, could have unleashed the demoniac

---

1. Tolstoy, *War and Peace*, Epilogue.

forces that were eventually produced by the *Führer.* Yet Hitler's fate hung on a thread many times. Ever some little incident saved him; always in the minds of the chief actors there existed meaningful alternatives.[1] Whatever our view of the necessity of these events today, the key question is in how far necessity could have served either as a guide to action or for the prediction of events in 1933. Similarly, Spengler's analysis of the British political development contains many challenging observations. He has not explained, however, why it was the Fronde and not the state which triumphed in the seventeenth century.

This demonstrates the essential characteristic of historical necessity. No matter what we may think of its compelling quality, it ever appears to man in the guise of freedom. There always seem to exist alternatives, between which one can choose, and without such alternatives life would be unthinkable. This is perhaps the profoundest meaning of the union of the categorical imperative with historical necessity in Kant.[2] Necessity as a guide to action is useless, even for a pragmatist. The number of historical figures who died believing themselves to have failed, and yet represented the future of their culture, is legion, as is the number of those whose pinnacle of temporary success merely served to hide the historical hollowness of their position.

The question of conceptual historical necessity can be safely left unsettled, then, for it is prejudged by our experience of freedom. Freedom is not a definitional quantity, but an inner experience of life as a process of deciding meaningful alternatives. This, it must be repeated, does not mean unlimited choice. Everybody is a product of an age, a nation, and environment. But, beyond that, he constitutes what is essentially unapproachable by analysis, the form of the form, the creative essence of history, the moral personality. However we may explain actions in retrospect, their accomplishment occurred with the inner conviction of choice.

This is not to say that Spengler's view of the development of the culture, through youth, maturity, to decline and death, is without merit. To life belongs death, in history as in individuals. No culture has yet been permanent, no striving completely fulfilled. It is not given to man to choose his age, or to the statesman the condition of his time. But the form taken

---

1. See Gisevius, *To the Bitter End*, Vol. II, Ch. 1.

2. This, however, cannot serve as the ultimate reconciliation of this inconsistency in Kant. See *post* Ch. "History and Man's Experience of Morality."

by the particular period, the meaning given to life, is the task of each generation. Man can find the sanction for his actions only within himself, not in the discovery of purposes in phenomena.[1] It is a responsibility correctly seen by Kant as a duty, since even inactivity postulates an absolute norm.[2]

And so we come to the final problem in Spengler, that of youth and age. Can one ascribe organic periods to cultures? In how far is the analogy to organic experience valid? It seems certain that to man the problem of age is closely tied to a physiological state. After a certain period of life, the knowledge of a limit becomes ever more definite, the inexorability of development in the light of one's past inevitable. The knowledge of the transitoriness of existence is responsible for much consistency in action, and gives rise to the tragedy of the man who must live out an essentially meaningless belief, only to give content to his past. This is the drama of Rubashov in *Darkness at Noon*, and of Ivan Karamazov, who confesses not indeed because he committed the murder, but because the crime was implicit in his previous life, which could acquire meaning only through this sacrifice.

Yet age is not exclusively a physiological state. Life exhibits an eternal recurrence of problems, the settlement of each conditioning and weakening the ability to respond to others.

It is a dilemma in which abstract argument cannot go much further.[3] The physiological analogy is not tenable with cultures, yet the existence of civilizations may be conceived as a succession of dilemmas. Toynbee correctly analyzed the Challenge-and-Response element, but turned it into a mechanistic method for material salvation. It appears that the solution of each problem takes away something of the ability to experience its inner meaning, gradually lessening the intensity of the response. The League of Nations was a dream, the United Nations is merely a technical clearinghouse, perhaps therefore of longer duration as its inner idea is dissipated. Ageing in a culture may well be the gradual solution of the problems immanent in its existence, their death a form of disenchant-

---

1. On this point see also Schweitzer, *The Philosophy of Civilization*, p. 271 *et seq.*
2. For full discussion of these generalities see *post* Ch. "The Sense of Responsibility."
3. See *post* Ch. "The Sense of Responsibility" for limitation of a theory of action, which attempts to derive its attainability from phenomenal reality.

ment.[1] Abstract argument can give no aid, because the fact of existence forces a position towards life regardless of the state of the culture in which one lives and because the very certainty of transitoriness can enable man to give a meaning to his existence.

All the cultures Spengler treats have disintegrated. It is of no avail to charge pessimism. Immortality cannot be achieved by postulate. But behind the physical decay that seems the lot of everything existing emerges a level of meaning which embodies a type of attainable permanence. In its death each culture bequeathed forms to the successor which, whatever Spengler's assertion, were the condition precedent to all subsequent problemation and the foundation of future greatness.

Mommsen has stated it well: "We are faced with the end of the Roman Republic. For half a millennium we observed her ruling the countries of the Mediterranean. We have seen her collapse in politics, in morals, in religion, and in literature, not through the violence of external events, but through a gradual inward decay. The world which Caesar found contained much of the noble heritage of past centuries and an infinite abundance of pomp and glory, but little spirit, still less taste. Above all, the joy had gone out of life. It was indeed an old world; not to be made young again even by the genius of Caesar's patriotism. The serenity of the dawn cannot return until darkness has set in and night has reigned supreme. But nevertheless he brought to the sorely harassed peoples on the Mediterranean a tolerable evening after the sultry noon. And when in good time, after a long historical night, the day of new peoples dawned again and young nations in free self-fulfillment began to move towards new and higher goals, there were among them quite a few in which the seed strewn by Caesar had borne fruit and which owed him, as they still do, the distinctive character of their nationality."[2]

Perhaps this is the only immortality a culture has a right to require.

Thus Spengler's philosophy of history, with its challenging intuitions and broad vistas, represents an attempt at the resolution of the enigmas of existence. He clearly realized the necessity of an explicit metaphysical foundation for the apprehension of History as Intuition.

Though his philosophical assumptions do not always stand up under

1. See *post* Ch. "The Sense of Responsibility" for development of this concept.
2. Theodor Mommsen, *The History of Rome*, Vol. VI, p. 614. (German edition, Verlag der Weidmannschen Buchhandlung). My translation.

analytical criticism, and though alternative interpretations can be offered for some of his data, Spengler's poetic imagination pointed the way towards insights of profound and compelling beauty. The world-as-experience represents a construction which takes full cognizance of the organic factors of existence. There is considerable merit in his articulation of the two possible modes of cognition and existence, Destiny and Causality, Time and Space. The interdependence of religion and natural science constitutes a poetic vision of great depth. However, Destiny cannot merely consist of vegetation, and all activity implies purposes. No mere assertion of necessity can relieve a culture from the responsibility of giving its own meaning to its own existence.[1] Whatever the tragedy of life, its content constitutes the creation of an individual soul; the reaction to its immanence contains the essence of personality.

Spengler thought that he had resolved this problem by a postulation of alternatives. But at each aspect of his philosophical exposition, this dilemma has accounted for a lack of consistency and his inability to account for a wide range of phenomena. It is strange that a Transcendentalist should have found no deeper meaning in history than its mere manifestations.

And so the poetic beauty of Spengler's psychology presents a challenge for other minds and new approaches. The dilemma of the relation of Necessity and Freedom remains, to guide our quest for the meaning of history, the purpose of life.

---

1. See *post* Ch. "The Sense of Responsibility." Also Appendix, "The Concepts of Meaning."

CHAPTER III

HISTORY AS AN
EMPIRICAL SCIENCE:
TOYNBEE

Introduction

Toynbee attempted to transcend Spengler's metaphysical limitations by an assertion of purposiveness. He argued that history did not reveal an organic process, continuously and inevitably reproducing new manifestations of power, but a willed development of responsive growth, its fatality a testimony to man's failure, not to a tragedy of unavoidable death.

History, in Toynbee's scheme, exhibits a constant alternation of dynamic creativity and static torpor. The embodiments of activity are civilizations, beings of "the highest order and self-contained,"[1] which alone constitute "intelligible fields of study."[2] They do not represent organic entities with determined life spans, but merely a relation, the common field of action of their component political communities. Their life presents a succession of problems, each a challenge to undergo an ordeal. If the successful response creates an overbalance, which in turn presents itself as a challenge, then the civilization grows through a dynamic rhythm of continuous problemation.

This is accomplished under the guidance of a minority which leads the uncreative majority by mimesis, a social drill, and the charm of its inspiration. Yet creativity contains its own nemesis in an idolatry of past successes, and mimesis is doomed to break down because of its mechanicalness. The creative minority, sensing the rift in society, turns itself into a dominant minority and rules by force. The uncreative majority and the barbarians beyond the borders secede, forming the internal and external proletariat. The rift in the body social parallels a schism in the soul, from the tensions of which a universal state appears the immediate solution. But an

---

1. Toynbee, *A Study of History*, Vol. VI, p. 45.
2. Toynbee, *op. cit.*, Vol. I, p. 57.

unsuccessful series of responses has doomed the civilization. Its inner meaning is, however, salvaged by the higher religion which the internal proletariat creates on the ruins of the collapsing universal state. After a violent interregnum, the universal church becomes the chrysalis from which a new society may spring by the process of apparentation-and-affiliation.

The approach of the study, which bases itself on the "well-beloved method of making an empirical survey,"[1] leads Toynbee into inner contradictions. An empiricist will always be faced with the validation of those normative concepts for which history offers no necessary proof, and phenomena no universal rule.[2] The formulation of historical laws implies a conception of necessity, not to be evaded by a mere postulation of purposiveness. Against a background of twenty-one civilizations that either have collapsed or exhibit all the symptoms of decay, Challenge-and-Response, with its accompanying doctrines of Withdrawal-and-Return, becomes not a negation of inevitability, but its mechanistic description. Moreover, an empirical survey has a tendency to consider mere surface phenomena as equivalent, since the inner interpretative meaning must constitute a metaphysical resolution.[3]

Toynbee compounds this by imposing a normative pattern on a comparative study of civilizations, all of which are conceived as philosophically contemporary and functionally equivalent. A Platonic identification of political action with appropriate types of souls results, and an affirmation of a supra-mundane plane of history that embodies the true fulfillment of existence.

It will be our task to analyze the validity of an attempt at finding solutions to problems of inner experience in the causal manifestations of life. We must determine the degree of reality that can be ascribed to analogies from mythology or the New Testament. This will bring us face-to-face with our basic enigma: Does history or life exhibit a master plan the understanding of which offers a key to the dilemmas in our souls, or does the solution reside in an inner reconciliation? Must we look outside or inside ourselves for a motive force to apprehend the essence of history as a guide to action? Can a metaphysical pattern be utilized in a study that professes to find its proof in the first instance in empirical data?

---

1. Toynbee, *op. cit.*, Vol. IV, p. 261.
2. As Kant shows.
3. See *post* Appendix, "The Concepts of Meaning."

Metaphysics [1]

Every philosophy of history must sooner or later face the problem of what constitutes the motive force of directed life. Spengler had opted for an organic immanence that ruled all happenings. Toynbee could not face the dilemma in this form. He argued that life presented a series of challenges, the response to which revealed a personality and whose solution was therefore unpredictable. Yet this assertion of freedom clashed with his empirical data that indicated almost certain decay for each civilization.

Toynbee tried to solve this difficulty by considering history as the realization of a divine plan, in which "the seeds which the sower sows are separate seeds; and every grain has its own different destiny ... Yet the seeds are all of one kind, and they are all sown by one sower in the hope of obtaining one harvest." [2] Growth and decay merely hide an underlying unity through which God reveals Himself to mankind. Life presents an alternation of activity and decay, of Integration and Differentiation. While events seem superficially recurrent, history actually operates in the fashion of a wheel, the circular motion of which serves as the condition for progress. [3]

The disintegration of civilization merely exhibits the condition for a higher experience, for the vision of the supra-mundane reality which is of and beyond this world, the City of God, which emerges out of the ashes of the human City of Destruction. [4]

This is the concept of Transfiguration, which transforms the events of this world into incidental appearances in a divine scheme, and which considers true peace that inner state of blessedness which comes with the recognition of limits. Yet how can God's realm be in this world and not be of it? What is the relation of God's immanence to His transcendence? [5]

---

1. Toynbee's metaphysical doctrine is nowhere explicitly stated. In order to give it the most complete presentation, I have utilized Dante's philosophy, which seems closest to the implied concept of Toynbee, and applied it to the concept of Transfiguration, which is the key of Toynbee's cosmology.

2. Toynbee, *op. cit.*, Vol. III, p. 390.

3. Toynbee, *op. cit.*, Vol. IV, p. 34.

4. Toynbee, *op. cit.*, Vol. VI, p. 167.

5. Toynbee answers the problem with two similes, one geometrical, on the nature of the relation of a square to the side of a plane of a cube, the other geographical, based on a temporal superimposition of successive layers of settlements on the same site. Neither is completely satisfactory. The geometrical simile merely proves the feasibility of constructing such a relation,

Dante has poetically resolved the philosophical problems raised by Toynbee.[1] Man participates in a divine plan and, insofar as he is God's creature, is incapable of greater perfection. The cognition of the First Intelligence (self-evidence of certain axioms) and the affection for the first objects of desire (the pure love of God) express the divine imprint. But man is also fallen from Eden. He has tasted the fruit of good and evil, a sin both because of its timing and the overstepping of limits. Man's fall has been so deep, the corruption of his nature so extensive, that unaided he would be totally incapable of transcending his fallen state. Humanity attains the possibility of grace only through the majesty of Christ's sacrifice. Its existence reveals an unceasing struggle for the self-realization of a will corrupted by desire. Reason, "the virtue that counsels,"[2] constitutes the agency by which the will is determined into its proper direction.

The potentiality to love God expresses man's true essence; the misdirection of this feeling contains the fatedness of existence. Inward blessedness exhibits the reflection of God's love and that of all true believers and serves as the condition for immortality. Yet this love cannot achieve the full implications of its immanence in the mundane sphere or by merely rational conditions. Only Paradise sees the complete union of will, desire, and reason. There everything coalesces in the all-embracing love of God. This is the true meaning of Piccarda Donati,[3] whose symbolic appearance in the moon expresses both Volition and Necessity and to whom Dante's rational query regarding the justice of degrees of bliss appears essentially meaningless. That, too, is the import of the ability, peculiar to the blessed, of reading each other's thoughts. In Paradise, indeed, the "virtue that counsels" has become superfluous, at least in its directing connotations. Knowledge is now instantaneous, belief no longer subject to either buttressing or argument. Everything merges in a total unity brought about by the radiance of an all-illuminating grace.

This exhibits the assumptions of Toynbee's metaphysical doctrine, which suffers from an overly utilitarian argumentation and a lack of explicit

not its existence. The geographical analogy illustrates the truism that every physical object is part of a larger whole. Toynbee, *op. cit.*, Vol. VI, pp. 159–62.

1. It must be repeated that this represents my construction of the spirit of Toynbee's metaphysics.

2. Dante, *Purgatorio*, Canto 18.

3. Dante, *Paradiso*, Canto 3.

formulation. God's love, identical with that of man's love for Him, expressed in the feeling of brotherhood, constitutes the condition for the experience of Transfiguration, the connecting link between mundane and supra-mundane reality.[1] The conception of transcendence is given symbolic expression by Christianity in God, the Father, the aspect of immanence in God, the Holy Ghost. Christ, the Son of God, who sacrificed Himself to attain blessedness for His own, represents the connecting link to the human heart, however great the logical difficulty reason finds in the Trinity.[2]

His metaphysics enable Toynbee to impose a normative pattern on historical events. He validates the attributes towards life which characterize a disintegrating civilization in terms of Christian theology.[3] For this reason the Stoics' philosophy of Detachment violates the imperative of the brotherhood of man based on God's love.[4] Therefore, Socrates' death loses meaning, since it represented a futile reaction to the schism in the Hellenic soul and attempted to transfer its field of action forward on a merely mundane plane. This, too, explains the moral sanction implicit in such statements as "the criminality of militarism,"[5] the "still greater treasure rejected" by the Jews,[6] whose inability to accept Christ doomed their civilization.

Toynbee's metaphysical assumptions permeate his concept of a culture's growth. Primitive humanity represents a Yin state of integration, the condition precedent to a further advance in the divine scheme of things. The creative minority contains the saints, in whose soul a spark of the divine has kindled a response and who constitute the "virtue that counsels," in Dante's terms, towards the uninspired majority. Man's fall from grace has resulted in that perversity of human nature which prevents direct illumination, forcing recourse to a mimesis doomed by its mechanicalness.[7] At the end of this development stands the City of Destruction, a testimony to man's present inadequacy but also a token, through its creation of a universal church, of potential fulfillment.

---

1. Toynbee, *op. cit.*, Vol. VI, p. 164, though it must be said that Toynbee can do no better than derive God's love by a syllogism.
2. Toynbee, *op. cit.*, Vol. VI, p. 162.
3. See *post.*
4. Toynbee, *op. cit.*, Vol. VI, p. 132.
5. Toynbee, *op. cit.*, Vol. IV.
6. Toynbee, *op. cit.*, Vol. IV, p. 263.
7. See *post* for further dependence on Dante.

Toynbee, however, did not merely attempt to probe deeper layers of meaning than Spengler, but conceived himself in the tradition of the British Empiricists. He asserted that history revealed its immanence to the application of the proper methodology, to the patient classification of data. Such an approach, however, is totally inconsistent with Toynbee's philosophical basis. A mere empirical analysis of history is impossible,[1] the regularity observed in phenomena constituting a metaphysical assumption of order. An empiricist is unable to find purposiveness in history, since all regularity implies at least the necessity of constant conjunction.[2] A historical "law" always denies the unique experience or the creative act, reducing both to agents of an inexorability that constantly produces new surface manifestations of success and power.

For success constitutes the final lesson that historical phenomena teach man. Each accomplished fact, each surviving political organization, testifies to a method of prevailing, represents an answer to the pragmatic query "What works?" A mere collection of historical data—though it can never be constructed free from the metaphysical postulation inherent in selectivity—will always represent a negation of freedom and an assertion of determinism. The alternatives that accompanied the willed performance are forgotten and only the deed remains, a testimony to its fatedness. Failure constitutes the only sin known to history in an empirical and pragmatic approach.

Toynbee, however, does not succeed in constructing an edifice based on empirical considerations. His conclusions are precisely what one would expect in the light of his philosophical assumptions and theological convictions. A pragmatist should have been careful about a method that yields an answer so obviously in line with his preconceptions.[3] Nobody better illustrates the nemesis of the "egocentric illusion"[4] than Toynbee, who castigates it so violently. Love is not immanent in historical data, but constitutes a resolve of the soul. History is not a book designed to illustrate the New Testament, nor do Christ's sayings embody truisms for "successful"

---

1. See *post* Ch. "The Concepts of Meaning."

2. Hume, *An Enquiry Concerning Human Understanding.*

3. Particularly as Toynbee refuses to accept the race theory of material progress because it fits in with preconceptions of age.

4. Toynbee, *op. cit.*, Vol. I, p. 153.

conduct. But the superimposition of an empirical method on a theological foundation, with data conceived as proving moral validity instead of the postulates deriving from a transcendental experience,[1] yields precisely this result. It never becomes clear whether the Pharisees are condemned because of their failure to recognize Christ's moral superiority or because of their lack of political perspicacity in failing to respond properly to the wave of the future. Similarly, Toynbee sways uneasily between rejecting militarism for its ethical deficiency or its "suicidalness."[2]

A normative pattern for the evaluation of laws derived empirically represents a logical inconsistency.[3] The connection between moral action and material success cannot be found in manipulatory, technical laws and led Kant to the postulation of God as the guarantor of the *summum bonum*.[4] Empirical analysis compares phenomenal manifestations and seeks a recurring pattern. Value judgments concern themselves with the inner meaning, the noumena of existence, the consequence of our experience of freedom.

It is impossible to find a guarantee for the realization of religious faith in the appearance of historical phenomena. Such a guarantee would reduce ethics to rules of prudence.[5] A violator of the moral code would in this view be not a knave, but a fool. Freedom is not achieved by the mere assertion of a purposiveness that itself becomes but a manifestation of historical law, classifiable as a mechanistic technique for blessedness. The salvation of souls and the growth and decay of civilizations are not connected by a causality denoted by immediate reward and punishment. The wheel of existence may utilize its circular motion to progress along virgin ground. Yet no civilization has yet succeeded in this endeavor, and decay has marked their advance, even in Toynbee's terms. And so the very conception of virgin ground constitutes the longing of a soul, the hope of a fulfillment, for the attainment of which we must look into ourselves and not attempt to coax it out of history by conjuring its phenomena.

---

1. See *post* "Conclusions."
2. Toynbee, *op. cit.*, Vol. IV, p. 365. See also *post* "Conclusions."
3. See *post* Appendix for criterion.
4. See *post* Ch. "History and Man's Experience of Morality" (Kant).
5. See *post* Ch. "The Sense of Responsibility."

Two strands of thought can be distinguished in Toynbee's philosophy. The biological approach regards history as an evolutionary process, its recurrence of growth and decay a testimony to man's efforts to turn himself into Superman. This view dominates Toynbee's analysis of the genesis of civilizations and their growth. The theological conception sees in history the realization of a divine plan to teach man the essential meaninglessness of temporal success. All typical attitudes towards life fail, save the recognition of the supra-mundane plane of reality, which denies the substantiality of all worldly endeavor. This is the tendency of Toynbee's analysis of the breakdown of civilizations and their disintegration.

Toynbee's postulation of freedom is therefore deceptive. The biological approach reduces Challenge-and-Response to a mechanistic description of the immanent *élan vital.* The theological view considers purposiveness merely God's tool to teach man his impotence on the mundane plane. This is compounded by the empirical method, which moves with great patience through a vast amount of historical data. But data belongs to the past and is therefore ruled by necessity. Freedom, on the other hand, cannot be derived as an attribute of reality but only through an inward experience. History's purpose represents a metaphysical assumption, not a necessary conclusion from historical events.[1]

This becomes very noticeable in Toynbee's analysis of the genesis of civilizations. Challenge-and-Response, the interaction of race and environment, is conceived as the key factor in a civilization's birth. But this theory becomes a meaningful assertion of purposiveness only if the analysis concerns itself with the imponderability of the response. This is precisely what an empirical method cannot do, however. Its chief concern is not the uniqueness of the response but the generality of the challenge. Toynbee carefully classifies all possible challenges, conceived as qualitatively equivalent and varying only in intensity. This, however, reduces Challenge-and-Response to but a restatement of the environment theory.[2] These are the problems raised by this phase of *A Study of History.*

Toynbee's philosophy of history begins with a query: What are the

---

1. See *post* Ch. "History and Man's Experience of Morality" (Kant).
2. See *post* "Conclusions."

smallest meaningful entities which a historian may study? An examination of England's past leads Toynbee to the conclusion that every nation belongs to a larger unit which sets the framework for its endeavors. Consequently civilizations, not states, are the social atoms with which a philosophy of history must concern itself. For this reason, too, relations between states have a completely different import than contacts among civilizations. Relations between states represent the mechanism of a society's growth. Contacts among civilizations reveal the process of apparentation-and-affiliation by which new civilizations rise on the ruins of the old. Toynbee distinguishes only two completely independent civilizations among his twenty-one specimens.[1]

Toynbee considers the civilizations intelligible fields of study because they are the representatives of the evolutionary rhythm that permeates existence. Here his biological approach comes to full expression. The dynamic activity of civilizations is but a prelude to a new level of integration which in good time will serve as the jumping-off point for a fresh advance. Their common task serves as the condition for the comparability of civilizations. For this reason, Toynbee rejects the view that any one civilization can represent an ultimate stage of development. This assumption derives from the egocentric illusion which equates the influence of a civilization in its growth phase with the total meaning of history. It reflects an attitude which considers its point of observation as normative instead of accidental, a method discarded by the physical sciences since the Copernican revolution.[2] Moreover, the integration of the world into a Western pattern is confined to the economic and perhaps the political plane. The contributions of the Syriac civilization to Western ideation, the edifice of Chinese philosophy, the profundity of Sumeric astronomy all testify to levels of achievement which make the attribution of ultimacy to any one civilization meaningless.

Toynbee therefore disagrees with the periodization of history into ancient, medieval, and modern. Civilizations do not reveal stages of an uninterrupted progress but a common effort, the success of which can be judged only by the attainment of a new level of integration. All civilizations

---

1. Toynbee, *op. cit.*, Vol. I, p. 131. The Egyptian and the Andean civilizations are the unrelated civilizations.

2. Toynbee, *op. cit.*, Vol. I, p. 160. See obvious reliance on Kant and even more pronouncedly on Spengler.

are consequently philosophically contemporary. Compared to the life of the earth, the difference in age between civilizations becomes negligible, the youth of the species in terms of its own time-scale apparent.[1]

The uncertainty about the outcome of the evolutionary process prevents an evaluation of the intrinsic merit of civilizations.[2] This is compounded by the insignificance of any achievement compared to the common goal.[3] Toynbee utilizes the analogy of a one-way street to illustrate the philosophical equivalence of civilizations. The direction of the street forces dynamic activity and prevents reversing or even stopping the vehicle. Nevertheless none of the twenty-one civilizations which have entered the thoroughfare has succeeded in passing out by the further exit. Fourteen have reversed, in violation of the rule, and seven exhibit various stages of breakdown.[4] The furthest points of penetration lie so close together that an evaluation either absolutely, or in terms of distance from the exit, becomes a philosophical impossibility.

Civilizations thus represent intelligible fields of study and genera of a species in an evolutionary process. Their relation in time constitutes an aspect of the deepening of religious ideation,[5] but does not result in successive stages of a uniform advance. They are philosophically equivalent, functionally contemporary, and allow a comparison for the determination of the laws governing historical processes.

If the civilizations represent genera of a new species, what accounts for their genesis? Toynbee endeavors to locate a principle which distinguishes primitive societies and civilizations in order to find a clue for the solution of this problem. He rejects the view that the possession of institutions, or the articulation of the division of labor, can serve as a criterion. These occur in very elaborate form in all types of historical existence. Toynbee finds the distinguishing feature in mimesis, a generic feature of social life, defined as "the acquisition, through imitation, of social 'assets'—aptitudes or emotions or ideas—which the acquisitors have not originated for themselves, and which

---

1. Toynbee, *op. cit.*, Vol. I, p. 17 (for Toynbee's assumptions as to the age span of the earth).

2. This statement from Toynbee, *op. cit.*, Vol. I, p. 175, is in flat contradiction with the whole tendency of Vol. V and Vol. VI. See "Conclusions" for discussion.

3. This assumes that Toynbee is aware of the goal and presents another inconsistency in an empirical scheme.

4. Toynbee, *op. cit.*, Vol. I, p. 176. See also *post* for discussion of this inconsistency.

5. See *post.*

they might never have come to possess if they had not encountered and imitated other people in whose possession these assets were already to be found."[1] Mimesis is a social drill, its direction towards the past characteristic of primitive societies, its utilization for new creativity the mark of civilizations.

This raises the question whether the difference between civilizations and primitive societies is permanent and fundamental. Toynbee's metaphysical assumption of cyclical progress determines the reply. Since all existence exhibits not only a process of growth but testifies to a mode of evolutionary survival, civilizations can represent merely the most recent stage of historical development.[2] The transformation of Sub-Man into Man, which must of necessity have occurred in a social environment, is postulated by Toynbee as having been accomplished under the aegis of primitive societies.[3] This testifies to a level of dynamic creativeness far surpassing any achievement of the more recent species of civilizations.

The present static condition of primitive societies is therefore deceptive. It does not exhibit uninspired torpor but the last stage of Integration. Mankind's task is likened by Toynbee to the climbing of a mountain of vast extent, surrounded by ledges. The exertion required for climbing its steep sides issues forth in a feverish activity that sometimes produces strength sufficient for reaching the next ledge, but more often results in a loss of the grip and a drop to the death on a lower level.[4] The limitations of the human vision confine it to scanning only one perpendicular and one horizontal surface. The exhausted figures on the ledge are therefore frequently mistaken for paralytics and the climbers as the apprehension of activity. But reflection will reveal that the figures on the ledge could have attained it only by prodigious efforts and that many ledges below must be strewn with the corpses of failures of a previous dynamism.

The difference between primitive societies and civilizations is neither fundamental nor permanent, then, but the accident of a time and place of observation. The present static condition of primitive societies merely calls to mind past motion, just as the activity of civilizations will cease when Man has been turned into Superman.[5]

Toynbee's biological approach overrides any mere postulation of purpo-

---

1. Toynbee, *op. cit.*, Vol. I, p. 191.
2. Which in this view becomes almost indistinguishable from biological processes.
3. Toynbee, *op. cit.*, Vol. I, p. 192.
4. Note correspondence of this picture with Dante's Mount Purgatory.
5. Toynbee, *op. cit.*, Vol. I, p. 194.

siveness. History is an evolutionary process operating by alternate stages of Integration and Differentiation. The genesis of civilizations testifies to a mutation from the static condition to creative effort. This holds true even in cases of apparentation-and-affiliation. With respect to the internal proletariat, the dominant minorities are static by definition. The secession of the internal proletariat reveals the dynamic reaction which changes the torpor into activity and the Integration into new Differentiation. The births of civilizations form particular beats of a general rhythmic pulse of the universe.[1]

This explains the nature of the genesis of civilizations but not their particular appearance at a definite time. What are the factors that lift these entities out of the stream of humanity? What accounts for the long interval of Yin before the climb up the precipice commences? True to his empirical method, Toynbee examines all possible causes before drawing conclusions. He finds the negative factor which retards activity in the *vis inertiae*, the "cake of custom," the inherent tendency towards stability. This serves as the foil for the creative act, the condition to be overcome before Differentiation can set in.

Two obvious alternatives present themselves as the positive factors. The mutation can be postulated as the consequence of some special quality of the human beings who have succeeded in making the transition. The change may, on the other hand, be attributed to a specially favorable constellation of environmental conditions.[2] Neither hypothesis is tenable according to Toynbee.

Race is a construction of human prejudice, another facet of the egocentric illusion, for which no scientific criteria can be found. Its general acceptance in the West derives from the Protestant concept of predestination, which considers material success an indication of divine sanction and ascribes an insuperable deficiency to all disbelievers. It is reinforced by the racial theories developed from de Gobineau, whose primary concern had not been the validation of natural phenomena but political polemic. Against the self-evidence of the first assumption can be set the fact that race feeling represents a relatively recent Western phenomenon. In the medieval period the potential equality of all humanity constituted a cornerstone of popular belief. Moreover, no connection can be established between the pigmenta-

---

1. Toynbee, *op. cit.*, Vol. I, p. 204. Note the similarity of this concept with Spengler and its inconsistency with the emphasis on pure volition.
2. Toynbee, *op. cit.*, Vol. I, p. 208.

tion of the skin and the creative tendency that issues into the Yang state.[1] An empirical survey indicates that all races except the Negro race have at one time or another produced a civilization. The simile of the climbers on the precipice proves,[2] however, that this deficiency need not be inherent but may result from the comparative youth of the species.

The environmental theory fares no better. Its only conclusive proof, according to Toynbee, would involve an examination of all conditions that are claimed to be conducive to the genesis of civilizations and a determination of whether they were so operative wherever they occurred.[3] Such an empirical survey will reveal a wide variety in the geographical or climatic conditions that attended the genesis of civilizations. Though the Egyptian and Sumeric civilizations developed in a river basin, not every river of similar extent—such as the Colorado River—has produced a civilization. Again, though the Eurasian and Arabian steppes have produced nomadism, the American prairie and the Argentine pampas have not served as an obstacle to the birth of civilizations.

If both the race and environmental theories are discredited, what does account for the genesis of civilizations? Toynbee finds the solution in a combination of the two factors. Race, while not itself the cause, represents the manifestation of an immanence that the philosophers call *élan vital* and the mystics God.[4] The environment again constitutes an omnipresent obstacle thwarting this force and challenging it to battle. The interaction between race and environment, and God and the Devil, exhibits the plot of the Book of Job, of Goethe's Faust, of life, and of history.

The genesis of civilizations is not due to one factor, but to several. It results not from an entity but a relation. The interaction that causes the Yin state to change to Yang is the theme of much of the profoundest mythology.[5] An encounter between superhuman entities constitutes the plot of the theological versions as well as the scientific assumptions.[6] The encounter between

---

1. Toynbee, *op. cit.*, Vol. I, p. 227.

2. For a discussion of empirical proof by simile, see "Conclusions."

3. Toynbee, *op. cit.*, Vol. I, p. 253. For a discussion of the conclusiveness of such a proof, see "Conclusions." That these environments might yet produce civilizations is indicated by Toynbee's assertion that the Minoan island empire was not repeated in Indonesia. Recent history may have demonstrated the weakness of this argument.

4. Toynbee, *op. cit.*, Vol. I, p. 270.

5. For the validity of conclusions from mythology see "Conclusions."

6. Note the reliance of this argument on Spengler's metaphysical postulate.

Yahweh and the Devil is the story of Genesis, repeated with the same inherent meaning in the New Testament as the pattern of Redemption. The catastrophic impact of stars in space serves as the matrix on which physical science constructs its image of the origin of the universe.[1] Both accounts agree in conceiving the encounter as a rare and unique event with consequences of unimaginable portent.

The plot begins with a perfect state of Yin.[2] The perfect knowledge of Faust, the perfect goodness of Job, the perfect innocence of Adam and Eve can change into Yang only through the intervention of an external agent. It is the task of this factor to supply the inner creative force with that stimulus most likely to evoke the most potently creative response.[3] This essentially expresses the function of the climatic factor in certain variations of the environment theory.[4]

In mythology, the intrusion of the Devil into God's realm supplies the impetus for the transition to the Yang state. The Lord and Satan make a wager, which is then tested on a human agent. Faust, Job, and Adam represent those civilizations on the ledge who have just attained their feet and commenced the climb with a full awareness of the dangers of an ascent that brooks no stopping and in which death represents the only alternative to the achievement of the next level. However, mythology and theology make the attainment of the ledge inevitable, the winning of the bet by the Devil out of the question.

Does this mean that God has cheated the Devil and bet without risking anything? That would negate the essence of the encounter and could not therefore produce its vast consequences. Toynbee replies that the Devil's intervention suffices to disturb the equilibrium but cannot achieve a new level of integration. God, who has been yearning for an opportunity for fresh creation but could find none in the perfection of His previous effort, is now enabled to restore the equilibrium on a new and higher plane. In this act of creation, no demon can participate.[5]

On the mundane plane, the human protagonist constitutes the theater

---

1. Toynbee, *op. cit.*, Vol. I, p. 274.
2. The operation of Challenge-and-Response is described at such length because it is central to Toynbee's argument and will be utilized to illustrate limitations of his method. See *post* "Conclusions."
3. Toynbee, *op. cit.*, Vol. I, p. 278.
4. This contradicts previous approaches to that theory. See *post* "Conclusions."
5. Toynbee, *op. cit.*, Vol. I, p. 284.

for this activity, and his ordeal accomplishes itself in three stages. The first stage finds symbolic expression in the assault of the tempter and changes the state of Yin to Yang, from harmony to discord, from rest to motion. With awareness of the fatedness of a course from which there is no return begins the second stage, the crisis. The momentary rebellion at finding oneself but a tool in God's hands is transcended by the peace of reconciliation. This enables man to achieve victory through defeat, peace through suffering. Man resigns himself into God's hands and thus reverses the rhythm again—from motion towards rest, from storm to calm, from Yang back to Yin. God stands revealed not as a hard taskmaster, nor the cause of suffering, but as the all-embracing love which made the new level of integration possible.[1]

Toynbee's positive factor, then, that explains the genesis of civilizations and the emerging differentiation is the relation of Challenge-and-Response. Life presents a series of problems, each a challenge to undergo an ordeal. No calculation, however prudent of quantitative phenomena, can serve for the prediction of historical events. For nobody can know the "unknown God,"[2] the reaction of the protagonist when the ordeal actually occurs.

Despite this analysis of the imponderability of the response, Toynbee engages in an extensive analysis of the historically effective stimuli to determine the range of possible responses. An examination of the genesis of civilizations leads to the "law" that their birth results not from unusually easy, but from difficult environments, frequently in response to changes in climate (for example, the genesis of the Egyptian or Sumeric civilizations). Though, at first blush, the related civilizations do not seem to constitute a reaction to an environment, closer reflection indicates that their response is not to the physical but to the human environment. The internal proletariat's will to secede testifies to the dominant minority's will to repress, the final breaking away to the intolerability of the challenge. Moreover the geographical location of the affiliated civilization usually presents a greater stimulus than the physical locus of the parent civilizations. Both the physical and human environment, then, can provide the challenge that attends the genesis of civilizations.

The intensity of the response represents a function of the severity of the

---

1. Toynbee, *op. cit.*, Vol. I, p. 298.
2. Toynbee, *op. cit.*, Vol. I, p. 302.

stimulus. Ease is inimical to civilizations.[1] The stimulus of hard countries led to the superiority of Brandenburg over the Rhineland, of the Yellow River basin over that of the Yangtse, and the triumph of New England over its rivals in the colonization of North America.

Dynamic activity testifies to the direction of mimesis towards the future, achieved by breaking of the "cake of custom." For this reason new ground provides a stimulus by the removal of the weight of tradition.

The stimulus of blows and pressures accounts for the rejuvenation of many political entities, for the virility of border provinces. France underwent a regeneration through the military catastrophe of 1871, as did Prussia under the impact of Jena and Austerlitz. The dominant position enjoyed by border provinces within the civilizations results from the tempering they undergo in the constant challenge as guardians of the marshes. The history of the growth phase of the Holy Roman Empire exhibits a continuous shift of the center of gravity towards the border regions, its decline a reversal of that tendency.[2] Neither the Ottoman nor the Austrian Empire survived the relaxation of their mutual pressure in the contest for the Balkans.

Thus Toynbee distinguishes responses due to the stimulus of hard countries, to the stimulus of new ground, and the stimulus of blows and pressures.

If an increase in the severity of the stimulus yields a correspondingly successful response, can this process be continued indefinitely? Toynbee denies this and postulates an optimum challenge, defined as the Golden Mean, of sufficient intensity to elicit the maximum potential of creativity, though not so oppressive as to be stifling.[3] The "law of compensation" expresses his mechanical formulation of this principle. It states that an excessive challenge by either the physical or the human environment must be compensated by an alleviation of the alternate factor.[4] Such was the case of Switzerland and Holland, both of which mastered a prohibitive physical environment in exchange for the lessening of the human pressures.

The concept of the Golden Mean raises formidable problems in methodology. For how is a challenge proved excessive? The unsuccessful response

1. Illustrated by examples from the *Odyssey*, Capua, Roman Campagna. For limitations of this methodology see *post* "Conclusions."
2. Toynbee, *op. cit.*, Vol. II, p. 166. For a discussion of Toynbee's data see *post* "Conclusions."
3. For a discussion of the essential meaninglessness of this adaptation of an Aristotelian concept, see *post* "Conclusions."
4. Toynbee, *op. cit.*, Vol. II, p. 274.

to a particular challenge may merely indicate a lack of inner reactive ability. Toynbee offers two approaches. An excessive challenge can be proved by a relation in three terms, of which, in comparable conditions, the Golden Mean of severity produced the optimum response.[1] Toynbee's second proof examines the abortive civilizations, which collapsed soon upon attaining birth under the formidableness of their challenges. Thus the Far Western civilization of the Celtic Fringe experienced a brief bloom which for a time indicated that the style of Christianity might be set from Ionia instead of Rome. Irish missionaries ranged far over the Continent, and Scotus Erigena represented merely one example of brilliant Celtic learning. Yet the dual challenge offered by the superior discipline of the Roman Church and the impact of the Scandinavian *Völkerwanderung* was too severe. The Synod of Whitby (A.D. 664) settled the issue and led to the isolation of Ireland from the rest of Christianity. The invasions by the Norsemen had hardly been overcome when Henry II invaded the Celtic Fringe with papal sanction. These two successive blows presented a challenge of such severity that an effective response proved impossible, and thus the Far Western civilization, whose inception was so promising, proved abortive.

The concept of Challenge-and-Response represents an affirmation of purposiveness in history. Its distinguishing characteristic is the creative imponderable that prevents the prediction of the reaction to the ordeal. The level of integration of Yin is disturbed, and the dynamic activity (Yang), of which suffering represents man's lot, leads back to the inner reconciliation with God and the recognition of His love.

Thus Toynbee's metaphysical assumptions find expression in his doctrine on the genesis of civilizations. But the initial dilemmas remain unresolved. The empirical method imposes a success pattern which makes the recognition of God's love dependent on the new level of integration achieved on the higher ledge. But no civilization has yet managed this precipice, and the assertion of the purpose of history as an inner reconciliation represents a metaphysical resolve, not a datum of history. The immanence in all activity of the *élan vital* makes Challenge-and-Response little more than the mechanism of an inexorable immanence. Moreover, the

---

1. Toynbee, *op. cit.*, Vol. I, p. 290. For illustrations see pp. 291–322. This argument, of course, does not really resolve the original dilemma, since all terms mutually define each other.

pragmatic approach results in an analysis of response almost exclusively in terms of challenge, which represents at best a refinement of the environment theory. Empiricism and noumenal experience continue as logical antinomies.[1] Thus God's purpose is derived syllogistically from a normative pattern based on Toynbee's conception of a fair wager.

Toynbee's distinction between discrete phases of Yin and Yang raises many problems. If integration represents organic being, and Yang purposive creation, must those two stages operate successively? Life never seems to exhibit perfect states of either absolute Integration or absolute Differentiation. It appears likely that the static condition of primitive societies results from the same egocentric illusion that considers one civilization the acme of all achievement. Similarly, the dynamism of civilized life does not represent a purposiveness that completely transcends tradition, the organic factor.

Spengler resolved the problem of Necessity and Freedom by postulating alternative modes of behavior, in separate realms. History was ruled in its main tendencies by an immanent Destiny, not to be influenced by human volition. Toynbee, on the other hand, argues for successive stages in an evolutionary, biological process ruled by mimesis. But is this social drill not based on a uniformity in history for which no warranty can be found in empirical data? It seems that drill is hardly a preparation for the creative individual whose appearance is conceived as of "almost unimaginable rarity."[2] These are the problems to consider in the subsequent development of Toynbee's philosophy.

The Growth of Civilizations

The growth of civilizations in Toynbee's scheme does not exhibit an immanent inexorability, but a process of increasing self-determination, with breakdown the penalty for an unsuccessful response. Just as the genesis of civilizations results from the reaction to the challenge of disequilibrium, so growth reveals a series of successful responses to recurring challenges. The loss of the capacity for successful response, or the appearance of an excessive challenge, mark the stage of breakdown. The difficulty of uniting the metaphysical assumptions with the empirical method reappears. Toynbee's crite-

---

1. See *post* Ch. "History and Man's Experience of Morality" (Kant).
2. Toynbee, *op. cit.*, Vol. III, p. 272.

rion for growth is etherealization, the transfer of the field of action from the macrocosm to microcosm. Toynbee the theologian ascribes this to an inward state. Toynbee the empiricist can, however, find it only in a physical extent that perforce becomes its own environment. Similarly, Toynbee sways between considering breakdown the consequence of a deficient response or of an insuperable challenge. The incommensurability of the realms of theology and biology appears in every aspect of Toynbee's analysis.

Once the genesis of civilization has been accomplished and the dangers inherent in birth overcome, must their subsequent development follow a uniform pattern? Does every civilization which avoids being abortive exhibit identical symptoms of growth? Toynbee denies the necessity of uninterrupted growth and distinguishes a third specimen of the genus, the arrested civilizations, as an illustration.[1] All the arrested civilizations have been petrified in response to a challenge of such severity that its solution required a *tour de force*. The entire strength of the society was required for responding to this oppressive stimulus, a task achieved only at the price of pegging the civilization at a level of inflexible readiness for one crisis.

Such was the case of the Polynesians, who had responded to the challenge of the Pacific Ocean with an intensity just sufficient for the attainment of an equilibrium. They succeeded in crossing the vast spaces but never with any margin of safety, until the tension went slack and their civilization degenerated on the forgotten islands of the Pacific.

This, too, is Toynbee's conception of the history of the nomads, whose existence results from a successful response to the recurrent challenge of desiccation.[2] The drought forces the cultivators of the soil to either withdraw to more fertile regions or launch themselves on the inhospitable steppe, no longer the domesticators of plants, but of animals. Manifestly the latter is a higher art, more comparable to industrialism than to agriculture. It substitutes the indirect utilization of vegetation for the planting of crops. By means of grazing animals, the sparse produce of the steppe is transformed into food and clothing. This involves a division of labor and a hierarchy of specialization articulated into the nomad, his animal auxiliaries (the dog, camel, *et cetera*), and the herds of cattle. The survival of the group depends on a finely tempered adaptation in an environment

---

1. Toynbee, *op. cit.*, Vol. III, p. 3.
2. Toynbee, *op. cit.*, Vol. III, p. 12.

which leaves no margin for lax discipline and severely limits the range of possible responses.[1]

The explosion of the nomads into settled areas results from a further increase in the severity of the environment, destroying the narrow balance of survival. Alternatively, the nomad may be pulled out of the steppe by a vacuum in the neighboring society. The transformation of a nomadic community from a master of the physical environment on the steppe to a lord of the human environment of a civilization constitutes the superlative challenge of this stage of development.[2] The nomad attempts to respond to this stimulus by treating his human subjects as he would his cattle and changes from a herder of cattle to a herder of men. This was the reaction of the Avars, who collected their Slav prisoners into flocks and placed them in a vast semicircle around the Hungarian plain.

But while the composite society constituted by the nomads and their flock represents the most efficient mode of survival on the steppe, their division of labor the condition of everybody's survival, the nomad acts as an incubus in an environment of fields and cities. The organization of society into nomads and indigenous human cattle is economically unsound and parasitic. From shepherds keeping their flocks, the nomads turn into drones exploiting their working bees. This accounts for the ephemerality of nomad empires established on a base of sedentary people. The virtues that led to the nomad's early successes, self-reliance and physical toughness, atrophy in an environment that no longer provides the necessary stimulus. The degeneration of the conquerors is paralleled by an increase in stature of the sedentary settlers, to whom the existence of foreign domination constitutes a constant challenge. The end of nomad empires is like their beginning, violent, sudden, total.

Some nomad conquerors, such as the Osmanlis, succeeded in the *tour de force* of imposing a lasting empire on a sedentary population, but only at the price of arresting their own civilization. Catapulted out of the steppe into the Balkans by the pressure of the Mongols, the Osmanlis' political beginning was auspicious, for they provided that universal state which the Balkan offshoot of Orthodox Christianity had been unable to

---

1. These passages are presented at such length because they represent the happiest examples of a successful use of the empirical method, as well as Toynbee's practical application of Challenge-and-Response.
2. Toynbee, *op. cit.*, Vol. III, p. 22.

achieve for itself. The duration of the Ottoman Empire was, however, the result of a successful response to the extraordinary challenge constituted by the human environment.[1] The Osmanlis remembered that successful utilization of animal flocks depended not only on the relation of the shepherd to the herd but also on the employment of animal auxiliaries: the dog, horse, and camel. This lesson they applied to their Balkan empire. Instead of animals they took advantage of human auxiliaries, recruited forcibly from their Christian subjects. The employment of slaves as soldiers and administrators, the Janissaries in the Ottoman case, has been the *tour de force* by which all successful nomad empires over sedentary people have maintained themselves. This response had two consequences. By excluding the Osmanlis from any administrative and political responsibility, their moral fiber degenerated, in the absence of any effective stimulus. The Janissaries could maintain their efficiency only as long as their numbers were small, in itself a *tour de force*. Eventually the loss of public spirit by the ruling Osmanlis led to a dilution of the Janissaries, and the arrested civilization represented by the Ottoman Empire expired as the "sick man of Europe" in 1918.

Thus the history of nomad empires illustrates the manner in which civilizations become arrested, through the excessive challenge of either the physical environment, such as the steppe, or the human environment, exemplified by the impact of sedentary populations.[2]

Two corollary conditions characterize arrested civilizations: caste and specialization. Survival in a severe environment is purchased only at the price of that proficiency in one excellence which stifles creativity in all other fields. The Centaur, the man grown to the horse, represents the outsider's view of the nomad raider. It contains the symbolism of the return to animalism, which constitutes another facet of the arrested civilization. Their reactive ability has become concentrated on one challenge, which is indeed mastered, but which first reduces and then prevents the proper response to the inevitable new challenges inherent in existence. Utopias, by definition attempts to peg societies at a certain level, exhibit most clearly this tendency towards caste and specialization. The arrested civilizations thus disprove both the uniformity of the civilizations' development as well as the necessity for constant growth.

---

1. Toynbee, *op. cit.*, Vol. III, p. 27.
2. For other illustrations see Toynbee, *op. cit.*, Vol. III, pp. 22–79.

If growth is not the necessary concomitant of a civilization's existence but depends on a balanced response to a series of challenges, what is its nature? Toynbee again bases his answer on mythology. Aeschylus' *Prometheus Bound* contains his symbolic representation of the conditions attending growth. Having attained dominance over Olympus, Zeus is chiefly concerned with maintaining his mastery. Any change can merely detract from the absoluteness of his power. Yet Zeus did not achieve his eminence unaided. His Titanic ally Prometheus, the apprehension of creativity, the embodiment of the *élan vital,* works constantly for progress against arrest and represents thought against force. No amount of physical compulsion can avail to wrest Prometheus' secret from him, and in the end there is reconciliation. Zeus admits the creativity as a condition for his own survival. He had not been what he seemed.[1]

Toynbee sees in Aeschylus' trilogy a poetic chronicle of Hellenic history. Just as Zeus avoided the fate of the arrested civilizations by being galvanized into activity by Prometheus, so Hellas' growth testified to a series of successful responses to recurrent challenges. The first challenge, offered by the barbarian highlanders, evoked the response of mastery over the brigands. This victory decided that Hellas should be a world of cities and agriculture, not of villages and pasturelands. The limit of maximum density of population supportable by agriculture proved to be inelastic, however. The Malthusian problem served initially as a stimulus for overseas expansion. But the impact of Hellenic imperialism evoked the reaction of greater unity among the Mediterranean peoples and set an effective limit to Greek colonization.

This challenge of overpopulation was finally solved by Athens, which became the "education of Hellas."[2] Under its guidance, Greek expansion was transformed to indirect methods, with commerce and production the key methods of continuing survival. Aeschylus' trilogy serves as a testimony to the intensity of the Athenian response.

Growth—in Toynbee's scheme—stands revealed as a process of successful responses to recurrent challenges. The optimum challenge is that which provides a stimulus for a response that carries the civilization

---

1. Toynbee, *op. cit.,* Vol. III, p. 117. For a discussion of this method of utilizing mythology, see historical proof; see *post* "Conclusions."
2. It is doubtful whether Pericles meant his reference to Athens as the education of Hellas in an economic sense.

beyond the point of exact balance—the condition of the arrested civilization—into a continuing disequilibrium. The step from genesis to growth exhibits a repetitive, recurrent rhythm in which equilibrium constitutes breakdown.

Growth represents one aspect of the process of evolution, accomplishing itself through ever greater self-articulation and progressive mastery over the environment. Yet what criteria exist for evaluating the growth of a civilization? Does mastery over the environment mean the external relations of the civilization or its inner self-determination?

Increased control over a civilization's human environment, expressed in terms of geographical expansion, is rejected by Toynbee as a criterion of growth. Expansion seems to exert a stifling effect on the ability to respond creatively. The most archaic forms of Christianity exist in the Catholicism of Quebec, the Coptic Church of Abyssinia, and the Fundamentalism of the Mississippi basin.[1] The "law" that geographical expansion retards social progress further explains the philological phenomenon that the most archaic forms of the language usually occur at the furthest distance from their origin.

Why should the era of greatest expansion coincide with the period of decline? Toynbee argues that the "social radiation" obeys the same laws as light waves.[2] During the period of growth a civilization emits its influence in a ray of uniform consistency, with cultural, political, and economic manifestations merging into a meaningful whole.[3] The period of decline witnesses a diffraction of these rays into their component parts, allowing absorption of the desirable emission. Since the resistance to the acceptance of an alien cultural pattern is much greater than the reluctance to take over alien techniques, the decaying civilization usually succeeds in making its influence felt on the economic, sometimes on the political, rarely on the cultural plane.

Increasing command over the physical environment cannot serve as a criterion of growth for Toynbee, since it represents merely another emanation of the egocentric illusion. In the present stage of Western civilization, a conception of history as a uniform development of increasing technical mastery fits too precisely the prejudices of the age to be objectively consid-

---

1. This is, of course, in direct contradiction to the doctrine of the stimulus of new ground.
2. For the danger of arguing from physical phenomena see *post* "Conclusions."
3. This leans rather heavily on Spengler.

ered.[1] Moreover, the division of history into periods distinguished by technological labels, such as Bronze Age, Iron Age, *et cetera*, has no standing in empirical data. At every stage the new technique can only have been the property of the creative few, from whom it was acquired by the rest of mankind through mimesis and by a very gradual process. Thus, there probably never existed a Paleolithic Age.[2] Moreover, no support can be found in history for a necessary connection between technical proficiency and a civilization's growth. The transition from the Paleolithic to the Neolithic Age witnessed an improvement in technique accompanied by a degeneration of wisdom, ideation, and style.[3]

The interregnum between the collapse of the apparented and the appearance of the affiliated civilization also exhibits a deficiency in inward stature, despite a superior technique. Such was the case of Rome. The improvement in agricultural techniques made large-scale agriculture profitable and resulted in the introduction of plantation slavery in the Hellenic world. The destruction of the free peasantry and the consequential rise of a parasite proletariat in Rome served as an incubus which in time strangled the Hellenic civilization. Finally, the technological improvement in military weapons is relatively constant, proceeding in inverse ratio to the civilization's growth.

Increasing command over the environment does not disclose any criterion for progress, but it does reveal the condition precedent to technological advance. Toynbee finds this in the law of progressive simplification,[4] which states that growth attends a continual economizing of means. The operation of this law can be observed in the development of script, which proceeds from the pictograms of Chinese to the hieroglyphics of Egypt, culminating in the alphabet. In this Syriac invention, the introduction of auxiliary words has enabled Western languages to surpass in simplicity, while equaling in expressive power, the Arab verb of many aspects.

The progressive simplification of fashions parallels the economy of hypothesis for the explanation of natural phenomena. The Copernican sys-

---

1. Though this argument limits inference from universal assent, it can hardly be utilized to disprove the thesis of uniform progress.
2. This argument holds good only for the origination of the technique and says nothing about the condition after its general acceptance.
3. Toynbee, *op. cit.*, Vol. III, p. 173.
4. Toynbee, *op. cit.*, Vol. III, p. 174.

tem replaces the Ptolemaic, accounting in far simpler terms for the same range of phenomena. Einstein, again, has provided a theory which synthesizes the laws of gravity, radiation, and magnetism.[1]

This simplification does not, however, reveal a negation or omission, but the liberation of energy for higher tasks.[2] Its human representatives are Socrates, who in a Platonic dialogue transfers his attentions from the physical to the psychic sphere by means of an inner experience,[3] and Gandhi, whose appeal for the return to handiwork expresses the symbolism of a spiritual plane. In its deepest sense, the process of etherealization exhibits a shift of this field of activity from the macrocosm to the microcosm. Toynbee's criterion of growth then applies to a progressive internalization of the field in which Challenge-and-Response occurs. The growing civilization tends to become its own environment, and the subsequent ordeal takes place within its own body.

Thus in Hellenic history the earliest challenges were offered by an external environment, the Achaemenians and the Thracian barbarians.[4] But with the decisive defeat of the last Syriac power, Carthage, and the subsequent conquest of the European barbarians, the external factor grew ever less important. The conflict shifted to the internal field, where the bitterness of the antagonism between the Oriental plantation slaves and their Roman masters equaled in intensity the passions engendered by the Punic Wars.

Similarly, in the West, the external challenge of the Norsemen preceded the domestic problem of the replacement of the feudal system by an organization of sovereign states. The most recent stage of Western history exhibits in the phenomenon of Bolshevism the ultimate proof of its absorptive power. Marxism, which transferred Russia's capital to Moscow as a symbolic repudiation of the West, has been forced by its emphasis on technique and electrification into the pattern of Western civilizations. Thus the challenge of Communism, as also Gandhi's, who ever draws his inspiration for economic self-sufficiency from Europe, is an internal problem of the Western civilization.[5]

---

1. Toynbee, *op. cit.*, Vol. III, p. 181.

2. This is another illustration of Toynbee's normative pattern.

3. *Phaedo*, pp. 96–97.

4. Toynbee, *op. cit.*, Vol. III, p. 197. This contradicts the earlier assertion that overpopulation, an internal factor, constitutes the earliest challenge.

5. Toynbee, *op. cit.*, Vol. III, p. 216. For the weakness of this argument see *post* "Conclusions." Toynbee here confuses an alien inspiration with an area of activity.

Growth, for Toynbee, constitutes a pattern of the progressive etherealization of Challenge-and-Response. The external factor constantly diminishes in importance, the necessity of self-articulation becomes more pronounced. Growth is a process of increasing the range of self-determination, of a transfer of the field of activity from the macrocosm to the microcosm. History represents the chronicle of that effort.[1]

If growth exhibits an increase of self-determination, by what mechanism does it accomplish itself? Toynbee examines two common arguments: the theory of the atomistic independence of individuals and the conception of society as a biological organism. He refutes the former by referring to the *Odyssey*'s description of the Cyclops and the postulate that language and therefore thought can be developed only in society. Toynbee dogmatically denies Spengler's conception of the culture as a super-organism, without adducing any supporting data except the assertion that man can act only as an individual, not as part of an organism.

For Toynbee, society represents a community of individuals, each of whom constitutes a discrete field of activity. The areas at which the various fields of action intersect contain the political and social institutions of each civilization. A field of action obviously cannot serve as a source of action. A relation merely provides the common ground for the encounter of several forces. Society serves as the medium of communication for the interaction of its components.

Toynbee considers creativity the attribute of suddenly inspired individuals. They arise with unpredictable rarity and express the essence of evolution, the force that changes the state of Yin into the activity of Yang. These men of genius push back the vistas of human intelligence and serve as the guideposts on the road of history. Their illumination is achieved in a mystic ecstasy which transforms the essence of their soul and indicates the necessity for fresh creation. They represent the future state of Yin, and an intrinsic superiority comparable to the eminence of the civilizations over primitive societies.

The appearance of these "saints," "geniuses," or "supermen" presents[2] society with a dilemma. Though they are the leaven which galvanizes society into activity, the uncreative majority can follow them but with difficulty. The most satisfactory leadership would rely on the direct illumination of

---

1. Note the dependence of this concept on Hegel.
2. Toynbee, *op. cit.*, Vol. III, p. 243.

the mass by contact with the saints. This, however, can be achieved only at the end of the process, at the new level of integration.[1]

Thus social drill, mimesis, replaces inspiration, utilizing an existing faculty by merely changing its orientation. This generic feature of social life is henceforth directed towards the creative minority, no longer restrained by the "cake of custom." Mimesis constitutes a shortcut fraught with danger, for the mechanicalness of its drill might be channeled into immoral directions. Yet it reveals the only condition for social growth, its risk the problem of mortality.

The saint cannot achieve his mystic ecstasy in society, however. Only in solitude can he attain through suffering that clarity of vision, that inner tempering which enables him to lead his people out of the wilderness into the Promised Land. This is Withdrawal-and-Return, the plot of the fables of many civilizations, the story of the foundling who grew to greatness, the tale of the rebirth of the agricultural God, Christ's sojourn in the wilderness.

The intuition that the withdrawal obtains its moral sanction from the return to this world exhibits Christianity's moral superiority over Hellenism. Life is action, and a transformation of the microcosm must work itself out in the macrocosm.[2] The Greek philosophers considered withdrawal as the ultimate state of bliss. Plato's captives return to the cave with a heavy heart. Christianity, on the other hand, sees the test of the ordeal in the quality of the return, that will lead the captives towards the light.

Here Toynbee's mythology of the genesis of civilizations recurs. The state of Yin is disturbed in the microcosm, which suffers its crisis in solitude and whose inner reconciliation enables the macrocosm to participate in creativity. Growth exhibits beats of the universal rhythm, of which Withdrawal and Return represent subsidiary pulsations. Peace results from activity, reconciliation from suffering, harmony from discord.

This is the meaning for Toynbee of the lives of Dante, Hindenburg, Saint Paul, and almost all creative personalities.[3] This, too, describes the role played by Athens in the second part of Hellenic history and by England in the third chapter of the Western development. At a time when most Greek

---

1. Note correspondence with Dante's concept. See *post.*
2. Toynbee, *op. cit.*, Vol. III, p. 235.
3. Toynbee, *op. cit.*, Vol. III, pp. 217–333. For the essential incommensurability of most of Toynbee's illustrations see *post* "Conclusions" (Discussion of Methodology).

poleis were engaged in overseas expansion, Athens withdrew into isolation and there developed a solution to the most serious Hellenic problem, that of overpopulation. Basing her greatness on a commerce achieved by specialization and manufacture, Athens signaled her return to the Greek scene by throwing down the gauntlet to the Achaemenian Empire. For over two hundred years Athens' role was the exact antithesis of its previous condition of apparent hibernation. The institutions developed during the withdrawal proved their superiority over their Spartan counterpart, which had broken down while Athens became the "education of Hellas."

Similarly, England's insular position enabled her to find the solution to the most serious challenge of the seventeenth-century Western civilization. By breaking down feudal barriers within her domain and substituting democratic government for aristocratic dominance, she achieved the transformation of an agricultural to an industrial society. When the Glorious Revolution brought England's return to the European scene, the Continental powers found there a model for their adaptation of Italian transalpine efficiency to nation-states.[1]

This, Toynbee believes, may be Russia's role in the Western world. The early Communist tendencies of absolute isolation may well constitute that withdrawal which finds the proper response to the all-pervasive Western challenge of nationalism. Brought by technology into the Western pattern, Russia will perhaps return to serve as the creative minority in the next stage of Western development.[2]

Growth accomplishes itself through the agency of a creative minority, the withdrawal of which results in an inward tempering and which becomes effective through its return. It leads by mimesis, a social drill, in the absence of the direct inspiration which will be attained at the next level of integration. Life presents a series of problems, each a challenge to undergo an ordeal. Yet each problem is essentially unique, each response singular. Moreover, the successful solution of one problem exposes the civilization to a new challenge, the nature of which is largely determined by the previous response. Spengler asserted that each culture possessed a soul, which revealed itself in the selection of its appropriate symbolism and which contained the key to the understanding of the culture's history. This Toyn-

---

1. Toynbee, *op. cit.*, Vol. III, p. 377 *et seq.*
2. It is difficult to see how Russia can serve as the creative minority of a civilization which meets Toynbee's every criterion for disintegration. See *post* "Conclusions."

bee denies. He opts for a willed direction, based on a series of overbalances, each successful response creating a fresh challenge. Differentiation is achieved by growth, not through a determined immanence.[1]

The growth of civilizations, in Toynbee's scheme, exhibits that purposiveness which his metaphysical assumptions postulate. The dependence of Toynbee's concepts on Dante is striking. Toynbee's precipice resembles nothing so much as Dante's Mount Purgatory. The direct mutual illumination in the new state of Yin parallels the ability of the denizens of Dante's Paradise to read each other's thoughts.

Yet again the empirical method leads to the logical inconsistencies and the philosophical difficulties observed previously. If etherealization exhibits the liberation of energy for higher tasks, then this assertion finds no warranty in historical data. Higher and lower—as Kant already pointed out in his "Refutation of Ethical Hedonism"[2]—do not constitute categories of empirical experience, but normative patterns of rationality. On the other hand, empiricism sees etherealization as merely a technical transfer of a field of activity brought about by the physical expansion of the civilization.

In fact, Toynbee sways uneasily between his theological conception of inner self-determination and the etherealization which is merely a product of the civilization's growth (environmental). Toynbee the empiricist sees the problems of Western civilization as consequences of a technological mastery (though the inconsistency implicit in at one point postulating that an improvement in technology accompanies simplification, and at another considering Gandhi's return to the spinning wheel as a symptom of a yearning for simplicity, cannot be overlooked). Toynbee the theologian views the criteria of growth as emanations of a soul's self-articulation. What is the connection between these realms of Necessity and Freedom? Do arrested civilizations result from an insuperable challenge or a deficient response?[3]

Toynbee's criticism of Spengler is curiously inept. Surely Spengler's assertion of a culture as an organism did not imply that the culture and its component individual constituted two mutually exclusive entities. Spengler would not deny that all activity presupposes individual volition. The crucial question is, however, whether this personal volition represents an immanent, inexorable Destiny which implicitly structures thought or

---

1. Toynbee, *op. cit.*, Vol. III, p. 377.
2. Kant, *Critique of Practical Reason, op. cit.*, p. 111.
3. See *post* "Conclusions" for further developments of this point.

whether it serves as the cause of a civilization's development. Toynbee offers no definite answer to this question. He denies the concept of a culture's soul, but his differentiation by growth resembles the quibble of psychologists of whether a child's personality is formed before birth or begins to develop from the first days. It seems that after the first challenges are surmounted, the subsequent problematic aspect, in Toynbee's terms, is set in ever narrower limits.[1]

The dilemma of Necessity and Freedom stands unresolved. The inadequacy of utilizing history as a technical proof of normative concepts has become more apparent.

The Breakdown of Civilizations

The breakdown of civilizations can never for Toynbee contain the sanction of an unavoidable fatality. If growth is a process of progressive etherealization, breakdown must result from a failure of self-determination. A challenge that does not evoke a successful response constantly faces a failing civilization with its threatening presence. Under its impact the reactive capacity of the civilization becomes exhausted; the creative minority loses its charm for the uninspired majority. Mimesis breaks down and society degenerates into antagonistic classes. To escape these tensions of the now dominant minority, a universal state develops as an instrument of repression. The internal proletariat gives expression to the frustration in its soul by the creation of a universal church, the repository of the meaning of history. His metaphysical dilemma ever accompanies Toynbee on his journey through history. The difficulty of uniting normative concepts with empirical deduction becomes more pronounced. If all civilizations have collapsed or exhibit symptoms of breakdown, how can the necessity of a society's decline be consistently denied? Why is Christianity of absolute validity in a cosmology which produces higher religions as the accidental consequence of social breakdown? These are the questions that dominate Toynbee's analysis of the breakdown of civilizations.

All civilizations that have heretofore existed have either broken down or

---

1. The fact that Toynbee's mimesis is very close to a concept of the soul will be developed; see *post* "Conclusions."

exhibit all symptoms of decay.[1] An empirical survey cannot draw conclusions from this phenomenon until all possible theories have been examined. Toynbee rejects the argument that the decline of civilizations results from a general ageing of the earth, with an assertion of the relative youth of the species in terms of its life span.

The racial theory presents no greater difficulties. Based on Plato and Aristotle, it insists that all creative advance results from the infusion of virile blood into static civilizations, all decline from the degeneration of this race. Thus the Renaissance is conceived as due to the Lombard invasions, the beneficial effects of which took several centuries to appear. Nevertheless, according to Toynbee, empirical data fails to support this thesis. The bloom of the Risorgimento occurred without any preceding barbarian invasion.[2]

What of the cyclical theory? Does the repetitive movement of the stars find its counterpart in human history? At first blush, Toynbee's assumption of an elemental rhythm that expresses itself in alternate states of Yin and Yang, and Withdrawal-and-Return, lends support to this thesis. Toynbee denies that this constitutes a correct inference. Though the shuttle that weaves the web of time moves up and down, its movements serve as the condition for the creation of a meaningful pattern.[3] The wheel must turn in order to advance. Withdrawal and Return, Yin and Yang, do not disclose senseless cycles, but requisites for the liberation of the Promethean *élan* of creativity.[4]

Breakdowns of civilizations do not result from the operation of cosmic forces, then, but from factors within human control. Yet what criteria for the evaluation of decline exist? Toynbee again examines the relation of the civilization to its physical and human environment.[5]

Loss of control over the physical environment does not cause the break-

---

1. Toynbee wavers on the question of Western civilization but on the whole seems to include it among the decaying societies.

2. This seems an unhappy choice for the refutation of the very likely untenable race theory. The Risorgimento is hardly comparable in creative effectiveness to the Renaissance.

3. Toynbee, *op. cit.*, Vol. IV, p. 35.

4. This argument does not, however, refute the necessity of a civilization's decline. However purposeful the movement of the shuttle in objective terms, subjectively it involves the growth and decline of civilizations. See *post* "Conclusions."

5. These arguments are presented at such length because without some glimpse of his methodology, Toynbee's philosophy becomes meaningless.

down of a civilization. On the contrary, technique may improve in many fields long after the decline has set in. Wherever the command over the physical environment does diminish, it exhibits the consequences, not the cause, of social breakdown. The ability to construct roads did not decline after Marcus Aurelius, but Roman willingness to do so degenerated. The technical knowledge for draining swamps existed throughout Rome's history, yet the capacity to respond to this continuing challenge suffered and so the Campagna became, in time, malaria-ridden.

Loss of command over the human environment also fails to qualify as a criterion for the breakdown of civilizations in Toynbee's scheme. Indeed, the early stage of decline reveals a great increase in the mastery of the human environment. As the breakdown proceeds and the inner strength of society dissipates itself in domestic strife, the barbarians beyond the borders cease to be charmed by the civilization's creativeness and overrun large areas. This, again, is a result, not a cause, of the inner decline. The barbarians' appearance on the civilization's geographical field heralds the beginning of the time of troubles from which in time a new civilization emerges.

Similarly, Toynbee denies that the impact of an alien civilization may cause a society's breakdown. An alien civilization succeeds in making its domination effective only in the advanced stages of social breakdown. A society that has undergone a prolonged "Time of Troubles," without being able to create a universal state, may welcome an alien intrusion that affords relief from the intolerable warfare. This was the service performed by the Osmanlis for the Orthodox Christian civilization, which had broken down in the Bulgar wars of the eleventh century. The internecine warfare of the subsequent centuries had not given way to the peace of a universal state, and in these circumstances the Ottoman Empire represented a relief from an oppressive situation. This, too, according to Toynbee, seems the condition of Russia, Japan, and India, all of which achieved universal states under Western inspiration.[1]

Its human environment may absorb a society in two ways. The more painful process of apparentation-and-affiliation really represents a victory through defeat, for the inner meaning of the civilization is salvaged through the agency of a universal church. The total absorption into an alien civilization, on the other hand, results in the atrophy of all cultural activity.

---

1. Toynbee, *op. cit.*, Vol. IV, p. 89.

In either case the human environment's intrusion follows social breakdown, and does not cause it.

If the breakdown of civilization does not result from loss of command over either the physical or human environment, what does account for the high incidence of fatalities among civilizations? Toynbee finds part of the answer in the faculty of mimesis. This social drill, the consequence of man's inability to absorb directly the inspiration of the saints, represents a shortcut fraught with dangers. Just as increased technological efficiency increases the responsibility of the engineer, so the faculty of mimesis becomes dangerous if directed outside the path charted by the creative minority. Mimesis is ever threatened by its mechanicalness. Tradition provides ordinarily the best guarantee for the safe direction of mimesis. The civilization, however, has broken the "cake of custom,"[1] and is therefore forced to live dangerously, the breakdown of mimesis its ever present threat.

Their dependence on mimesis exposes creative personalities to many dangers. The leaders may become infected with the hypnotism they deliberately instilled in their followers. This will transform the purposeful advance into robot-like activity.[2] The loss of creativeness destroys their claim to leadership. The magic charm evaporates and the multitude, which heretofore followed unquestioningly, mutinies. Power replaces inspiration as the social tie. The exercise of force constitutes an abuse of trust which eventually dooms its perpetrators. The failure of the Promethean *élan* leads to a loss of harmony. The society articulates itself into classes and dissipates its strength in inner conflict.[3]

The intractability of institutions provides another obstacle to the uniform growth of civilizations. The precept that the best-adapted methods yield maximum results, contained in Christ's saying that new wine should not be placed in old bottles,[4] can be successfully applied only in a family. Society, however, as the common ground of many persons' field of action, severely limits the range of possible adaptation.

Social readjustments have to contend with the *vis inertiae* that attempts at all times to keep the structure static. Creative forces can overcome these

---

1. Toynbee, *op. cit.*, Vol. IV, p. 128.
2. See *post.* This, according to Toynbee, is the condition of the arrested civilizations.
3. See *post* "The Disintegration of Civilizations."
4. Toynbee, *op. cit.*, Vol. IV, p. 133. See *post* "Conclusions."

tendencies by gradual adjustment, by utilizing old institutions for new purposes or by violently eliminating the inelastic structure. The violent removal of the obstruction is revolution, a process of retarded mimesis, the intensity of which is proportional to the anachronism to be overcome. Social enormities utilize old institutions for purposes they were never meant to fit. If the response accomplishes itself through adjustments, growth is assured. Revolutions, too, may assist growth by removing impediments to progress, though the resort to force ever constitutes a moral blight. Enormities are the very embodiments of social breakdown, however, their perversion of institutions resulting in that rigidity of outlook which characterizes arrested and declining civilizations.[1]

Toynbee ascribes a large measure of the inconstancy of human fortunes, the recurrent growth and decline of civilizations, to the nemesis of creativity. Creative responses to successive challenges are extremely rare. Indeed, it seems that the successful solution of one problem severely limits the reactive capacity to the next ordeal. The insight and uprightness which enabled the Pharisees to guide Jewry in its Babylonian captivity failed them when faced with the greater treasure of a supra-mundane kingdom promised by Christ.

This, too, is the motif of the Attic drama which ascribes the sudden change in human fortunes to the envy of the gods. Herodotus' fable of the ring of Polycrates exhibits the sudden negation of being brought on by divine disfavor. But in the legend of the end of Croesus emerges a deepening of the understanding. And in Aeschylus the total collapse of all human aspirations results not from the aberration of a fickle Deity, but from a deficiency in the soul of the sufferer. Sin, not envy, dooms human endeavor. The sinner's blight follows an inner alienation from the divine love, which makes him unworthy to continue as God's instrument. The nemesis of creativity constitutes one aspect of this drama of the doom of man, with God's role merely passive, revealing the inevitable consequence of sinful conduct.

This aberration accomplishes itself in two possible modes. The passive fault consists in resting on one's oars, in considering one's achievements a summit instead of a stepping-stone, in worshipping Time instead of eter-

---

1. For illustrations see Toynbee, *op. cit.*, Vol. IV, pp. 137–245; for discussion of incommensurability of illustrations, see *post* "Conclusions."

nity. The adoration of a glorious past tends to induce passivity towards the tasks of the moment. The exaltation of the creature, in place of the Creator, characterizes the arrested civilizations. This is idolatry, the replacement of the constantly true by the ephemeral.

The active aberration exhibits the denial of limit, that rushes headlong into disaster, the psychological condition of being spoilt by success, with annihilation as its consequence.

Toynbee distinguishes several forms of idolatry. The idolization of an ephemeral self led Jewry to disaster. After having divined a truth of eternal validity in the sublimity of the One True God, Israel fell into the error of conceiving its temporary spiritual eminence as an eternal divine sanction. Worshipping a past greatness, which had been sterilized by the self-adoration of the "Chosen People," Jewry was unable to accept the greater treasure offered to it by Christ. Thus Israel atrophied while Christianity was preached by Galileans and accepted by Gentiles.[1]

Similarly, Athens had become the "education of Hellas" in the fifth and sixth centuries. But this magnificent success blinded Athens to the import of new problems. The inadequacy of the polis organization as a stable base for further Hellenic growth was the most pressing challenge of the fourth-century Hellenic civilization. Athens could react only by attempting to assert a military hegemony, and the limit of her physical strength was quickly reached. The poleis were finally transcended by peripheral powers, Macedonia and Rome, whose prospects had initially seemed much less bright than those of Athens. Moreover, the glory of its philosophy evoked such an idolization that the divine truth preached by Paul fell on deaf ears in Athens.[2]

Enormities result from the idolization of an ephemeral institution, exhibited by the limitations of the Greek city-states, whose constant warfare led to the breakdown of the Hellenic civilization. Even after disintegration had run its course and the barbarians had occupied Rome, Justinian attempted to invoke the ghost of the Roman Empire for Belisarius' campaign in Italy. This futile effort so depleted the resources of Anatolia that the Sassanid Empire succeeded in annexing most of Byzantium's

---

1. Toynbee, *op. cit.*, Vol. IV, p. 263.
2. Toynbee, *op. cit.*, Vol. IV, p. 273. This illustrates Toynbee's confusion of the normative and the empirical. See *post* "Conclusions." Further illustrated pp. 274–303.

eastern territories and caused the breakdown of that civilization.[1] Similarly, the Parliament of Westminster is performing functions for which it is organizationally unsuited. The representation of territorial units is the most effective democratic device in an agricultural society. The complexities of modern industrialism, on the other hand, require a Parliament based on a corporate structure. Yet the worship of this ephemeral institution will in all likelihood prevent England from finding a solution to this twentieth-century challenge.

The arrested civilizations testify to the final nemesis of idolatry, the idolization of ephemeral techniques. They possess biological counterparts in those organisms, whose overly successful adaptation to an environment has accounted for their retardation on the evolutionary scale. In the industrial sphere, an initial technological advantage is often purchased at the price of flexibility, exemplified by the gradual decline of Manchester's commercial position. The excessive reliance on an ephemeral military technique leads to that sudden collapse of an apparent colossus, of which David's encounter with Goliath constitutes the mythological intuition.[2] Thus Toynbee has accounted for three types of idolatry: the idolization of an ephemeral self, an ephemeral institution, and an ephemeral technique, all manifestations of the passive form of the nemesis of creativity.

If idolatry exhibits the sin of resting on one's oar, the active nemesis of creativity accomplishes itself through dynamism in three stages. It begins with the psychological condition of being spoilt by success. The consequent loss of mental and moral balance results in a blind impulse that tempts the soul to attempt the impossible.[3] Here, too, Toynbee distinguishes several forms.

The suicidalness of militarism derives from an arrogance in the exploitation of success, which fails to appreciate the limits of its own physical strength. The hatred of the subject populations is compounded by the fear of all neighboring states, whose decision to end the constant state of insecurity leads to the inevitable extermination of the militarist. This was the case of Assyria, which escaped the nemesis of the idolization of an ephem-

---

1. Toynbee, *op. cit.*, Vol. IV, pp. 320–404. This contradicts an earlier assertion that the Bulgar wars caused the breakdown of the Orthodox Christian civilization.
2. For other illustrations see Toynbee, *op. cit.*, Vol. IV, p. 423–465.
3. Toynbee, *op. cit.*, Vol. IV, p. 258.

eral technique, but whose recurrent resort to force caused a coalition of all neighboring societies to wipe it off the face of the earth.

The careers of Charlemagne and Tamerlane reveal sharply the suicidalness of militarism. Their position as guardians of the civilization's marshes had placed great opportunities within their grasp. The importance of border provinces derives from the stimulating effect of their exposed position. The response to this challenge may carry the margrave into barbarian territory and thus vastly expand the civilization's geographical extent.[1] Regarded from another point of view, the articulation of the marshes exhibits an aspect of the process of etherealization. By assuming the task of military defense, they liberate the energies of the civilization for other tasks and continued creative endeavor.

Tamerlane and Charlemagne failed to perform their proper function. They diverted their energies into the body of their own civilization, and commenced a civil war, the only issue of which could be social breakdown. The Iranian civilization did not long survive Tamerlane's onslaught, and Western Europe was saved from a similar fate only by the weakness of Charlemagne's sons and the fresh challenge presented by the Norsemen.

The intoxication of victory[2] constitutes a special instance of the "active" nemesis of creativity in Toynbee's scheme. Rome's secular and spiritual history exhibits its symptoms. The victory over Hannibal so slackened Roman military discipline that the next century saw a series of defeats at the hands of outmatched powers.[3] In the spiritual field, Gregory had brought the church out of the depth of disrepute into which it had fallen in the previous generations. But the initial successes against the empire caused the papacy to lose its sense of proportion. The alliance with the Sicilian Norsemen sanctioned a use of force that inextricably involved the church in the affairs of this world. The fight to the death against the Hohenstaufen ensued, symbolizing that idolization of an ephemeral self that ever contains its own nemesis. Innocent III's seeming preeminence only served to hide an inner weakness, of which the Babylonian captivity was to bear witness before the end of the century.

Thus, the nemesis of creativity contains two possible aberrations.

---

1. Toynbee, *op. cit.*, Vol. IV, p. 491. This contradicts the concept that expansion is a symptom of decay.
2. Toynbee, *op. cit.*, Vol. IV, p. 505.
3. Toynbee, *op. cit.*, Vol. IV, p. 506. This seems a better illustration for the passive aberration.

The passive sin of resting on one's oar expresses itself in the idolatry of the ephemeral. The active failure to recognize limits proves the saying that "those who live by the sword shall perish by the sword." The inevitable penalty in both cases is death.

Toynbee's concept of the breakdown of civilizations is a necessary product of his metaphysical doctrine. If growth discloses a successful response to recurrent challenges, then breakdown must constitute the penalty for a failing self-determination. The necessity of decline is a function of a degenerating purposiveness, not of a cosmic inexorability. The mechanicalness of mimesis, the intractability of institutions, and the various aspects of the nemesis of creativity serve as the criteria by which to evaluate social breakdown.

Yet no aspect of Toynbee's philosophy can free itself from the difficulties and inconsistencies of his metaphysical assumptions. To assert that civilizations break down as a result of some failure of willpower on the part of its members is not refuting the doctrine of organic necessity. For surely Spengler, too, would admit that individuals constitute the entities of action. The key problem resides in the dilemma of human volition as the cause or the result of breakdown. This failing response may itself constitute the manifestation of an immanent decline.

Toynbee's ambiguous postulation of purposiveness is compounded by his theory of society as a common field of activity. If the intractability of institutions results from the difficulty of modifying overlapping, dynamic fields, then the individual's freedom of action is severely limited. The only portion left for purposiveness would be that part of a person's sphere outside the common field. This, in relation to the total range of interaction, must be, of necessity, small and insignificant. Thus, Toynbee substitutes a mechanism for an organism, an immutable causality for an immanent destiny.[1]

The difficulty of uniting the metaphysical assumptions with an empirical method constantly recurs. For what is the meaning of sin in a pragmatic context? It never becomes clear whether Toynbee condemns the Athenians for failing to understand the profounder truth represented by Paul or for a faulty analysis of the wave of the future.

No support can be found in historical data for the denial of the inexora-

---

1. On this point see quotation cited *post* "Conclusions."

bility of the decline, in the face of the collapse of every heretofore existing civilization. The postulation of a One True God in Christianity, though a logical consequence of Toynbee's theology, rejects the very pattern of recurrence necessary to establish a historical law. For a God cannot be both exclusive and the accidental result of a civilization's decline.

The deficiency of moral standards implied by the use of force may be well founded in theology, yet the only criterion empirical data admits is failure. And so Toynbee's ultimate proof resides in technical excellency, his final standard of values in the ability to prevail.

The Disintegration of Civilizations: Schism in the Body Social

The breakdown of civilizations issues into disintegration if the capacity to react to challenges becomes permanently stultified. The sense of frustration in the body social leads to an articulation into classes, the ever more violent conflict of which dissipates the strength of the civilization.

The analysis of the disintegration of civilizations represents the culmination of Toynbee's philosophy, the revelation of his metaphysical doctrine. Out of the ashes of the City of Destruction emerges a profounder level of world experience, the supra-mundane level of reality. The period of breakdown had prevented the creative forces of the civilization from realizing their potentialities. Though this static condition exhibits a level of integration, its duration is ephemeral. Since it was attained outside of God's plan,[1] this type of Yin cannot last. Against this negation of creativity, the secession of the internal proletariat constitutes a dynamic reaction. Yin changes to Yang again. Humanity proceeds on its journey up the precipice. The universal church, which salvages the purposiveness in life, gives content to the void in the soul and reveals truths of eternal validity.

Toynbee's metaphysical dilemmas are ever present, however. How can the accidental consequence of social breakdown embody the meaning of history? How can an empiricist evaluate the possible inward reactions to a state of disintegration? Indeed, what does the soul's anguish matter except as it embodies itself institutionally? Toynbee's empiricism forces him to

---

1. Or the sanction of evolution. Toynbee sways between the biological and the theological interpretation of history.

consider permanence a criterion for inward fitness. This raises the key problems of his philosophy. Does the growth and decay of civilizations contain the moral sanction of history, from which man can learn rules not only for moral but at the same time of successful conduct? Does salvation or hope reside in phenomenal appearance or inner experience? It is Kant's query again, the original dilemma restated, containing our metaphysical standard for the interpretation of Toynbee.[1]

If breakdown reveals a failure of self-determination, must it inevitably lead to disintegration? Toynbee turns to his "well-tried empirical method" for a solution. Just as birth did not necessarily involve growth, so breakdown does not inevitably lead to collapse. The alternative of disintegration is petrification, a state of creative impotence. Its dominant political form is a totalitarianism which accentuates the timeless evenness of existence, under which philosophy and art languish, but natural science continues to grow.[2]

Growth reveals a process of differentiation. The uniqueness of each challenge as a function of the previous response determines the civilization's specific development and artistic style. The opposite holds true for disintegration. There, the failure to meet the problem results in the continuous confrontation of the same challenge. The unhappy soul[3] struggles in vain, dissipating its inner strength in the futile attempt to escape defeat. For each unsuccessful response causes an increment in the formidability of the challenge and a loss of capacity to respond. Therefore, every disintegration accomplishes itself through standardization, expressed in a universal state, a universal church, and a *Völkerwanderung*.

Toynbee finds one criterion for disintegration in the existence of a schism in the body social, an articulation into incompatible social groups. To be sure, the growth phase was also characterized by class distinctions.[4] But its organization was hierarchical, the common devotion to values constituting the social bond, the distinction into classes revealing merely a technical division of labor. But now the claim of leadership has evaporated and the creative minority rules by force. The application of power makes a violent

---

1. For full discussion see *post* "Conclusions" and Appendix, "The Concepts of Meaning."
2. Toynbee, *op. cit.*, Vol. V, p. 10. This relies heavily on a combination of Spengler's Caesarism and the fellah state.
3. Toynbee, *op. cit.*, Vol. V, p. 13. This is another instance of Toynbee's use of the word *soul* for a civilization. See *post* "Conclusions."
4. Toynbee, *op. cit.*, Vol. V, p. 15.

response in the uncreative majority which forms the internal proletariat. And beyond the civilization's border, an external proletariat threateningly faces the dominant minority.

Any attempt to heal the schism in the body social is doomed to failure, for the loss of creativeness prevents any except makeshift solutions. Toynbee believes that the Marxian philosophy accurately describes the condition of a civilization moving towards collapse amidst an ever greater accentuation of class oppositions. But the Old Testament strain in Marx also pointed the way towards a means of transcending this conflict. For the vision of the classless society transcends economic aspirations and expresses man's longing for a Promised Land that reconciles all striving. Oppressors and oppressed will vanish and harmony will reign everywhere. This intuition of peace through suffering, of happiness through agony, does not represent for Toynbee a bridging of the schism but its immanent purpose.[1] This is palingenesia, the new level of integration.

Schism-and-palingenesia appears, like Withdrawal-and-Return, as another beat of the elemental rhythm, of which Yin and Yang represent phases. It exhibits the mechanism by which the condition of dynamic activity maintains itself. The schism represents the withdrawal. The dominant minority, which clings to its position against all equity,[2] has forced society into a static mold. The secession of the internal proletariat constitutes a dynamic response, the disturbance of the uneasy equilibrium. It withdraws to work out the solutions of the next phase of development. Its agony is shared by a small group of inspired personalities, the new creative minority, which utilizes the faculty of mimesis to control the mass of the internal proletariat. In relation to this dynamic group, the dominant minority merely constitutes an enormity.

When the work of creation has proceeded and found its institutional embodiment in the universal church, palingenesia ensues, the apprehension of a deeper meaning, the condition of a fresh advance.[3]

Each component of the disintegrating civilization develops a distinctive institution in response to the challenge of decline. The internal proletariat creates the universal church, the dominant minority founds the universal state, and the external proletariat forms itself into barbarian war-bands.

---

1. Toynbee, *op. cit.*, Vol. V, p. 28.
2. Toynbee, *op. cit.*, Vol. V, p. 26.
3. This is the return phase.

Each institution moreover allows for the articulation of an active and a passive set of attitudes.

Its monopoly of force enables the dominant minority to create the universal state as a response to the challenge of the internecine warfare of parochial states. Toynbee distinguishes three characteristic human types as products of this military success: the conqueror, exemplified by Alexander, the hangman, and the wastrel. The wastrel exemplifies the tremendous increase of the material scale of life brought about by territorial expansion. He appeared in the Roman aristocracy after the defeat of Hannibal and in the pyramid builders of Egypt. The hangman is a familiar figure of the dominant minority of decaying civilizations, represented by Titus in the Hellenic civilization and ranging from the princes who consigned the Anabaptists to the pyre[1] to the Nazis in the Western civilization.

Yet the dominant minority also produces different and nobler individuals. The universal state brings peace to a suffering humanity after the intolerable "Period of Contending States." Though its existence is ephemeral, the universal state in full bloom develops administrators whose unselfishness and devotion to duty hides the inner weakness of all institutions. This was the condition of the Roman Empire in the second century, when the excellence of its civil service achieved the deceptive bloom which really was that society's Indian summer. Similarly, the changing ethos of the dominant minority in the West in the twentieth century has replaced the blatant exploitation of colonial areas with at least a lip service to the welfare of the indigenous population.

The ethos of the administrator develops from the dominant minority's most spiritual creation, the school of philosophy. It transforms the Roman wolf into a Platonic watchdog.[2] It weaves into the texture of the disintegrating society those moral precepts which represent the only enduring results of its existence. Yet the universal state is beyond salvation. The union between the dominant minority and philosophy is never complete. The original sin of militarism constantly reappears, not to be avoided by even the most high-minded rulers, such as Marcus and Julian.[3]

---

1. Toynbee, *op. cit.*, Vol. V, p. 41. This seems to date the disintegration of the Western civilization several centuries before even Spengler.
2. Toynbee, *op. cit.*, Vol. V, p. 39.
3. Toynbee, *op. cit.*, Vol. V, p. 79 (f.n.). See *post* "Conclusions" for discussion of this concept.

The schools of philosophy express an attitude born of frustration, a reaction to the inadequacies of life. Their ideal is Detachment, the contemplation that knows no social responsibility,[1] the withdrawal which is conceived as an end, the return which exhibits an inner sacrifice. They find refuge from the oppressive present in an assertion of determinism, of which the triumph of astrology in the Hellenic and Babylonian worlds furnishes the most notable examples.[2] Philosophy does not represent the ultimate answer to the inner void of the civilization. It may, however, assist the dialectical formulation of the only true solution, the higher religion. Finally, when disintegration has run its course, only the universal church remains as the chrysalis of a new civilization, into the body of which the dominant minority merges and disappears.

Toynbee conceives the internal proletariat as the product of a state of mind, not of an economic condition. It is inspired by a consciousness of having been deprived of its rightful place in the community, of being in but not of a society, of being unwanted and useless. Its resentment inspires a constant application of repressive measures which only serve to accentuate the rift.

All declining societies contain an internal proletariat recruited from three distinct sources: the disinherited and uprooted members of its own body social, the partially disinherited components of alien conquered civilizations, who are exploited in their native environment, and the doubly disinherited conscripts from subject populations whose exploitation involves their transplantation.[3] The destruction of the Hellenic peasantry by the introduction of the *latifundia* is paralleled in the West by the pernicious consequences of the enclosure movement. The indigenous Syriac internal proletariat of the Hellenic civilization has its counterpart in the Indian component of the Western Great Society.[4] The institution of slavery blighted both civilizations.

All the typical reactions of the dominant minority to the pervasive sense

---

1. This criticism of Detachment seems contradicted by the very existence of Plato and Aristotle's political philosophy, which indicates some concern with the affairs of this world.
2. Toynbee, *op. cit.*, Vol. V, p. 58, considers Cartesianism the Western counterpart of determinism.
3. Toynbee, *op. cit.*, Vol. V, p. 66.
4. There seems no warranty for including India and other colonial dependencies in the Western society. The only connection between India and the West is on the technical (economic) and political plane. This, in Toynbee's terms, is a consequence of Western disintegration, not of Indian inclusion in the Western civilization.

of futility manifest themselves in the internal proletariat as well. The arbitrariness of the rulers evokes the rebellion of the oppressed. The "violent" response, however, cannot succeed because of the dominant minority's monopoly of force. Out of the bloody suppression of the slave rebellions in Sicily and the peasant and Anabaptist revolts in the West emerges an alternative response. The gentle attitude, exhibiting a provisional recognition of limits, issues in a religion which is at once faced with the crucial dilemma of its existence. It must decide whether to use its hold on the hearts of the internal proletariat for the satisfaction of immediate political aims or whether to confine itself to the satisfaction of the greater spiritual wants.

Judaism chose the first alternative. Its nemesis became the futile search for a Messiah to actualize a parochial state. But Christ set Christianity firmly on the other path. His reprimand of Peter exhibits a final level of transcendental reconciliation, which guaranteed the eventual triumph of Christianity.[1] Similarly, Jewish survival was not assured until the realization that the Kingdom of God was not an external state and that man must abstain from all attempts to promote the divine plan.[2]

The spiritual superiority of the internal proletariat over the dominant minority becomes apparent in their comparative institutional embodiments. The universal state is a child of militarism; the universal church exhibits a new level of inner reconciliation. The dominant minority's gentle response issues in a philosophy which preaches Detachment as the highest state of bliss and an idolatrous religion of self-worship in the form of the Divus cult.[3]

Toynbee finds most of these symptoms of disintegration in the Western civilization as well. The dominant minority has failed to solve the problem of the internecine warfare of parochial states, the increasing violence of which multiplies the internal proletariat. Its gentle response is a meaningless theosophy, a re-emerging astrology, and the idolatrous adoration of nation-states.

The internal proletariat, on the other hand, after its unsuccessful violence in the Peasants' Revolt, has learned in many respects the ways of gentleness. The Quakers illustrated by their prosperity that "the meek

---

1. Toynbee, *op. cit.*, Vol. V, p. 75.
2. Toynbee, *op. cit.*, Vol. V, p. 76.
3. This is a good illustration of Toynbee's normative concepts.

shall inherit the earth" and that "honesty is the best policy."[1] The violence
of Marxism has been tempered until it has been transformed into a like-
ness of the dominant minority's totalitarian worship of the state. But the
miracle of Christianity represents the deepest manifestation of Western
gentleness. In the souls of races but a generation removed from slavery,
Christianity has been revitalized and again becomes a living force. The
hold of the neopagan dominant minority is visibly lessening and hope
again flows through the branches of Western Christendom.[2] Toynbee
expressed the belief that this tottering civilization, which has been reduced
to its present state by the intoxication of victory over physical nature, may
become the first to escape its nemesis, to find peace through gentleness and
life through Christ.[3]

The external proletariat constitutes itself in response to the flagging
inspiration of the civilization. During the growth phase the barbarian's
mimesis had been directed towards the creative minority's cultural
achievements. The area of contact between the two societies had been
fluid, the extent of cultural radiation determined by the civilization's inner
energy. But the emergence of the dominant minority sees a secession by
the barbarians who now form the external proletariat. The boundary
becomes fixed, and the two antagonists face each other across a *limes* in an
uneasy truce before the inevitable clash.

The external proletariat may continue to adopt the civilization's still
superior technique, but the inner relationship has ceased, and conflict is
the unavoidable climax. For the external proletariat possesses effective
means of physical resistance. In contrast to the internal proletariat, the
majority of its members are outside the dominant minority's direct control.
Moreover, the dominant minority is exposed to all the nemesis of creativity, while the external proletariat experiences constant additions in strength
from the ranks of the ever more disgruntled barbarians.

Violence is therefore the most typical reaction of the external proletariat.
Its institutional embodiment is the barbarian war-bands, whose penetration of the civilization's territory heralds the beginning of the interregnum.
The external proletariat's religion reflects its change of outlook. The religion of primitive mankind exhibits a worship of the community in all its

---

1. Toynbee, *op. cit.*, Vol. V, p. 174. See *post* for discussion of this argument.
2. Toynbee, *op. cit.*, Vol. V, p. 193.
3. For other illustrations, see Toynbee, *op. cit.*, Vol. V, pp. 76–194.

manifestations, of which procreation and military defense are the most important. Thus the goddess of fertility constitutes the primary religious symbolism of the earliest stage of development, while the god of destruction plays a very subsidiary role. The emergence of a military frontier, however, engenders a social revolution. The energies of the community are henceforth directed towards conquest, with a consequent inversion of the relative importance of the procreative and destructive activities. The god of war appears as the Divinity towards which the worship of the external proletariat begins to be directed, a testimony to its choice of the attitude of violence.

Even this period is not without its creativeness, however. The Homeric poems testify to a profundity of vision which was to be repeated in the English and Scandinavian epics.[1] The external proletariat's conquests achieve permanence only after the barbarian war-bands have accepted the universal church of the internal proletariat and under its gentle guidance created a new civilization. And so the history of the external proletariat, too, reveals the ultimate victory of gentleness over violence, the attainment of peace through strife. The City of Destruction appears as ephemeral as the universal state, and out of its ashes rises the inner meaning of history, to which even the barbarians must bow, the universal church.

The analysis of the disintegration of civilization exhibits the happiest application of Toynbee's pragmatic method. For the inner contradictions of his metaphysical pattern are here at a minimum. Whatever the cause of society's breakdown, its issue into disintegration discloses that inevitability, that "standardization,"[2] for the apprehension of which an empirical approach is ideally suited. All disintegration proceeds through the agency of a dominant minority, a seceding internal proletariat, and invading barbarian war-bands. The schism in the body social becomes ever wider, the frustration in the soul unbridgeable. The possible reactions to this dilemma are limited and confined to alternative violent or gentle responses. However, only the gentle responses contain the seeds of creativeness; only the universal church possesses a future.

Yet even here, Toynbee's normative pattern and its irreconcilability with the historical data emerges. The truth of the universal church seems in the final analysis merely founded on its future, the evil of the repressive meas-

---

1. Toynbee, *op. cit.*, Vol. V, p. 233.
2. Toynbee, *op. cit.*, Vol. V, p. 13.

ures of the universal state on their futility. "Honesty is the best policy" becomes, in Toynbee's interpretation of the Quakers, primarily a maxim of prudent conduct. It is not apparent whether an inner attitude or a physical location characterizes the internal proletariat. Though Toynbee's emphasis on purposiveness makes him opt for the proletarization by willed secession, the account of the proletariat's recruitment supports the theory of geographical accident. The miracle of Christianity may cause its embodiment in the universal of a second decaying civilization, but this can have no bearing on the fate of the Western civilization. For the essence of a universal church is the supra-mundane plane of reality. Its full meaning is only realized after disintegration has run its course and barbarian war-bands toppled the City of Destruction. Christianity could then become the chrysalis—in Toynbee's scheme—of a new civilization. But its conception as the material salvation of the West repeats that very sin for which Toynbee castigates Athens, the idolization of an ephemeral self.

The Disintegration of Civilizations: Schism in the Soul

The mere description of the institutional manifestations of disintegration can never, for Toynbee, exhaust the essence of that process. Just as growth was revealed as a rhythm of progressive etherealization, independent of the material conditions of command over the environment, just as breakdown resulted from failure in the capacity to respond successfully in recurrent challenges, so disintegration hides a deeper meaning. The schism in the body social represents merely a symptom of that profounder schism in the soul which is the real cause of society's collapse. The growth phase of the civilization had witnessed a consistent directedness in all fields of behavior, feeling, and life.[1] But with disintegration, the possible reactions become polarized into inconclusive alternatives. A choice between the active and the passive option is the only freedom left to the soul which has lost its creativeness and which participates, either as villain or victim, in the social disintegration.[2]

This aspect of Toynbee's philosophy results in a total breakdown of his method. The state of a soul is approachable in terms of empirical analysis

---

1. Toynbee, *op. cit.*, Vol. VI, p. 375.
2. For discussion of this ambiguity see *post* "Conclusions."

only in its institutional embodiments. The interpretation of their inner meaning must remain a metaphysical construction.[1] An attempt to derive historical laws from a categorization of states of mind which are really emanations of theological viewpoints cannot claim to base itself on the surface manifestations of phenomenal appearance. The full implications of Toynbee's concept of the Promethean *élan* reveal themselves. Its immanent working had always seemed to contradict the purposiveness postulated by Challenge-and-Response. It now appears that any conscious attempt to change the present condition constitutes the sin of Archaism or Futurism, the penalty for which is disintegration. We are back with Hegel's "whatever is, is right." We have not really transcended Spengler. The problem of Freedom and Necessity remains unsolved.[2]

Disintegration reflects the schism in a soul, which has destroyed its creativity and whose collapse is approaching amidst mounting frustration. Every aspect of life exhibits this inward dilemma; no part of society can escape it. Yet since the problems faced by each component vary, the schism will reveal itself in a different form in the typical reactions of each class.

Toynbee distinguishes several symptoms of inward frustration on the planes of behavior, feeling, and life. On the plane of behavior, the loss of creativity evokes the alternatives of abandon and self-control, each an attempt to coax out of nature the inspiration which has been wantonly destroyed. While the dominant minority endeavors to recapture the charm of its youth, either by giving rein to the passions or by their strict control, the internal proletariat seeks a substitute for the lost art of mimesis. The lack of leadership accentuates the inner helplessness of the mass. Its alternatives are truancy and martyrdom, a shirking of responsibility made possible by the breakdown of discipline or a conscious quest for a death that will finally end all uncertainty.

On the plane of feeling, the reactions occur to a reversal of the Promethean *élan* by which growth had accomplished itself.[3] The sense of drift exhibits the passive response, a resignation to the enigmatic universe which under either the aspect of Chance or Necessity accentuates the impotence of man. When the failure is viewed subjectively, the sense of sin

---

1. See Appendix, "The Concepts of Meaning."
2. For full discussion see *post* "Conclusions."
3. Toynbee, *op. cit.*, Vol. V, p. 380.

appears, a recognition of an inward failure to master life, an admission of inadequacy, the condition for salvation.

The breakdown of growth is accompanied by a cessation of the differentiation which had produced the civilization's style. The sick soul loses its sense of form and gives vent to a feeling of promiscuity, expressed in the blending of incompatible values, the emergence of a cosmopolitan language, the syncretism of religion and philosophy. Yet the profounder souls of each society sense a profound meaning in the loss of style, an apprehension of unity behind the growth and decay of ephemeral institutions. The sense of unity conjures a Cosmos of eternal validity out of the chaotic appearance of the phenomenal world.

On the plane of life, the transfer of the field of action from the macrocosm to the microcosm, the etherealization, is replaced by two pairs of alternative modes of behavior. On this plane, however, there exists an option between a pair of violent and a pair of gentle responses, between the attempt of realizing one's aspirations on the material level or the apprehension of a deeper truth transcending mere appearance. Archaism and Futurism constitute the violent options, a projection of longing in Time, the quest for a Utopia which evades the challenge presented by the change in spiritual climate.[1] The doom of this endeavor causes a violent eruption of the pent-up frustration and seals the doom of the society. When all material hopes are disappointed, the gentle response re-emerges, the recognition by man of his limits, the humility which transcends itself, the faith that moves mountains. Detachment and Transfiguration,[2] the bliss of contemplation and the salvation through God's love, appear, the guarantee, at the eleventh hour, of the continuation of the meaning of life.

Any society contains creative personalities, agents of dynamic activity, embodiments of the new level of Yin. But a disintegrating society offers no obvious field of activity for leadership. Mimesis has broken down, and attempts at revitalization are bound to be tentative and uncertain. As the schism in the soul of the civilization becomes wider, the inspired individuals appear in the role of saviours, their effectiveness determined by the attitude of life they represent.[3] For gentleness will always triumph over violence, peace over discord, faith over materialism. God's love, the motive

1. Toynbee, *op. cit.*, Vol. V, p. 383.
2. Toynbee, *op. cit.*, Vol. V, p. 391.
3. Toynbee, *op. cit.*, Vol. VI, p. 175.

force of the universe, shines as a beacon of mercy through the gloom of collapse.

Abandon and self-control constitute Toynbee's conception of the reactions of a soul which attempts to claim the sanction of nature for the absence of its creativeness. Abandon ascribes the loss of its inspiration to the inner separation from a state of nature and attempts to recapture its youth by giving free rein to all spontaneous appetites. Its representatives are Thrasymachus and Alcibiades in the Hellenistic civilization, Rousseau and Machiavelli in the West.

Self-control, too, claims the sanction of nature. Salvation from the intolerable present is sought in disciplining the base emotions, in the melancholy rejection of the world, of which Marcus Aurelius and Savonarola furnish the outstanding examples.[1]

Truancy and martyrdom represent the alternatives by which a leaderless mass seeks to find a substitute for the loss of direction induced by the collapse of mimesis. Just as in an army the relaxation of discipline offers a moral excuse for the shirking of danger, so truancy in a disintegrating society appears as an alternative to the purposiveness which has become oppressive. This was the reaction of Sparta and Athens at a time when only unity could prevent a Roman hegemony over Greece. This, too, is the meaning of the "irreligious toleration" of the West, which has cut itself off from its spiritual heritage and substituted a secular idol, in the form of the national state, for the spiritual basis of this greatness.

Yet the spectre of defeat may cause other minds to attempt to salvage their ideals by courting death without any hope of material reward. Socrates refused all chances to play truant and met a martyr's death. In its hour of trial, the Christian church steadfastly refused the very tempting and very easy escape of formal allegiance to the Divus. The blood of her martyrs furnished the condition of her eventual triumph. As an indication that the spirit of the martyrs is yet with us, Wolsey and More chose death rather than the ignominy of truancy.[2]

Toynbee turns next to an examination of the impact of disintegration on the plane of feeling. The loss of the Promethean *élan* of growth faces the soul with the very negation of existence, from which the sense of drift and the sense of sin represent antithetical methods of refuge. The feeling of

---

1. Toynbee, *op. cit.*, Vol. V, p. 403.
2. Toynbee, *op. cit.*, Vol. V, p. 411. For a discussion of these illustrations see *post* "Conclusions."

drift appears as the consequence of an idolatry of Necessity or Chance, a sin which inevitably leads to breakdown. Necessity and Chance are correlative as the expressions of a soul which represents its defeats subjectively as blind disorder and its objective operation under the aspect of inevitability. The West has worshipped Chance since *laissez-faire* was elevated into an ethical principle. But fate, too, has been the subject of adoration. The Calvinist doctrine of predestination, the counterpart of the Hellenic Tyche, introduced determinism into the lives and fortunes of human beings.[1]

But while an idolatry of fate may serve as an opiate in instilling in the soul an acquiescence in a disaster assumed to have its root in external circumstances, its counterpart, the sense of sin, acts as a powerful stimulus. Man turns inward for an explanation of his failure and attempts to make himself worthy of receiving God's grace. The road from an unconquerable Necessity to a conquerable sin is the saving truth which prevented Judaism from rushing headlong into disaster through the idolization of an ephemeral self.[2] The Hellenic civilization had to discover this great truth slowly, but the West was fortunate in growing out of the chrysalis of a higher religion. Nothing illustrates the perversity of human nature better than the Western hostility to its noble heritage, the repudiation of which may well doom the Great Society. Only by repenting can Western man save himself from the nemesis of his fate.[3]

A sense of promiscuity appears as the passive substitute for the sense of style which has disappeared with the breakdown of society. Toynbee finds its influence in all spheres of activity and in all social classes. The dominant minority exhibits the most pronounced tendencies towards promiscuity. Its military technique is usually an amalgam of the successful methods of neighboring civilizations.[4] An extensive dilution accompanies the expansion of the army, the insatiable requirements of which are the consequence of the campaigns for attaining the universal state. Common military service vulgarizes the dominant minority. The lack of inward strength forces the dominant minority to follow the immediate trend. When Christianity was small and without popular support, the persecutions of Rome were

---

1. Toynbee, *op. cit.*, Vol. V, p. 430. For the lack of inner relationship between Tyche and Calvin, see *post* "Conclusions." It would seem to fit much better under "Sense of Sin."
2. See *ante.*
3. Toynbee, *op. cit.*, Vol. V, p. 439.
4. Toynbee, *op. cit.*, Vol. V, p. 439. This, of course, may be the secret of their success.

persistent, if half-hearted. But once Christianity had achieved a position of eminence, the dominant minority reluctantly followed the internal proletariat's lead, by announcing its own conversion.[1]

The dominant minority's barbarization matches its vulgarization. The establishment of a military frontier across which the external proletariat ever threatens to erupt testifies to a barbarian war-band's feat of arms. Since the moral fiber of the dominant minority is steadily degenerating, the balance along the *limes* inclines in the barbarian's favor. The attempt to solve this challenge by enrolling the barbarian war-bands in the universal state's military service ends with the dominant minority a prisoner in its own house. This was the case in Rome, and may occur with the Indian army, the large majority of which is recruited from the external proletariat.

Vulgarity in art and manners is a concomitant of disintegration. The Western artist consciously turns his back on his great tradition, as did his Hellenistic predecessor. Negro dances and a Byzantian architecture constitute expressions which must remain ever foreign to the souls of a true Western creator, dooming their present improvisators to sterility.[2] In the field of language, the sense of promiscuity reveals itself in the replacement of a local distinctiveness by a general confusion of tongues.[3] The requirements of communication in a universal state lead to the emergence of a *lingue franche*, such as Aramaic and Latin in the Hellenic and English in the Western civilization.

Religious syncretism, too, is a manifestation of the sense of promiscuity which arises from the schism in the soul in an age of disintegration.[4] The history of all universal states exhibits a convergence towards a common type in both religion and philosophy. The Stoa dominated all philosophic discussion during Rome's last centuries, and there was little difference between the various religious cults.

The final manifestation of the sense of promiscuity is the syncretism between religion and philosophy which announces the impending triumph of the internal proletariat's universal church. Philosophy offers little more than the dialectical underpinning for the proper formulation of church dogma. The oppressiveness of the void in the souls of both the dominant

---

1. Toynbee, *op. cit.*, Vol. V, p. 456.
2. Toynbee, *op. cit.*, Vol. V, p. 481. Note dependence of this concept on Spengler.
3. Toynbee, *op. cit.*, Vol. V, p. 494.
4. Toynbee, *op. cit.*, Vol. V, p. 527.

minority and the internal proletariat, the similarity of their frustration, will of necessity issue in a common religious experience. Yet this identity of feeling cannot be maintained. The philosophies degenerate into mere superstition because their appeal is too exclusively directed towards the intellectual faculties. The universal church attains that depth of understanding which enables it to serve as repository of all the hopes and the guarantor of the fulfillment of the disintegrating civilization.

Since Toynbee postulates alternative responses to the frustrations of feeling, the sense of promiscuity cannot constitute the only reaction to the civilization's loss of style. While the blending of all forms during the period of disintegration exhibits to weak souls an immanent Chaos, the steadier spiritual vision may regard this trend as the revelation of an underlying unity.[1] The phenomenal world reveals flickering manifestations which only serve to hide the eternal truth just below the surface. The first intuition of the sense of unity arises through the appearance of the universal state. The Saviour with the Sword[2] strives for that unification of mankind which Alexander denoted with concordia. However, the violence of its creation seals the doom of the universal state. It is ever plagued by the militarism that created it, externally through constant warfare and internally through the intermittent persecution of its minorities. Its inner contradictions cause the collapse of the universal state and bring to naught the enterprise of the Saviour with the Sword.

The apprehension of unity remains, magnified in the hearts of the members of the internal proletariat, whose specific national existence has been destroyed. The religions of even primitive societies reveal the truth[3] that the terrestrial plane can never satisfy man's striving for universality, expressed in a solidarity of the savage's soul with the tribal god in a super-human dimension. Mundane reality cannot achieve the unity of brotherly love without the common recognition of the Kingdom of God. The gradual realization of the importance of the celestial plane is strengthened through the oppression by the universal state. The tribal god, whose initial function had consisted of the protection of physical existence, now becomes the sole guarantee of tribal individuality, the chief hope for deliverance. Since conditions clearly do not warrant the expectation of

---

1. Toynbee, *op. cit.*, Vol. VI, p. 1.
2. Toynbee, *op. cit.*, Vol. VI, p. 178.
3. Toynbee, *op. cit.*, Vol. VI, p. 13.

liberation, the apocalyptic vision of a God arises whose judgment contains the moral sanction of history. The immediate attainment of material hopes is renounced, though the ultimate realization of the exclusive validity of the supra-mundane plane still awaits a profounder vision.

Two conceptions of unity permeate the universal state, derived from its political organization. The omnipotence of the ruler leads to the exaltation of the transcendence of God, and the uniformity of justice to the postulation of the Supremacy of Law. The dominant minority is acutely conscious of the potency of Law, which constitutes not merely an engine of administration, but a force in itself.[1] With the exaltation of Law, the personality of God grows progressively fainter. This was the condition of the Achaemenian Empire, of Babylon, and of the West since the triumph of physical science.[2]

The other representation of the unity of the universe as the work of an omnipotent God, with the Law as merely an emanation of God's will, discusses the typical reaction of the internal proletariat. The various tribal gods of the subject internal proletariat tend to develop a standard type, for they are now all alike exposed to the oppression of the same human monarch. In the contest of the gods of the internal proletariat, the most exclusive God usually triumphs, for in His exclusiveness resides the proof of His living existence, and in His jealousy the certainty of maintaining an unimpaired identity. Thus Yahweh outran all competitors for the soul of the internal proletariat of the Hellenic world, enabled by Christianity to develop its apprehension of the unity of One True God into a universal church.[3]

On the plane of life, Toynbee distinguishes the same incompatibility of reactions that the planes of behavior and feeling exhibited. Here, however, two pairs of violent and gentle response arise, each containing an antinomy of possible attitudes. Archaism and Futurism constitute the violent pair. Archaism Toynbee defines as the attempt to remount the stream of time in the hope of attaining the happy condition of a happier period, which now appears as the Golden Age. It operates in the same fields as promiscuity, conduct, art, language, and religion. But while promiscuity reveals a spontaneous feeling resulting from the loss of style, Archaism represents a conscious effort, strenuously pursued, of re-creating institu-

---

1. Toynbee, *op. cit.*, Vol. VI, p. 18.
2. Toynbee, *op. cit.*, Vol. VI, p. 19.
3. Toynbee, *op. cit.*, Vol. VI, p. 49.

tions of a happier time. In politics, the reintroduction of the Roman censorship in 250 is paralleled by the veneration accorded to the English kingship.

Archaism in art expresses itself in the neo-Gothic building style of the West, in the adoration by the Renaissance of the past. In the field of language, a *tour de force* results. The frantic attempt to purge all words of foreign origin from the language does not take into account the complete interdependence of all Indo-European languages and constitutes the confession of a defeated soul.[1]

Archaism is doomed to futility. It fights against the "impetus of Life—an elemental force which [it] can never arrest,"[2] and attempts to re-achieve an irretrievable past. The frustration of the endeavor leads its practitioners to resort to violence and thus hastens their defeat. When Archaism has come to the full realization of its impotence, an abrupt turn in direction occurs and the soul plunges into the equally hopeless but more deeply meaningful way of Futurism.

Where Archaism attempts to remount the stream of Time, Futurism rushes headlong in the opposite direction in its flight from an intolerable present. This attitude is even more contrary to human nature and consequently requires a *tour de force* of a still higher pitch. Futurism in the field of manners reveals itself in the adoption of outlandish dress and manners, of which Kemal Ataturk's and Peter the Great's reforms furnish Toynbee's outstanding examples. Its institutional manifestations proceed on the assumption that the organs of social life can be remade by fiat. Thus Hitler rearranged the German administrative map, and Peter the Great westernized Russia.[3]

Futurism "fares better than it has any right to expect."[4] It constitutes the reaction of a transplanted internal proletariat, prevented forever from returning to its former state. Goaded into physical revolt by the dominant minority's oppression, it sets an apocalyptic vision before its eyes to take courage in the desperate enterprise. Its fulfillment will be nothing less than an inversion of the present order, a change of roles between the slaves and the masters. This was the Jewish reaction to the Roman and Persian

---

1. Toynbee, *op. cit.*, Vol. VI, p. 63.
2. Toynbee, *op. cit.*, Vol. VI, p. 97. This concept is discussed in *post* "Conclusions."
3. Toynbee, *op. cit.*, Vol. VI, p. 109. These examples seem to prove the success of Futurism.
4. Toynbee, *op. cit.*, Vol. VI, p. 101.

occupations, and the conjuring up of a Messiah who would transform the agony into bliss by the establishment of an Israeli Commonwealth. The mundane world remains the center of hope. It took the catastrophic defeats of the Maccabees to teach Jewry the lesson of deeper spiritual insight,[1] the recognition that the True Kingdom of God does not lie in This World. This intuition is Transfiguration, the apprehension of the supra-mundane plane of reality.

The practitioners of Archaism and Futurism appear on the scene as saviours with the time machine.[2] They arise in all classes of the disintegrating society. The external proletariat develops its saviour-archaists, who seek to return to the happy days before the civilization's impact and whose reaction is violence. The dominant minority also produces saviour-archaists. When they act in the field of foreign relations, their policy results in a fiasco, such as Justinian's attempt to revive the ghost of the Western Roman Empire. When they attempt to remedy social conditions, they are disowned by their own class, for the internal proletariat's loss has been the dominant minority's gain.[3] These outlaw saviours include frequently some of the noblest souls of the dominant minority. They are joyously received by the internal proletariat, whose vague ideology attains form under their influence. The disappointment of the internal proletariat's futuristic hopes is given meaning by these outlaw saviours. The City of Destruction is transcended, the City of God brought into view.[4]

Archaism and Futurism reveal the pair of violent responses to the emptiness of life; Detachment and Transfiguration furnish the gentle variations in Toynbee's scheme. Just as the experience of the impracticability of Futurism leads to self-transcendence, so the frustration of Archaism issues in the philosophy of Detachment.[5] The sorrow of a disintegrating society is evaded by a withdrawal from life, a quest for salvation through meditation. It finds bliss in a will-less resignation, an escape from existence in which death appears as welcome oblivion. Detachment implies not only a rejection of life, but a love of its negation. As an intellectual achievement, Toynbee considers this philosophy imposing, but its moral consequences are

---

1. Toynbee, *op. cit.*, Vol. VI, p. 131.
2. Toynbee, *op. cit.*, Vol. VI, p. 213.
3. Toynbee, *op. cit.*, Vol. VI, p. 237.
4. Toynbee, *op. cit.*, Vol. VI, p. 241. Toynbee included Lenin in the category of outlaw saviours.
5. This contradicts his previous assertion that Archaism leads to Futurism.

repulsive.[1] For Detachment implies a purging of all passions, of pity and love, as well as the baser emotions.

The Stoic ideal of indifference to suffering, repeated in Buddhism, involves the reason for the defeat of Detachment. By appealing to the head to the exclusion of the heart, the Philosopher tears asunder what God has joined together.[2] For failing to divine this truth, the philosophy of Detachment is superseded by the mystery of Transfiguration.

The Philosopher masked by a king[3] represents Toynbee's conception of the creative personality of this attitude of life. The ambiguity of his position dooms the Philosopher's endeavor. The universal state in which such individuals appear is the product of force, and the sin of violence ever haunts its steps. Even if the sword is temporarily sheathed, internal tensions will force its reappearance. Indeed, the Platonic philosophy implies the necessity of the use of force. Though basing the Republic on a recognition by everyone of the division of labor, Plato negates this lip service to popular consent by uniting the executive and the military. The Philosopher's direct inspiration can reach but a few; leadership of a social organization must always rely on mimesis. The Philosopher masked by a king cannot provide the real saviour of society. By acting politically, he trespasses on the king's proper field of ruthless deeds while the king stultifies himself in attempting to practice Detachment.[4] His acts of violence turn him into a Saviour with the Sword. Detachment offers no ultimate solution to the schism in the soul and only Transfiguration remains, the experience which contains the true meaning of history.

When the soul's quest for relief from the tensions of disintegration has been stymied at every turn, there emerges a deeper level of historical existence, the recognition of the Kingdom of God.[5] Christ Crucified will always constitute a stumbling block for futurists, because He offers no guarantee of material reward. He will remain foolishness for the philosophers who cannot grasp the reason for a return to the world after such a hard-won withdrawal. The Kingdom of God, of which Christ Crucified is King,

---

1. Toynbee, *op. cit.*, Vol. V, p. 132.
2. Toynbee, *op. cit.*, Vol. VI, p. 138.
3. Toynbee, *op. cit.*, Vol. VI, p. 242.
4. Toynbee, *op. cit.*, Vol. VI, p. 259. This seems to confirm Spengler's two worlds, world-as-history and world-as-nature. See *post* "Conclusions."
5. Transfiguration has been fully explained *ante*; see "Metaphysics."

nevertheless has meaning, though its dimensions are not commensurable with any mundane criterion. It exists in This World though is not of it, extending into Eternity and the Infinite, in a supra-mundane, spiritual sense.[1]

The connecting link between the two planes is Christ Jesus, exhibiting both a divine and a human nature. Yet how can these two natures be present in a single person? Toynbee assumes that the accessibility of the divine essence depends on the possession of a faculty common to God and man. Since love is man's noblest faculty, its absence in God would make Him a spiritually inferior being (*quod ad absurdum*). Thus the very emotion which the philosophers attempt to excoriate guarantees the realization of God's purposes. Love, flowing from God to man and evoking an answering response that on earth runs in the channel of a feeling of brotherhood, constitutes the essence of Transfiguration, the assurance of the supra-mundane plane.[2]

The Kingdom of God contains the hope for salvation from the schism in the soul, the sole condition for inward peace. The only Saviour whose claims Toynbee considers of eternal validity is the God Incarnate in man.[3] He arises in all civilizations, though in various guises. In the Hellenic world He first appeared as a blind Necessity which offered no hope and found no lasting acceptance. The demi-god who endures human suffering reveals a profounder understanding. But the longing of humanity has concentrated on the God who appears as a man, on the Fatherhood of God, whose love was so great that He sacrificed His son to give blessedness to His own.[4] For salvation can only be attained by suffering, and the Saviour-God must experience the depths of human agony. This represents the symbolism of Heracles and Orpheus, of Tamus and Osiris, of Attis and Christ. Yet Toynbee applies a final criterion. Though all these gods suffered on behalf of humanity, the ultimate merit of the sacrifice resides in the spirit in which it was endured. Of all the gods incarnate in man, only Christ meets this test. His death is not suffered in resignation or in sadness but reveals that transcendental love with which God loves This World, "so that whosoever believeth in Him should not perish but have everlasting life."

---

1. Toynbee, *op. cit.*, Vol. VI, pp. 156–62. Toynbee discusses at length how something can exist in This World though not be of it. See f.n. *ante* section "Metaphysics."

2. Toynbee, *op. cit.*, Vol. VI, p. 166.

3. Toynbee, *op. cit.*, Vol. V, p. 259.

4. Toynbee, *op. cit.*, Vol. VI, pp. 272–75. Toynbee engages in a long syllogism on the question of the Son's birth, whether by procreation or adoption. For discussion see *post* "Conclusions."

The road to Christ, to the Kingdom of God, contains the only lasting hope of mankind, the true purpose of history, the condition of eternal life. "The member of a disintegrating mundane society who has taken this road has a surer hope, and therefore a deeper happiness, than the merely 'once-born' member of a mundane society that is still in growth; for he has learnt the saving truths that 'the Most High hath not made one world, but two,' and that the human wayfarer who still finds himself a sojourner in This World is not on that account beyond the pale of the Other World but is travelling all the time within the domain of the Kingdom of God and is at liberty to live as a citizen of that omnipresent commonwealth here and now, if he is willing with all his heart to pay allegiance to Christ the King and to take upon himself those obligations of citizenship which Christ has consecrated by voluntarily fulfilling them in person. This entry into the Kingdom of God is a second birth; and, for the 'once-born' denizen of This World, the discovery that it is possible to obtain this freedom is like finding treasure hid in a field, or finding one pearl of great price."[1]

Toynbee's journey through history ends with a paean of mysticism, a rejection of This World, a hope for salvation through Christ. The theological foundation of his philosophy appears in full clarity. The defeated soul of a disintegrating civilization has exhausted all alternatives for healing its schism. Finally the "truth" emerges that true blessedness is not attained in This World, but results from a recognition of the Kingdom of God, of infinite extent and eternal duration. This is Transfiguration, an emanation of God's love, the apprehension of the supra-mundane plane of reality. Its achievement and the recognition of the subsidiary importance of This World does not constitute an act of truancy but a withdrawal according to a plan in which God, incarnate as man, the Saviour, leads humanity towards a New Jerusalem.[2]

The reliance on Dante is obvious. With Transfiguration the pilgrim has reached Paradise. Now his mind is at one with the love of God, and terrestrial bonds fall away. Here everything is bliss, with will and necessity harmonized, with Time at a standstill and Space no longer an obstacle. The greater "truth" appears to man, of the insignificance of mundane affairs, of the transcendental reprieve which God gives to those who repent.

But the nobility of this conception is marred by an empirical method

---

1. Toynbee, *op. cit.*, Vol. VI, p. 168.
2. Toynbee, *op. cit.*, Vol. VI, p. 279.

which recognizes no mysteries and imposes its causal patterns on all spiritual manifestations. The alternative ways of behavior, feeling, and life are metaphysical emanations of a theological viewpoint, which will not be buttressed by any, however vast, amount of empirical data. Christ's moral superiority in the "Battle of the Gods" is derived from His readiness to sacrifice Himself. This, however, represents a value judgment, not a necessary conclusion from historical events.[1] The alternatives seem to fit all conditions of life, with no necessary relation to disintegration.[2] The supporting data includes such incommensurables as Hitler's abolition of the old administrative system, Peter's shearing off of beards, Japan's modernization, all as symptoms of a suicidal Futurism. Nothing could illustrate better the frustration of an empirical documentation that must ever confine itself to the mere phenomenal appearance, which reflects the noumena, the soul.

The assertion of purposiveness of the first five volumes has disappeared. Nothing can really save This World. Indeed, should it be saved? For only through the disintegration of civilizations, in Toynbee's terms, does man learn to know God.[3]

Conclusions[4]

Toynbee's philosophy represents an attempt to transcend the conception of history as an organism continuously reproducing new manifestations of

---

1. Unless, of course, one attempts to equate morality with success.
2. See *post* "Conclusions."
3. See *post* "Conclusions" for full discussion of these points.
4. Limitations of space have forced me to confine the discussion to a criticism of Toynbee's philosophical position and those concepts central to Toynbee's scheme. Therefore, I did not explore inconsistencies which do not affect Toynbee's central argument, such as Toynbee's hint that Russia may be the new creative minority of the West (a growth criterion) while spending considerable effort in implying that the West is in a stage of breakdown. A similar contradiction is the argument that geographical expansion accompanies breakdown if set against a previous description of the stimulus of new ground. Again, Toynbee proves that a civilization's influence over neighboring societies is greatest during the period of decline, while at the same time including India in the Western civilization because of her adoption of Western technology. These inconsistencies, while reflecting on Toynbee's exactness of thinking, do not, however, invalidate his central position. (For my criteria see Appendix, "The Concepts of Meaning." For other inconsistencies see my footnotes on previous sections.)

power. The inevitability of decline and the inexorability of a development through determined stages are replaced by an assertion of purposiveness. Challenge-and-Response represents the mechanism by which growth accomplishes itself, the intrusion of an alien element into the perfection of creation, the foil which evokes a new phase of activity. History exhibits a continual alternation of static repose and creativity, of Integration and Differentiation, of Yin and Yang.

All progress results from the civilizations, whose birth heralded a new stage in an evolutionary rhythm which permeates all existence. Civilizations are not organic beings whose destiny determines their history but merely fields of activity, the common ground of action of their constituents. Their dynamism expresses itself in the direction of their mimesis, a social drill, which serves as a substitute for the direct absorption of inspiration from the creative minority. Yet the process of growth is fraught with dangers. Mimesis breaks down because of its mechanicalness, and the creative minority succumbs to the nemesis of the idolatry of the ephemeral instead of the eternally true. Civilizations do not break down because of an inevitable fatality, but commit suicide.

The repeated failure to respond to a challenge leads to disintegration, the first manifestations of which appear as a schism in the body social. The creative minority substitutes force for charm, and evokes a correspondingly violent reaction from the seceding internal proletariat. The barbarians beyond the borders constitute themselves as an external proletariat whose constant threat across a military frontier gradually saps the energy of the dominant minority.

The schism in the body social is paralleled by a schism in the soul. All alternative ways of behavior, feeling, and life appear doomed. Then out of the collapse of material hopes arises the vision of the ultimate meaning of human suffering, the real embodiment of historical existence, the Kingdom of God, with Christ as King. The soul which had defeated itself on the mundane plane understands the immanence of God's love and, through repentance and humility, may win its way to salvation.

Toynbee's common-sense approach, which pretends to derive its conclusions from a vast and impressive collection of empirical data, hides great complexities. The incommensurability of his metaphysics and the empirical data, the logical antinomy of his position, present themselves at every stage of Toynbee's philosophy. The realm of theology and the field of natural laws can be reconciled only with extreme difficulty. Does history reveal the gradual unfolding of a divine purpose? Or is history a natural force, obeying well-understood laws of evolution, through which a rhythm of self-implementation appears for the discerning? Does history, finally, constitute merely the common field of activity of the constituent civilizations, its standard purposive self-determination, with disintegration the penalty for an inward failure?

These three questions exhibit Toynbee's conflicting tendencies. The assertion of purposiveness in the first two volumes is soon revealed as but the emanation of a biological evolutionary development which proceeds from Yin to Yang, from Integration to Differentiation. In these terms Challenge and Response constitute merely beats of an elemental rhythm and a description of the operation of inevitability, not a denial of its necessity.

Toynbee's metaphysical assumptions derive from a theology in the medieval tradition of Dante, in which love constitutes the motive force of the universe and This World is conceived as but the preparation for the Kingdom of God. For this reason he submits the evolutionary manifestations of the *élan vital* to a normative criticism which rejects militarism as an original sin and which judges all actions by their aptness for the attainment of the Kingdom of God. The criticism of the typical attitudes of a soul are less descriptions of the alternatives of a disintegrating society than the denial of the substantiality of all secular activity.[1] In the final analysis, only the Kingdom of God matters. Mundane success hides the inner hollowness of political institutions, the existence of which ever depends on violence.

The difficulties of Toynbee's position are compounded by the utilization of an empirical approach whose exhibition of deep learning tends to obscure its methodological shallowness. Empirical analysis relies on a recognition of recurrent situations. The formulation of laws requires a comparability of phenomena. The inner meaning of these manifestations

---

1. Toynbee's categories of Archaism, Futurism, and promiscuity lead to this conclusion. It is obvious that all activity must fit one of these classifications. For example, Toynbee castigates the Renaissance for its traditionalism and the modern West for its rejection of traditional art styles. Similarly, Peter's reforms in Russia, Japan's modernization, and Hitler's administrative reforms are criticized as symptoms of a suicidal Futurism, while the retention of the British king and the organization of the Parliament of Westminster on the basis of territory instead of corporations is described as the emanation of an Archaism doomed to self-destruction.

cannot enter into calculations; the uniqueness of experience constitutes a contradiction in terms. An empirical method is therefore unsuited for the demonstration of a theological view, which must of necessity rest on a transcendental experience. To be sure, a philosophy of history based on theology is feasible, as Bossuet and Niebuhr demonstrate. Yet their formulation derives, in the first instance, from a frank recognition of a normative pattern and a profound metaphysics.

Two consequences result from Toynbee's attempt to combine his theological and biological approach. Survival, which in an evolutionary development becomes the only criterion of inner fitness, is given divine sanction. Sin denotes the causality of which failure constitutes the phenomenal manifestation. Success represents the reward for moral action.[1] This Calvinist concept is, of course, not inconsistent with an assertion of purposiveness, for the only indication of God's favor in a world of dark uncertainties is the temporal eminence achieved by strenuous exertion.[2] It does, however, define morality in terms of ability to prevail and hardly differs from Spengler's concept of necessity as the sole guide to action.[3]

On the other hand, the impossibility of uniting general laws with the unique merit of Christianity issues in a rejection of phenomenal reality. All possible attitudes towards life are seen to fail in achieving that permanence which alone can indicate the attainment of the Kingdom of God.

---

1. For an example of the utilization in terms of mundane success of even the concept of Transfiguration, see the following quote: Toynbee, *op. cit.*, Vol. VI, p. 321. "What response to this challenge is Christian going to make? Is he going to look this way and that way as if he would run, yet stand still because he cannot tell which way to go—until the fire from Heaven duly descends upon the City of Destruction and the wretched haverer perishes in a holocaust which he has so dismally foreboded without ever bringing himself to the point of fleeing from the wrath to come? Or will he begin to run—and run on crying 'Life! Life! Eternal Life!'—with his eye set on a shining light and his feet bound for a distant wicket-gate? If the answer to this question depended on nobody but Christian himself, our knowledge of the uniformity of human nature might incline us to predict that Christian's imminent destiny was Death and not Life. But in the classic version of the myth we are told that the human protagonist was not left entirely to his own resources in the hour that was decisive for his fate. According to John Bunyan, Christian was saved by his encounter with Evangelist. And, inasmuch as it cannot be supposed that God's nature is less constant than Man's, we may and must pray that a reprieve which God has granted to our society once will not be refused if we ask for it again in a contrite spirit and with a broken heart."
2. On this point see Friedrich, *Inevitable Peace*, p. 111. Also Friedrich, *Politica Methodice Digesta of Johannes Althusius.*
3. See *ante* for my criticism of this concept.

Throughout Toynbee's analysis of the schism in the soul,[1] the tendency to reject all worldly ambition as sham becomes more pronounced. The doom of mutability, the transitoriness of existence, the unresolved mystery of the decline of civilizations all derive meaning from an affirmation of the eternal validity of the Kingdom of God.

The biological and theological view are found to be irreconcilable, after all. The *élan vital*, operating through Challenge-and-Response, leads a succession of climbers upwards on a precipice towards a ledge where the species becomes transformed into Superman and the inspiration of the mundane creative minority unnecessary. Yet the failure to reach successfully this new level of integration produces as a concomitant of disintegration the universal church, the repository of the only true meaning of existence. This implies that either the evolutionary process is a chimera, the very unattainability of which teaches man his limitations, or that the new state of Yin by definition excludes the necessary validity of the higher religions. No compromise between these two attitudes is possible. The pervasiveness of the elemental rhythm reduces the universal church to the incidental by-product of disintegration. The eternal applicability of Christianity denies the substantiality of worldly endeavor[2] and makes the precipice a stage of transitory futility. If man succeeds in transforming himself, he will never have known a higher faith.[3] The appearance of religion, again, signals the doom of worldly endeavor. What is the real tragedy in Toynbee, the birth of civilizations or their disintegration?

Toynbee has not resolved Spengler's antinomies but sharpened them by an insistence, whatever his denials, on a hint from God, expressed in success, regarding the merit of activity. The two realms of History and Causality, of Time and Space, of Destiny and Morality, remain incommensurable. For Spengler, too, had admitted a religious experience, but explicitly affirmed its distinctness from history, or, in Toynbee's terms, its rejection of mundane success: "My kingdom is not of this world. This is the final word which admits of no gloss and on which each must check the course wherein birth and nature have set him. Pulsation or tension, history or nature, politics or religion—here it is one or the other, there is no honest

---

1. Toynbee, *op. cit.*, Vol. VI.
2. In Toynbee's definition of Transfiguration.
3. Since religions only arise as by-products of the schism in the body social in Toynbee's scheme.

way of compromise. A statesman can be deeply religious, a pious man can die for his country—but they must both know on which side they are really standing. There is no bridge between directional Time and timeless Eternity, between the course of history and the existence of a divine world order. This is the final meaning of the moment in which Pilate and Christ confronted one another."[1] This, in the abrupt language of Spengler, expresses the full implication of Toynbee's concept of Transfiguration.[2]

Toynbee's methodology adds to these inconsistencies. It offers no support for the assumption of an *élan vital* manifesting itself in progress. It structures all historical appearances into a causality, the essence of which is expressed by temporal or spatial succession. Thus Toynbee ascribes the decline of the Holy Roman Empire to the gradual displacement of the ruling dynasty from the frontier marshes to the interior provinces, the reduced challenge of which impaired the intensity of the response. This seems to mistake what represented at best a manifestation of inner weakness[3] for its cause. Moreover, though the Hohenstaufen were perhaps instrumental in bringing about the nadir of the imperial position, and though their ancestral territories lay rather in the center of the empire, their doom can hardly be said to have resulted from a deficiency in reactive ability.

Again, Toynbee considers the sudden decrease in cultivation and prosperity upon crossing the German-Lithuanian frontier a demonstration of the existence of an excessive climatic challenge.[4] The very occurrence of an abrupt transformation should have cautioned Toynbee against postulating climatic change as the key factor, however. An examination of history, moreover, will disclose a variety of reasons for the deficiency in economic development of this border region between Catholic and Orthodox Christianity, the West and the Slavs.

Yet such a single-factor analysis is the logical consequence of the application of the methods of natural science to historical phenomena. Historical

---

1. Spengler, *op. cit.*, Vol. II, p. 216.
2. It may be interesting to compare Spengler's quotation with the following statement by Toynbee: "In fact, the philosopher-king is doomed to fail because he is attempting to unite two contradictory natures in a single person. The philosopher stultifies himself by trespassing on the king's field of ruthless action, while conversely the king stultifies himself by trespassing on the philosopher's field of loveless and pitiless contemplation" (Vol. VI, p. 259).
3. Though even this is a highly debatable point.
4. Toynbee, *op. cit.*, Vol. II, p. 304.

events represent unique occurrences, products of the impact of creative personalities on an organic environment to be analyzed causally only in their determined aspects.[1] Though Toynbee realized this in his theory, his emphasis is ever on a quest for the apprehension of immutable laws, of which his law of race or law of compensation furnish examples. The tendency is to consider all manifestations comparable triumphs over the mere postulation of the unpredictability of events. But comparability for natural science implies qualitative equivalence. Only quantitative differences exist for the empiricist.

This leads to a superficiality of classification which draws conclusions from mere surface phenomena. Thus, because a universal state preceded disintegration in most civilizations, each appearance of an inclusive political organization heralds the breakdown of its society. The empire of the Romanovs represents as certain a criterion for the decline of the Russian civilization as the appearance of Augustine's creation for the impending disintegration of Hellenic civilization. For this reason, too, the introduction of the Western alphabet by Mustapha Kemal, the abolition of the *Länder* system by Hitler, the administrative reforms of the French Revolution, the political creation of Peter the Great are all considered emanations of the same Futurism, equally doomed to self-destruction.

Since each disintegrating society has an external proletariat, all attacks from beyond a civilization's borders must fit this category. The Sassanid Empire's onslaught on declining Byzantism is paralleled by the incessant warfare in the Russian forest between the Khazar Empire and Scandinavian war-bands.[2] Again the "gentle" reaction, postulated by Toynbee as a possible attitude for the external proletariat, manifested itself on the one hand in the person of Atawulf and on the other in the appearance of Islam. It requires no extended argument to show that the only common feature of these phenomena is their occurrence outside the civilization's borders, a classification into which the Khazar Empire fit only with difficulty.[3]

Toynbee's analysis of the range of endurable challenges exhibits his

---

1. For full development see *post* Ch. "The Sense of Responsibility." Also Collingwood, *The Idea of History*, p. 169.

2. Toynbee, *op. cit.*, Vol. VI, p. 288.

3. Limitations of space prevent a multiplication of examples. Moreover, severe doubts are raised by the "gentle" response of some of the barbarian occupiers of Rome. Though undoubtedly there existed various degrees of severity, this is very far from proving an innate gentleness.

inability to make qualitative distinctions.[1] He refutes the theory of the excessiveness of the Hellenic challenge by the success of the Teuton response after the Celtic disaster. Similarly, Islam triumphantly met the challenge represented by the Roman intrusion into the Syriac civilization despite the abortive Jewish and Zoroastrian revolts. Yet it must be apparent that the only connection between these challenges is supplied by their Hellenic origin. The impact of Rome on the Celts occurred at the height of Roman power, aided by the proximity of the Po Valley to the center of its strength. It is at least debatable whether the Teutons could have successfully resisted the Roman challenge had it been offered under comparable conditions. The catastrophe of Judaism and Zoroastrianism also took place at a much earlier stage in historical development. Moreover, Islam hardly represented the response to a Roman stimulus. Yet Toynbee's empiricism allows him to distinguish challenges only by their origin and magnitude, not by their inner meaning. Similarly, Toynbee considers standardization through disintegration demonstrated conclusively by the uniform appearance of a dominant minority, an internal proletariat, and an external proletariat in declining civilizations. However, this proves merely an identity of outward form, not of inward problemation. The same uniformity is found during growth, which, according to Toynbee, always reveals a creative minority, an uninspired majority, and barbarians under the civilization's spell.

The process of Withdrawal-and-Return by which the creative minority accomplishes its growth in stature reveals all the difficulties of Toynbee's pragmatism. Its proof rests, in the first instance, on the life of Christ. Once postulated, the principle magically reveals itself in a vast variety of manifestations of creativity. Withdrawal-and-Return as an agency of growth implies, however, that the increment in creative leadership bears some relation to the temporary cessation from activity and is given effect by a return to the world. Of Toynbee's illustrations only Christ, Saint Paul, and other Christian figures meet the test. Hindenburg was, to be sure, in retirement when placed in charge of Germany's Eastern Front in 1914. Yet absolutely no evidence exists that his period of inactivity increased his military efficiency at Tannenberg, which derived from his intimate knowledge of his ancestral Masurian Lake District. Lenin unquestioningly was

---

1. Toynbee, *op. cit.*, Vol. III, p. 274.

smuggled back to Russia by the Germans. It is only fair to assume, however, that Russia's military collapse was infinitely more instrumental in giving the Bolsheviks their opportunity in 1917 than the Swiss exile of their leader. Mohammed's withdrawal to Mecca, Machiavelli's exile from Florence, Kant's seclusion in Königsberg, and the life of the Buddha constitute phenomena without any inner connection. Withdrawal-and-Return has become a technical classification of surface phenomena, a mechanistic description of definitional concepts.[1]

The empirical method breaks down completely when applied to such concepts as progress and purpose, which must ever remain metaphysical constructions. Toynbee attempts, through a pyramiding of metaphors, to make the transition from the biological to the theological realm. But analogies cannot serve as substitutes for demonstration. They assume the proof and merely illustrate the essential similarity of divergent manifestations. An empiricist, whose field of vision is restricted to a ledge and a precipice, has no warranty for postulating a continuity of geological strata. A pragmatist, who lets himself be instructed by his data, cannot assert that any vehicle will succeed in negotiating the exit of a one-way street in the face of uniform disaster, nor can he consistently claim that the breakdowns are due to a "reversal in violation of the rules." In empirical terms, if all automobiles have in fact reversed, that seems to be the rule. The loom of history may utilize the backward and forward movements of a shuttle to spin its design, but in subjective terms each downswing marks the end of a civilization, and the pattern will not be apparent until the end of time. Progress and purpose represent the resolution of a soul, the rebellion against transitoriness, the hope for permanence. No technical manipulation of empirical data can wrest an assurance out of phenomena, the final attainment of which man can only find within himself.[2]

Toynbee thought that he had transcended Spengler by an assertion of purposiveness. Life presents a succession of problems, each a challenge to undergo an ordeal. Challenge-and-Response, the interaction of race and

---

1. Machiavelli and Dante did not "return"; Kant neither "withdrew" nor "returned" but lived all his life in Königsberg. It might further be asked how withdrawal differs from the truancy which Toynbee condemns.

2. See *post* Ch. "The Sense of Responsibility." Also Appendix, "The Concepts of Meaning."

environment, the opportunity presented by the Devil to God for further creative activity reveal the mechanism by which freedom accomplishes itself in the world. The prediction of historical events is impossible, for the reaction of the protagonist to the ordeal must remain the unknown quantity.[1]

Freedom cannot be proved syllogistically, however.[2] An inner experience, again, remains inaccessible to the empiricist. Toynbee's actual analysis defines the response exclusively in terms of challenge. This constitutes but a restatement of the environment theory. For, after all, no environmentalist would claim—as Toynbee implies—that climatic or topographical conditions spontaneously produce civilizations in the manner of the Giants growing out of the earth.[3] Toynbee's analysis of challenges involves the same difficulties of Spengler's postulate of historical necessity as a guide to action.[4] For what constitutes a challenge? Toynbee replies: that which produces a civilization. A challenge is proved excessive by a comparison in three terms, of which the middle term represents successful adaptation. The Golden Mean exhibits that challenge which evokes the most potently creative act. Yet Toynbee here defines these concepts syllogistically in terms of each other and explains not challenge, but the fact of survival. Just as the "pleasure principle," just as the "necessary" dictum, Challenge-and-Response assigns conceptual quantities to past action.

Challenge-and-Response, to be meaningful as an assertion of purposiveness, would have to examine the personal in the response, the unique in the reaction to the ordeal. But this is precisely what Toynbee's method does not permit. His empiricism implies that every event can only result from a commensurate causality defined as challenge, classifiable as a phenomenon subject to well-understood laws. This is illustrated by his survey of the genesis of civilizations, postulated as the consequence of the stimulus of hard countries. It becomes apparent, however, that among Toynbee's twenty-one civilizations, all climates and all topographical conditions are represented. This indicates that it is not the challenge which structures the response, but the response which finds its challenge.

---

1. Toynbee, *op. cit.*, Vol. I, p. 302.

2. Toynbee's syllogism goes like this: A civilization is that which develops from a challenge. A challenge is that from which a civilization develops. This, however, merely shifts the problem of definition from "development" to "challenge."

3. Toynbee utilizes the same misstatement to refute Spengler.

4. See *ante* Ch. "History as Intuition" ("Conclusions").

Freedom is not the nice balance of external factors which will evoke the most suitable reaction, but an inner state which seeks its own stimulus. For what else can account for the decline of the Easter Islanders?[1] They had conquered the sea, if not with any margin of safety, and achieved a considerable cultural level. But then the ocean ceased to be traversed, and Easter Island disappeared into an oblivion from which it re-emerged as but a colonial dependency in the nineteenth century. Yet what happened? The severity of the sea did not change, the stimulus of the environment did not lessen. But the capacity to experience the ocean as a challenge, the inner state that had utilized the Infinite as a foil, did diminish, and therein lay the doom of Easter Island.

Toynbee recognized the purposive element, but the ambiguity of his method resulted in a definition of the operation of necessity. Freedom, however, is not to be found in the apprehension of external relations. Nor will it develop from an engineering into society of a maximum of alternatives. Freedom depends less on the existence than on the recognition of alternatives, not on a set of conditions, but an inward experience.[2]

The assertion of pervasive purposiveness led Toynbee to deny the existence of any organic factor in the development of civilizations. Societies do not represent organisms but the common field of activity of their members, the medium of communications of their constituents. Their growth is accomplished by mimesis, a social drill, through which the saints, as the apprehension of the new life, lead the uncreative majority on the road towards increased etherealization. Breakdowns exhibit a failure of self-determination, not an inexorable fatality. Sin constitutes the causality by which the nemesis of creativity accomplishes itself.

Yet again the mere postulation of freedom is not enough. Toynbee rejected the concept of a civilization's soul, but his empiricism merely issues in its definition. For what else is mimesis? Spengler, after all, had not used the word *soul* in a literal sense, but defined it as the "image of a counterworld which is our mode of visualizing that which remains eternally alien to the physical eye."[3] If social drill constitutes a generic feature of social life, if it exhibits those relations which require no formal institutions

---

1. Toynbee, *op. cit.*, Vol. III, p. 5.
2. See *post* Ch. "The Sense of Responsibility" for full development. Also Ch. "History and Man's Experience of Morality."
3. Spengler, *op. cit.*, Vol. I, p. 300.

because of their self-evidence, then Toynbee has merely shifted the emphasis from the manifestations of the organic aspect to a description of its operation.[1] How does mimesis differ from the beat of self-implementation by which Spengler's soul actualizes itself?

Toynbee ascribes the breakdown of civilizations to two contradictory factors: the nemesis of creativity and the mechanicalness of mimesis. This raises formidable difficulties in logic. If mimesis results from the inability of the uninspired majority to absorb directly the inspiration of the saints, then the "charm" of the leaders cannot reside in their creativity. How will the mass recognize the saints? Indeed, their appearance is itself an event of such "unimaginable rarity"[2] that a social drill, the efficacy of which must depend on a certain uniformity, can hardly develop from so uncertain a phenomenon. The breakdown of mimesis, moreover, is a mechanical failure and bears no relation to a deficient self-determination, Toynbee's usual criterion for decline.

Again, if the loss of inspiration by the creative minority accounts for society's disintegration and the secession of the internal proletariat, by what standard is that deficiency apprehended? If the uncreative majority possessed a criterion for creativity, it would not require mimesis. If mimesis constitutes the generic feature of social life, Toynbee cannot complain about its direction, and his attempts to describe breakdown in terms of purposiveness fail.

Toynbee maintains that compulsion replaces charm as the social bond in the early stages of breakdown. The philosopher masked by a king is doomed to frustration, for his efficiency depends on the implied threat of force. Mimesis, to be effective, must, however, rely on this threat.[3] Thus it appears that society's breakdown is, after all, inevitable, its fatality the function of the feature which distinguishes a civilization from primitive societies.

Toynbee replaces the theory of the organic nature of civilizations by the assertion that relations can possess no soul. This will hardly be contested. Yet he has not shown that civilizations represent no more than mere relations. His geometric analogy demonstrates the appearance of such a relation but not its existence. The question arises of what in the civilization constitutes the

---

1. Indeed, the choice of the word *generic* indicates an organic factor.
2. Toynbee, *op. cit.*, Vol. I, p. 275.
3. Toynbee specifically considers the reliance on mimesis as dooming the philosopher masked by a king. Toynbee, *op. cit.*, Vol. VI, p. 255.

common field activity? If they represent the medium of communication of their component political communities, then the original difficulty reappears in different form. For since the constituent societies are themselves merely relations, they manifestly cannot exhibit dynamic fields. If, on the other hand, civilizations represent the totality of their individual members, then the Withdrawal-and-Return by which Athens, Italy, and England grew in stature and the mimesis of the civilization's creative minority remains to be explained.

Toynbee can, in fact, never escape these difficulties. For since he leans to the conception of the civilization as the common field of action of the component political communities, he must perforce consider these units organic entities. This forms the basis for the assertion that Athens played truant at the crucial stage of Hellenic history.[1] This, too, is implied by the concept of the schism in the soul. It can hardly be maintained that each individual of the disintegrating society exhibits all these possible attitudes. The immanence of the organic factor constantly reappears. Toynbee rejects Futurism and Archaism, their necessary futility deriving from an attempt to arrest the "impetus of Life," which will not be denied.[2] The inevitable appearance, in twenty-one civilizations, of identical political organizations at each stage of development indicates a pervasive immanence not to be evaded by defining its necessity as sin.

The assertion of freedom stands revealed as the mechanization of inexorability. The attempt to impose an empirical method on noumenal reality could yield no other results. Differentiation by growth sets the limits of development as necessarily as Spengler's Destiny. For if each response automatically produces a new challenge, the range of possible reactions tends to become ever narrower and thereby more determined. The concept of society as a relation accentuates man's insignificance. "In the economy of social life men's power to order their affairs at will on a rational plan is narrowly restricted, since a society is not the chattel of any one owner, but is the common ground of many men's field of action; and for this reason a precept which is common sense in the economy of the household and practical wis-

---

1. It also is implied by Toynbee's concept that the idolization of an ephemeral self by Athens was so pervasive that the Byzantine empress of Athenian birth who was involved in the iconoclastic controversy exhibited the same perversity which once before had led the Athenians to reject Paul.

2. Toynbee, *op. cit.*, Vol. VI, p. 97.

dom in the life of the spirit is a counsel of perfection in social affairs."[1] This illustrates, any abstract exaltation of freedom to the contrary notwithstanding, the true implication of Toynbee's philosophy. Freedom is not to be apprehended by way of historical law. Inner experiences remain unsuited for a pragmatic method. Morality does not reveal itself in maxims of prudent conduct.

Yet the biological approach necessarily leads to such conclusions. In such a scheme, survival exhibits the ultimate test of inner fitness. Toynbee's criteria for ethical conduct are found to be based on their practical utility; permanence constitutes his ultimate test for historical endeavor. Immortality, however, is not a datum of history but an inward resolve. The concept of evolution contradicts its attainability. An unfolding of growth and decay has characterized all historical existence. Toynbee's reliance on transitoriness as a revelation of inward failure defeats itself, for life implies mortality. No stage of development, even in his terms, has lasted. Every civilization has either collapsed or exhibits all the symptoms of decline. Though the universal state precedes disintegration, etherealization precedes the universal state, and birth etherealization. Can temporal succession contain the causality of history? Is life the cause of death, or night of day?

Toynbee's causality recognizes no mysteries. It tends to wrest its assurance of immortality out of phenomena by conjuring their appearance. Its tool is an assertive syllogism that attempts to read divine purposes into historical events and submits even God to normative criticism. History exhibits unchanging laws, its rhythm apparent to the discerning, its morality success. Toynbee's approach to mythology illustrates the claims of a rationality that denies the existence of any reality outside of itself.

Fiction, historical treatment, and natural science represent qualitatively equivalent modes of apprehending an equally objective reality.[2] Their suitability for the description of phenomena is determined by the quantity of data. Thus natural science, with the manageability of its calculations, formulates general laws, while the manifold possibilities of everyday existence allow but the presentation of representative types in the form of fiction. History, as the mean, has as its most applicable style the comparable study. This explains Toynbee's approach to the New Testament and mythology. As representations of objective occurrences, they contain not

---

1. Toynbee, *op. cit.*, Vol. IV, p. 132.
2. Toynbee, *op. cit.*, Vol. I, p. 441 (Annex to IC).

only analogies, but actual maxims derived from real events. Thus Eden
represents a level of integration which through the intervention of the Devil
is changed to the activity of Yang. Therefore, Sabbath proves the nemesis
of creativity, when God in the perfection of the world found no further
outlet for His activity. For this reason, Toynbee has to engage in extended
argument to prove the essential "fairness" of God's wager with the Devil.
Love, as the motive force of the universe, must be a divine attribute, for its
absence would indicate a deficiency in God. Christianity will be saved
because God's nature has to exhibit at least the same constancy as man's.[1]

Yet what is Toynbee really doing? This is the magic attitude that wills to
escape the transitoriness of its existence by claiming this desire as a pattern
of objective reality. Mythology becomes practical ethics, a comprehended
mechanics, the key to eternal happiness. God obeys well-understood laws,
of "fairness," of "constancy," and of "love." What does humility mean in
such a context? Goethe said: "The noblest manifestation of Mankind is
shuddering awe." Toynbee, on the other hand, views the world as a
machine, capable of manipulation through a technical knowledge of the
levers Challenge-and-Response, Withdrawal-and-Return, and mimesis.

Mythology, however, describes an inner state, not an objective condition. It represents man's attempt to apprehend the fatedness of life and in
that recognition of necessity to transcend it. It expresses humanity's hope
and not its actualization, man's creative essence, not the material conditions of success.

In a world of determined phenomena distinguished by mortality, man
can give expression to his experience of a directed life only by keeping
before himself certain goals, not dependent on immediate success, as beacons to follow, or aims to attain.[2] When a skeptic suggests to Don Quixote
that perhaps his famous Lady Dulcinea del Toboso does not really exist, he
is perfectly willing to entertain this proposition. But at the same time, he
asserts that her material reality is much less significant than her exercise of
spiritual guidance. She serves as the condition of his prowess, as the motive
force of his activity, as the symbol of that purity for which alone the dream
of the Golden Age becomes worthwhile. Just as Dante's Beatrice lights the
road in the pilgrim's most desperate moments, so humanity tells itself its

---

1. Toynbee, *op. cit.*, Vol. VI, p. 321.
2. In Kant's description of the categorical imperative: "good in themselves."

aspirations in the quest for inward peace. For this reason—and not because of its correspondence to objective reality—is poetry truer than history, for it describes that which man imparts to organic necessity, the essence of his moral personality. Every individual has his Dulcinea or Beatrice and becomes a Don Quixote in the hopes of his creativity. Only he must learn that the Golden Age is the state of a soul, not in the first instance to be derived from the physical world.

And so poetry testifies to fatality overcome, to the goal of our quest, the hope of our fulfillment, the Infinite as certainty. The New Testament offers no causal proofs, nor prudent maxims. Its essence is inward tranquillity, the humility that does not attempt to define the limits of mortality and is expressed by Piccarda Donati: "In His will is our peace."[1]

This, too, constitutes the true substance of freedom. It resides in an inward experience of life as a process of meaningful alternatives. The content of existence cannot depend on social engineering or an apprehension of physical immortality. Man must act, and each action represents his biography, nonetheless irrevocable for being committed with a knowledge of transitoriness. Toynbee completely misunderstood the philosophical ideal of Detachment. It does not reject love, but affirms—in Kant—that man's rationality allows the self-determination to action out of a conception of the ultimacy of the moral personality, apart from any considerations of personal attachments. In the nobility of this sentiment[2] resides humanity's hope of self-realization, the possibility of transcending the determined inexorability of phenomenal reality, the apprehension of immortality, the inward recognition of limits—expressed as tolerance—before God.[3]

Toynbee's philosophy of history represents a conscientious and vast effort to resolve the dilemma of existence. He attempted to enlarge the area of human freedom by postulating a pervasive purposiveness. His conflicting approaches make an evaluation very difficult. The assertion of purposiveness is negated by the conception of history as an evolutionary pattern, in which survival constitutes the only test of inner fitness. The theological basis results in imparting a divine sanction into biological processes and leads to the Calvinistic implication of failure as a sign of sin.

---

1. Dante, *Paradiso*, Canto 3.
2. Which Toynbee calls "repulsive."
3. See *post* Ch. "History and Man's Experience of Morality." Also Ch. "The Sense of Responsibility."

At the end of the road stands Transfiguration, the recognition of the super-mundane plane of reality, the apprehension of the Kingdom of God.

Spengler had a vision of the world-as-experience but felt only the organic element. Toynbee saw in history a machine, but recognized theoretically the purposive factor. His failure, despite many brilliant empirical analyses, resulted from an attempt to look into the mere manifestations of history for a proof of their noumenal significance, from an effort to find a moral sanction in political events instead of within himself.

The problem of Necessity and Freedom remains unresolved. But a way has been pointed along which the two realms can be united. If freedom is not an attribute of external, objective reality, it must result from an inward state that imposes its patterns on phenomena. If morality is not denoted by successful activity, we must find better criteria for ethical conduct. The two realms of Freedom and Necessity are perhaps reconcilable through our experience of freedom in a however determined world. The meaning of history may appear as the emanation of man's moral personality.

We have come up to the problem of History and Man's Experience of Morality.

CHAPTER IV

HISTORY AND MAN'S EXPERIENCE OF MORALITY: KANT

Introduction: The Problem of Freedom and Necessity
in the Philosophies Preceding Kant

Spengler had a vision of the world-as-experience but instead of the uniqueness of events found the generality of phenomena. Toynbee had understood that man craves greater inward certainty than a mere exhortation to do the necessary. Yet his attempt to derive a sanction for moral action from an empirical analysis of historical events was doomed to fail. What then is the solution of our paradox? What is the import of freedom in a world of determined phenomena? If the meaning of life cannot be derived as an attribute of reality, wherein does it reside?

Over a hundred years before Spengler and Toynbee, in the provincial Prussian town of Königsberg, the problem of the meaning of life, the paradox of our experience of freedom in a world of causal laws, received its profoundest formulation. Kant was faced with the heritage of a philosophy which had reduced freedom and morality either to the technical knowledge of objective necessity or to a mere catalogue of pleasing perceptions. The opposition of Rationalism and Empiricism is analogous to the conflict between Spengler and Toynbee. Spengler's dictum that man's freedom consists of doing the necessary or doing nothing might have been uttered by Spinoza.[1] Toynbee's implication that survival embodies a mode of morality corresponds to Hume's concept of the pleasure induced by utility, of benevolence as an inherent trait.[2]

But Kant refused to admit the validity of these assertions. He affirmed that, besides the realm of necessity, there existed a realm of freedom as the repository of the meaning of occurrences. In part a reaction to Empiricism

---

1. Though, of course, giving it a different content.
2. Since survival is an indication of utility. See *post.*

and Rationalism, in part their synthesis, Kant's philosophy transcended both in reformulating the possibilities of human knowledge. And because possibility implies the notion of limit, and since metaphysics can be defined as tracing the boundaries of the knowable, Kant achieved a resolution of our enigma of the antinomy of Freedom and Necessity, in which metaphysical paradoxes are solved though not known by ethical postulates.

Kant limited knowledge to make room for belief. He maintained that the mind imposed certain forms on appearances as a condition for its cognitive action. By analyzing these categories which structure all knowledge, he made phenomenal reality the emanation of pure reason. But at the same time Kant asserted that reality was not exhausted by its appearances, that profounder levels of meaning existed, revealed to man in his aesthetic, theological, and, above all, moral experiences. The transcendental intuition of freedom opens vistas of the noumena, the things in themselves, which no causal analysis can ever reach. The meaning given to life discloses a personality whose moral sanction does not reside in specific attributes such as moderation or self-control but in the disposition of the will. The merit of conduct depends on its conformity to a rule which is not a law but a guide to action. Since nobody in the ultimate decisions of life can obtain a technical solution for moral dilemmas, but is forced to infuse his own spirituality into his problems, Kant's categorical imperative constitutes an affirmation of man's responsibility to give his specific meaning to his particular existence.[1] This finds expression in the concept of a universally legislating will which serves as both subject and lawgiver in a kingdom of ends and allows a morality of universal applicability.

The categorical imperative provides the framework for Kant's philosophy of history. If the transcendental experience of freedom represents the condition for the apprehension of the greater truth at the core of all phenomenal appearances, then its maxims must constitute norms in the political field. Peace is therefore the noblest goal of human endeavor, the affirmation of the ultimacy of man's moral personality. The essay "On Eternal Peace" contains an outline for the attainment of this task.

Kant's philosophy of history reflects his conception of peace as the final purpose of all human striving.[2] Here, however, the magnificent symmetry

---

1. See *post* my discussion of Sartre's and Schweitzer's criticism of Kant.
2. See Friedrich's concept that the problem of peace was the most central to Kant's thought, in *Inevitable Peace* and *The Philosophy of Kant.*

of Kant's thought weakens. If his "Idea for a Universal History" implies that our moral duty for peace enables us to form a conception of its historical attainability, then the inner relationship with the *Critique of Pure Reason* and the *Critique of Practical Reason* is maintained. Serious problems are raised, on the other hand, if Kant means that a hidden plan of nature inexorably compels humanity towards harmony, with human volition but a tool of nature's mechanism.[1] Necessity can never contain a sanction for moral action. Purposes—as the *Critique of Pure Reason* abundantly demonstrates—are not to be derived from phenomena. The *Critique of Judgment* illustrates that a conception of purposiveness in nature can be formed as the condition for mechanical law. Yet purposiveness does not mean a definition of purposes.[2] Though a demonstration of its impossibility would vitiate the command of the categorical imperative for peace, this does not logically imply the necessity for proving inevitability. Moreover, the possibility of the categorical imperative results from its very conception, not from its relation to empirical reality.[3] Theory and practice are united in the moral norm derived from a transcendental experience of freedom.

Withal a road has been pointed towards the resolution of our enigma of man's freedom in a world of determined phenomena. The meaning of life has been seen to constitute the emanation of a personality, not an attribute of reality. Morality derives its sanctions from the inward necessity of a universal rule, not from the objective necessity implied by a mode of survival. History—in one interpretation of Kant's essay—represents a challenge for the recognition of the ultimacy of the moral personality, expressed in the concept of peace and harmony as the goal of all strife, the purpose of all conflict.

The nature of Kant's philosophy cannot be made intelligible without a discussion of the doctrines that preceded him. The seventeenth century witnessed the final disintegration of the two pillars of the medieval concepts of universality: the Catholic Church and the Holy Roman Empire. Under the impact of the Reformation, through the religious wars and settlements of the sixteenth century, the Catholic Church had split up and

---

1. For the implication of inexorability see Kant, "On Eternal Peace," in Friedrich, *The Philosophy of Kant,* p. 453.
2. See Kant, "On Eternal Peace," in Friedrich, *op. cit.*, p. 458.
3. See Kant, *Critique of Judgment* (trans. Bernard), p. 25. See *post* for full discussion also of psychological difference for proofs of "impossibility" and "possibility."

given birth to several Protestant sects. The Holy Roman Empire, growing steadily weaker ever since the collapse of the Hohenstaufen dynasty, rent violently by the Reformation, was ruined in everything but name by the Thirty Years' War. A new era was dawning in Europe, an era of absolute sovereignty, dynastic monarchy, and nationalism.

This era needed philosophic justification. No longer were medieval doctrines of teleology, in which man and the universe were understandable only through an end, interpreted by the Pope in Rome, sufficient. The tremendous spirit of scientific discoveries in the early seventeenth century gave rise to a belief in the feasibility of an inquiry into causes. Thus there arose a new concept of Absoluteness, an Absolute determined by its essence, not by its end, and moreover discoverable by anybody by the mere application of the mathematical method to metaphysical problems. The pilot of nature was no longer God but reason.

Descartes was the founder of modern philosophy, setting the stage for later philosophical discussion. In his work "On the Method" he laid down the following four rules for abstract speculation. (1) To accept nothing but what is self-evident. (2) To resolve each problem into parts small enough to be individually examined. (3) To advance by a series of steps from self-evident premise to certain deduction. (4) To linger on each problem until all its possibilities are examined.

His central problem can be defined as an inquiry into the very possibility of knowledge. What relation exists between objective reality and our ideas about it? There is daily proof of the fallibility of sense impressions, and the possibility exists that some malignant demon might so warp the cognitive faculties that a rational knowledge of reality becomes impossible. Descartes escapes from this total solipsism by first asserting that, whatever the power of the deceiver, thought implies a thinking substance, and the reality of the "I" who thinks and doubts is thereby assured. Moreover, the intervention of an omnipotent God, who by definition cannot be a deceiver, guarantees the reality of the physical world. The Cartesian dualism posits two finite substances, thinking and extended, both of objective reality, with God, the Infinite Substance, as the middle ground and the assurance of certainty.

Descartes' attempt to attain knowledge through mere methodology raised many difficulties, however. God's existence was demonstrated by the very faculty the validity of which had been seriously brought into question. Moreover, if the Deity guarantees objective reality, *Cogito ergo sum* becomes a meaningless dialectic exercise. The trend of subsequent philosophical discussion was, however, established. Though Descartes' main concern was not moral philosophy, he strongly implied that virtue resulted from the right knowledge of an objective reality.

The unsatisfactoriness of the Cartesian dualism led to two strands of thought, each more consistent than Descartes, each utilizing one of Descartes' substances as the basis of its philosophy: the Spinozistic Pantheism and the British Empiricism. Spinoza opted for God. He denied that different substances of thought and matter existed. The universe, in all its manifestations, merely reveals God as the unity of all nature and its immanent cause. Matter and mind disclose but attributes of the divine, one viewed under the aspect of extension, the other as thought. In such a scheme, the experience of freedom becomes the emanation of the Deity as the only source of all motivation. Causality in the universe, purposiveness in events, can never, for Spinoza, serve as an explanatory principle. There are no actions, only happenings. Everything occurs by inward necessity, expressed by *conatus*, the tendency to persevere in one's own being. Moral sanction attaches to actions that support this effort; no other connotation of good and evil can be conceived.[1]

Virtue as the capacity for self-maintenance at the highest level is attained by man under the aegis of reason, which reveals God as the unity of all existence. The wise man will therefore realize that his advantage can best be served by surrounding himself with an atmosphere of peace, by repaying violence with kindness. An inner reconciliation ensues, a realization that nothing divine deserves contempt, but equally, that sympathy is not required as a source of motivation. Acting with enlightened egoism, the sage masters the passions which testify to his existence in nature and attains the power of self-determination in the bliss of a resignation into God.

Virtue is thus attained by knowledge, by understanding the inexorability of events, and by the correct evaluation of one's true advantage. The similarity to Spengler (and to Hobbes) is striking, however different their conclusions. Both agree that an inevitable necessity rules existence, for

---

1. Friedrich in *Inevitable Peace*, p. 149 *et seq.*, has characterized Spinoza as the logical philosophy of Calvinism.

which causality constitutes a shallow and inadequate explanation. Both find the key to comprehension in an intuitive grasp of the immanence that produces all occurrences.[1] Spinoza—just as Spengler—conceives the state as engaged in a fight for sheer survival, in which to keep promises on fancied moral grounds represents the only real sin. Freedom is the apprehension of an objective necessity to which man imparts but little.[2]

Yet the difficulties of a concept that required intuitive insight, backed merely by reason, were too great. An era of new scientific discovery, particularly in physics, seemed to demonstrate that the true source of knowledge was not the mind but nature, indeed that the mind is instructed by nature. Locke, founding the school of British Empiricists, conceived of the mind as a blank tablet endowed with a wax-like capacity of receiving sensory impressions. Thus the other implication of Descartes was developed, into an assertion of the primacy of the physical substance, into a rejection of any innate ideas.

Carried to its ultimate conclusion by Hume, this led to a total metaphysical skepticism. Knowledge was based on experience, reasoning revealed the habitual expectation of recurrent situations. Cause and effect constituted but the representation of a constant conjunction of events, so that the appearance of event A leads to the anticipation of event B. Yet one cannot postulate a necessary connection between A and B. Space and Time merely exhibit the result of certain regularities or juxtapositions of empirical entities. Thus innate ideas were non-existent, the concept of ultimate reality meaningless.

Hume's ethics reflect his metaphysical assumptions. Morality was based on a pleasing sensibility, the faculty of benevolence whereby humane impulses receive inward approbation. Social institutions depend in part on habit, in part on the pleasure derived from their utility. Thus morality became an attribute of external reality, however conceived, pleasure the only source of motivation. The similarity in the conclusions of the empiricists Toynbee and Hume illustrates the effect of metaphysical assumptions.[3]

---

1. Spinoza's sole criterion is inward certainty. See "Essay on Human Understanding."
2. See *post* Ch. "The Sense of Responsibility" for implication of Spinoza's concept of intellectual love of God, which makes this analysis provisional. The fact that Spinoza opted for peace and Spengler for strife reveals their personalities but is in no sense a logical necessity of their system. See *post.*
3. See *post* Appendix, "The Concepts of Meaning."

In each case survival is given moral sanction, conceived as an indication of utility by Hume, as an emanation of divine grace by Toynbee. But where Hume's metaphysical skepticism shrinks from ascribing ultimate purposes to phenomena, Toynbee's theological convictions enable him to find a divine imprint in historical events.

Kant's dilemma, then, is but a restatement of our original paradox: What is the meaning of this necessity that accomplishes itself under the mode of freedom? The rationalists had asserted the supremacy of reason, limiting freedom to the recognition of objective necessity, conceiving manipulatory knowledge as the only ethical criterion.[1] Their theory of knowledge was based on analytic *a priori* judgments, intuitively derived, which contained the whole truth within themselves and claimed their self-evidence as the objective pattern of reality.[2] Yet the attempt to achieve certainty by an analysis of innate ideas was doomed to failure, despite many great achievements of internal consistency. The rationalists were ever forced to abstract from the uniqueness of experience in order to achieve the minimal forms capable of intellectual manipulation. The problem of the objective existence of external reality and its relation to innate ideas was in this formulation insolvable. The irony of the rationalist position is best expressed by their ultimate recourse to an inward experience, subjective certainty, as the final criterion of the validity of their judgments.

Empiricism, on the other hand, faced the dilemma that, despite the acuteness of its analysis of ordinary thought, its judgments lacked the universality which forms the foundation of profound ideation. To base cognition on mere experience is to risk the overthrow of one's concepts with each new experience. In the field of ethics, conduct could obtain sanction only through a cataloguing of pleasing perceptions.

Kant was thus faced with the alternatives of freedom as a function of a mechanistic naturalism or morality as an enlightened hedonism. How, in a world obeying well-understood laws of causality, can reason give effect to the transcendental experience of freedom? What impact can moral maxims have on the unfolding of political events? What is the relation of history to man's experience of morality?

Kant decided that the problem was insoluble until the boundaries of the

---

1. For a distinction between objective and subjective or inward necessity, see *post* Ch. "The Sense of Responsibility."
2. Kant calls this a determinative judgment in his *Critique of Judgment.*

realms of Necessity and Freedom were defined. He asserted that a mechanistic description of nature did not preclude a conception of its transcendental immanence, to be derived, however, as a datum of inward experience, not as a category of reason. He limited knowledge to make room for belief. His political theory and consequent philosophy of history represent an emanation of his moral philosophy. Kant reconciled the antinomy between Necessity and Freedom by way of an inward state, a recognition of life as meaningful alternatives based on an explicit limitation of mere rational analysis. Man can find a sanction for conduct only within himself, not as an attribute of external reality.

Kant's metaphysics, expressed in his *Critique of Pure Reason*, thus serve as the basis for an understanding of his philosophy.

Kant's Metaphysical Theory

Kant addressed himself to his central problem of the implication of the transcendental experience of freedom by re-examining the metaphysical presuppositions of both the rationalists and the empiricists.[1] The rationalists had reduced freedom to a technical mastery of natural relations because their analytic judgments *a priori* had made impossible recourse to experience. The empiricists had approached morality as a problem of analyzing the pleasing perceptions of benevolence or utility because their synthetic judgments *a posteriori* had denied the possibility of universal validity. Yet experience without concepts is blind, while concepts without precepts are meaningless.

Kant solved this dilemma by what he termed his Copernican revolution. Perhaps the problem of how to achieve a relation between ideas and external reality, which had led Descartes and Spinoza to invoke God as the connecting link, one in the sense of guaranteed reliability and the other in the sense of all-pervasiveness, and which, on the other hand, had forced Hume into total skepticism—perhaps this problem was so intractable because its basic epistemological assumptions were incorrectly stated. Just as Copernicus, when he could not account for certain physical phenomena on the assumption that the sun revolved around the earth, was finally

---

1. "The Sense of Responsibility" will discuss what is implied by a transcendental experience.

forced to reverse this formulation, so Kant restated the dilemma of how the mind, which is abstract, can conform to concrete external reality.

He revolutionized metaphysics by insisting that, instead of the mind conforming to external reality, physical objects can only be understood if they conform to certain patterns and rules imposed by the mind. He emphasized, however, that reality in its entirety can never be comprehended. Man's knowledge extends only to phenomena in sensuous experience. Ultimate reality, the things in themselves, are not disclosed to the cognitive faculties. If this is true, then critical philosophy, by analyzing the essential structure of the thought processes, can attempt a definition of the forms by which external reality is apprehended by pure reason, and synthetic *a priori* judgment will be possible. These judgments state nothing less than that all phenomenal experience must conform to certain patterns, for the constitution of the human mind prevents cognition in any other context.

The distinction of reality into phenomenal (apprehended by pure reason) and noumenal (things in themselves and as such the object of speculative reason) does not, however, mean that knowledge of noumenal reality is impossible. Though pure reason is confined to phenomenal appearances, the noumena may reveal themselves to man by way of an inward experience. The realm of freedom appears as the transcendental condition of the realm of necessity. Thus Kant limits knowledge to achieve belief; thus he establishes the possibility of purposeful morality in a world of determined causality.

The validity of Kant's *Critique of Pure Reason* depends on his analysis of the framework within which phenomenal experience occurs.[1] Time and Space, in this sense, are not empirical entities nor properties of objects but patterns imposed by the mind on nature. Space is an absolute requirement to enable us to refer experiences to objects outside ourselves. The non-existence of space cannot even be imagined, though space without objects to fill it is conceivable. Similarly, substance constitutes a category imposed by the mind to account for the possibility of change, for unless a permanence in some respects is postulated, each modification would involve a new object.

Causality, again, reveals the condition which establishes the difference between objective and subjective cognition, between perception and

---

1. The following analysis is intended merely to indicate the general trend of Kant's argument. It is not meant to serve as an exhaustive discussion of the categories.

imagination. When events occur in a certain order, the mind attempts by an effort of will to reverse this sequence. If it fails, the objective reality of the experience is assumed, its fitness for causal analysis established.

Kant thus transcended Hume's skepticism by limiting man's field of knowledge to the world of natural occurrences, forced into patterns by pure reason. He affirmed, however, that the phenomenal world may only represent an inadequate portion of a reality the further reaches of which can never be apprehended by pure reason, but the existence of which speculative reason allows and practical reason postulates.[1]

The *Critique of Pure Reason* ends with a series of antinomies relating to the finite and infinite, to freedom and God versus causality. How can one speak of human freedom in a world of causal necessity? How is it possible to speak of God as a first cause, in the face of phenomena which require an antecedent cause for every other? Kant resolves this basic dilemma of existence by invoking his earlier distinction between phenomenal and noumenal reality. If the total reality is expressed in the phenomenal world, then indeed human freedom is meaningless and God as a first cause a logical inconsistency. If, on the other hand, there exists a noumenal reality beyond the phenomenal manifestations, then insofar as man is noumenal (a thing in itself), he may indeed achieve freedom, though as a physical phenomenon he remains subject to phenomenal requirements.

Pure reason can go no further than making room in its metaphysical scheme for the ultimate reality which may reveal itself to man in his theological, aesthetic, and moral experience. On the other hand, pure reason can show the weakness in the assumptions of both the rationalists and the empiricists. If phenomenal reality does not exhaust the totality of man's experiences, freedom cannot be derived from a recognition of naturalistic necessity. If sensuous experience is confined to the appearances of a profounder level of existence, the empirical world cannot contain a moral sanction. The experience of freedom in a determined environment is seen to be potentially meaningful after all. The meaning of life becomes the emanation of a personality, not an attribute of the empirical world. Purposiveness is not revealed by phenomenal reality but constitutes the resolve of a soul. Freedom does have a place in a determined universe.

The rigorousness and symmetry of Kant's method cannot be over-

---

1. See *post* for Kant's explanation of the noumenal reality.

emphasized. No other philosopher had a clearer grasp of the implications of our experience of freedom in a world of causality. He fully recognized the importance of a profound metaphysics for the apprehension of a total reality, which was not, however, exhausted by the categories of pure reason. Kant's metaphysics, which have traced the boundaries of human knowledge and at the same time opened vistas of an ultimate experience, serve as the condition for the apprehension of a morality that gives the profoundest expression to the intrinsic worth of the moral personality, the transcendental experience which connects man with the Infinite.

Moral Philosophy

"Two things fill the mind with ever new and increasing awe and admiration, the more frequently and continuously reflection is occupied with them; the starry heaven above me and the moral law within me. I ought not to seek either outside my field of vision as though they were either shrouded in obscurity or visionary. I see them confronting me and link them immediately with the consciousness of my existence. The first (the starry heaven) begins with the place I occupy in the external world of sense and expands the connection in which I find myself in the incalculable vastness of worlds upon worlds, systems within systems over endless ages of periodic motion, their beginnings and perpetuations. The second (the moral law) starts from my invisible self, my moral personality, and depicts me in a world of true infinitude which can be sensed only by the intellect. With this I recognize myself to be in a necessary and general connection not just accidentally, as appears to be the case with the physical world. Through this recognition I also see myself linked to all visible worlds. The first view of a numberless quantity of worlds destroys my importance, since I am an animal-like being who must return to its matter from whence it came to the planet (a mere speck in the universe) ... The second view raises my value infinitely as an intelligence, through my personality; for in this personality the moral law reveals a life independent of animality and even of the entire world of sense. This is true at least as far as one can infer from the purposeful determination of my existence according to this law. This is not restricted to the conditions of life but radiates into the infinite."[1]

Kant's ethics derive from the transcendental experience of the moral law, from a vision of the noumenal reality which constitutes the real essence of appearances. Freedom is an inward state which elevates humanity out of the world of necessity into the realm where man, in Dostoevsky's words, "perceives the divine mystery in things."[2] But what is the nature of the moral law? How can any content and universality be ascribed to it in the face of the intensely personal experience of freedom? Is morality expressed by conformity to explicit regulations, or by an inward state that gives meaning to its own maxims?

As in his *Critique of Pure Reason*, Kant rejects the views of both the rationalists and the empiricists. Objective necessity, naturalistically conceived, cannot constitute the essence of morality, for that would deny the direct experiences of freedom. Ethical hedonism is inadequate because it prevents the formulation of a universal rule. The happiness postulated by hedonism and the feeling of benevolence of Hume multiply motivations but suffer from the same defects as synthetic *a posteriori* judgments. The Epicurean concepts of higher (mental) and lower (physical) pleasures is meaningless in such a context. Intensity, not order, of enjoyment can serve as the only logical criterion for hedonism.

If neither Rationalism nor Empiricism provide a foundation for a universal law, how can humanity give effect to its experience of morality? Kant finds the answer in the very constitution of man. If everything in nature is created with a maximum of economy and the means chosen most apt, then happiness conceived as desire satisfaction cannot represent the purpose of a rational being.[3] Instinct would suffice for the achievement of pleasure in the hedonistic sense. But man is endowed with reason, and above all a practical reason that issues forth into action, and seemingly multiplies motivations. The faculty of rationality must consequently be designed to implement the moral experience.

But how can a personal experience contain a universal obligation? Just as the metaphysical dilemma was resolved only with the aid of synthetic *a priori* judgments, so Kant gives effect to man's experience of freedom by *a*

---

1. Kant, *Critique of Practical Reason*, in Friedrich, *The Philosophy of Kant*, p. 261.
2. For a discussion of the nature of this experience see *post* Ch. "The Sense of Responsibility." See *ante* "Introduction" for brief discussion of Dostoevsky.
3. This teleological concept depends on Kant's *Critique of Judgment*. See *post*.

priori principles that determine the will by their own inner necessity. Moral sanction consequently does not attach to such laudable qualities as moderation, self-control, or calm deliberation, for in villains these very qualities tend to accentuate evil. The merit of conduct is determined solely by the disposition of a will which acts out of a concept of duty expressed as respect for the moral law. This precludes inclination as a guide to action but prevents equally the definition of morality as a technical knowledge of naturalistic relations.

How, then, is the will determined by reason? In a holy will, which acts of necessity according to the moral law, such a determination is unnecessary. The human will, however, torn by desires, requires an imperative, a representation of a ground of action expressed by the word *ought.* It is a hypothetical imperative if represented as a means to an end, a categorical imperative if an end in itself. But the moral law stems from a transcendental experience, from a recognition of an ultimate reality beyond phenomenal appearances. It can therefore be implemented only by the categorical imperative, the maxims of which assure universality.

Kant's first formulation of the categorical imperative derives from the conception of the moral law determining the will by its own inward necessity from *a priori* principles. It states: "Act as if the maxims of thy action could become by thy will universal laws of nature." Morality in this sense results from a point of view which recognizes that by its actions it gives maxims of universal applicability. The difference between morality and expediency, between inward compulsion of duty and inclination, becomes immediately apparent. Kant cites the example of borrowing with the knowledge that its repayment is impossible. Whatever the expediency of this action, it is impossible to will it as a universal law of nature.[1] The key to an immoral action resides in the willingness to make an exception in favor of inclination to a moral law recognized as of universal validity.

Kant's second formulation relies on the distinction between the categorical imperative as an end in itself and the hypothetical imperative, in which the motivation is but a means. *"So act as to treat humanity, whether in thine own person or in that of any other, in every case as an end withal, never as means only."*[2] This concept expresses the recognition of the ultimacy of man's moral

---

1. For the discussion of this argument see *post.* It is not, of course, impossible to will this, but it is impossible to secure a reciprocal recognition of this volition.
2. Kant, "Fundamental Principles of the Metaphysic of Morals," *Critique of Practical Reason,* p. 47.

personality, the apprehension of tolerance which sets limits to one's activity out of respect for the divine in humanity. Its goal is the kingdom of ends, in which the autonomy of the wills precludes any personal inclination in the carrying out of moral laws. Here every man is both legislator of universal maxims and subject to the rules created by the autonomy of others. Here the dignity of man, flowing from an awareness of his responsibility to mankind, provides the foundation for a heteronomy of wills in whom the transcendental vision of freedom has kindled the spark that has led to the common experience of the moral law.

But how can the categorical imperative furnish a conception of its possibility? If man forms part of nature—as all experience indicates—he is ruled by causality. This raises a series of other antinomies. Man attempts to achieve morality, yet the goal is distant, and intuitively one feels the impossibility of its attainment. Man longs for the *summum bonum*—happiness commensurate with virtue—but no guarantee for a necessary connection exists in the phenomenal world. Duty seems the only motive that can guide humanity in its quest for morality.

Again Kant returns to the distinction in the *Critique of Pure Reason* between the noumenal and the phenomenal world. Insofar as man participates in the realm of necessity—as a phenomenon—he is indeed determined. But morality does not describe an order of nature, but has its origins in a mystic attitude within us.[1] Ethics testify to an experience which raises man above himself out of the world of senses, into the noumenal reality of the divine design. Freedom, the possibility of which speculative reason asserted, is now postulated by practical reason. The striving for perfection induced by the moral law implies immortality to give effect to an endeavor impossible of fulfillment in a finite time. God appears as the guarantor of the *summum bonum*.[2] The postulates of God, freedom, and immortality represent an assertion of the pervasiveness of man's moral experience. The transcendental experience of freedom overcomes all obstacles offered by the empirical realm. Theory and practice are united in the categorical imperative, the possibility of whose implementation derives from its very conception.[3] Through his moral experience—not through any analysis of

---

1. For interpretation of this attitude see *post* Ch. "The Sense of Responsibility."
2. N. Kemp Smith, *A Commentary to Kant's "Critique of Pure Reason,"* p. 575, points out that in later life Kant considered this an overly theoretical proof of God's existence and asserted instead that God speaks directly through the categorical imperative.

empirical reality—man attains a vision of a higher world order and of the meaning of occurrences.

This enables Kant to redefine Christianity on the basis of a transcendental intuition without attempting—like Toynbee—to claim the sanction of external reality for this effort. The moral law is holy and presupposes a will directly determined by its commands. Yet all man can achieve in this life is a rightful disposition arising out of respect for the law. The yearning for the bliss of holiness therefore postulates eternity. The order of nature can offer no happiness as an inducement for the performance of the moral law. But the Christian concept of the Kingdom of God opens vistas of a profounder plane, in which terrestrial striving dissolves in the blessedness of inward peace. In the same sense, Kant understands the biblical command of loving God and of loving one's neighbor as oneself. Pathological love cannot be commanded. But a feeling of respect for the experience of the moral law, a liking to do one's duty based on an *a priori* conception expressed in the categorical imperative, an approach to man as an end, these constitute the true meaning of ethical love.

Kant has come full cycle. His *Critique of Pure Reason*, by establishing the limits of knowledge, by the distinction between phenomenal and noumenal reality, left room for a significant moral experience. The transcendental experience of freedom gave meaning to the concept of a will determined to action by *a priori* considerations. The kingdom of ends emerged, and an affirmation of man's dignity as the goal of ethical activity.

The rationalistic formulation of Kant's ethical philosophy tends to obscure its profound visions. Morality is found to reside in a mystic relationship to a supersensuous world order, in a transcendental experience which alone makes the categorical imperative possible. For the necessity of the categorical imperative applies only to a specific attitude; its universality presupposes the prior experience of the moral law. This must be kept in mind in considering the criticism of Kant's ethics by Schweitzer and Sartre. Though they differ in their point of view, their arguments are remarkably alike. Schweitzer maintains that the validity of ethics issues from the necessity attending their thought.[1] Kant's moral philosophy achieves universality at the cost of vitality, according to Schweitzer. The content of the categorical imperative becomes so vague as to lose all meaning.

---

1. Schweitzer, *The Philosophy of Civilization*, p. 182 *et seq.*

Sartre restates this argument in practical terms.[1] He cites the case of a young Frenchman torn between the desire of joining de Gaulle's forces and thereby exposing his mother to possible German retaliation or staying and losing his self-respect. Kant's categorical imperative offers no solution to this dilemma, according to Sartre. Whatever the lad's decision, he would treat somebody, either himself or his mother, as but a means.

Despite the impreciseness of the example, it illustrates well the confusion involved in this interpretation of Kant's moral philosophy. Both Schweitzer and Sartre argue as if moral philosophy should be a manual of action supplying technical solutions to all the problems of existence. But the dilemmas of life are not to be reconciled by manipulation. Ethical conduct, to be meaningful, must reveal a personality, not a mastery of causal connections. Kant understood this and based his whole moral philosophy on a transcendental experience. This implies, however, that the categorical imperative can give conditions only to a prior moral experience. Its universality expresses a feeling of responsibility towards humanity, its obligation testifies to a vision of an ultimate reality.

The existentialists are right in their assertion that life involves action. But their demand that philosophy should offer absolute certainty tends to deny the uniqueness of the individual. The experience of freedom in a determined world implies that we can transcend necessity only by imparting our individuality to the inexorable unfolding of events. The existentialists' emphasis on activity, however, reduces man to an atom, buffeted by fate, doomed to whirl in concentric circles until a stable constellation is achieved through an understanding of causal laws. But this confuses a physical state with an ethical norm. Similarly, Schweitzer wants ethics to be a necessity of thought. This, too, expresses a quest for certainty in an uncertain world, a claim to wrest out of intellectual constructions an immortality which the experience of directedness denies. A necessity of thought cannot occur in a vacuum. The moral experience, again, reveals a task, not an inevitable development.

The young Frenchman's dilemma therefore was an aspect of the fatedness of existence, not a refutation of the categorical imperative. No other person can ever feel the soul's dilemma in the ultimate crisis of life. Man must solve his problems with dignity, but alone. The categorical imperative

---

1. Sartre, *Existentialism*, p. 28 *et seq.*

can guide an attitude only if preceded by a transcendental experience of freedom. But experiences are personal, and no outsider can possibly prescribe their content. Love is unique only to the lover. Philosophy can therefore never create an ethical system which constitutes a necessity of thought or provides technical solutions for all of life's problems. It is humanity's responsibility to give its own meaning to its own existence. The motive force for this activity issues in the first instance from an inward experience which teaches man his limits and his intrinsic worth.[1] This is the ultimate basis of human freedom, the condition for mankind's self-transcendence.

The transcendental experience of freedom serves as the foundation of Kant's moral philosophy; the categorical imperative provides the solution to the problem of reconciling universal applicability with personal experience. But Schweitzer offers another fundamental criticism.[2] The union of ethical and epistemological idealism in Kant implies—according to Schweitzer—that the noumenal reality which reveals itself as the moral law in men operates as the objective principle in the physical world as well. If the phenomenal world discloses but the manifestation of a transcendental reality, then the events brought about by causation are merely parallel appearances of occurrences which the intellect produces under the conception of freedom. Freedom and ethics thus become but a mode of necessity; an immanence rules all happenings, only the apprehension of which differs, but not its operation.

This is a profound analysis, though not a necessary one. The causality of the physical world represents a mode of apprehending phenomena, not a property of their occurrence. The experience of freedom constitutes man's intuition of an ultimate world order. But this does not mean that this transcendence is in fact the objective representation of the operation of noumenal reality. On the contrary, if noumenal reality is approachable only by an inward experience, the mode of its operation in the physical world must, of necessity, remain undecided.

Nevertheless, the tendency to equate man's experience of the moral law with the objective meaning of occurrences and thereby attribute an ethical sanction to phenomenal manifestations exists in Kant. It comes to expression in his philosophy of history, in which the duty to work for peace appears first as an emanation of the categorical imperative, only to stand

---

1. See *post* Ch. "The Sense of Responsibility."
2. Schweitzer, *op. cit.*, p. 186 *et seq.*

revealed as the objective principle governing historical events.

The next section will deal with the problems raised by such a conception, and by the attempt to equate history with man's experience of morality.

The Philosophy of History Derived from the Categorical Imperative

Just as Kant's metaphysical theory had given meaning to the transcendental experience of freedom, so his categorical imperative determines man's political duties. "Morals, when conceived as the totality of absolutely binding laws according to which we *ought* to act, is in itself practice in the objective sense. It is therefore an apparent paradox to say that one *cannot* do [what one ought to do] once the authoritativeness of this concept of duty is acknowledged." With this assertion of the absolute pervasiveness of the moral law begins the appendix to Kant's essay "On Eternal Peace."[1] No conflict can exist between theory and practice in the political realm any more than in the moral. The categorical imperative applies to all activity, in every field, its possibility postulated by its very conception.[2]

But what is the nature of the duty which the categorical imperative commands from *a priori* considerations? Kant finds the answer in the second formulation of the categorical imperative, that man must always be treated as an end, never as a means. In the domestic field, this implies the creation of a republican constitution, in which the categorical imperative is institutionalized in a general will.[3] In relations between states, this makes the attainment of eternal peace the statesman's noblest duty.

What validity can be ascribed to a duty which seems negated by all experience? The practical man will be ready to point out that the moral law rarely coincides with the volition for its performance. Yet empirical reality can never supply a criterion for motivated activity in Kant's scheme. If man denies his transcendental experience of freedom, then indeed public law is meaningless and eternal peace a chimera. If, on the other hand, the moral law constitutes man's connecting link with noumenal reality, then the realm of necessity appears as but a manifestation of the realm of freedom and no opposition can occur between theory and practice.

1. Kant, "On Eternal Peace," in Friedrich, *The Philosophy of Kant*, p. 454.
2. Friedrich, *Inevitable Peace*, p. 53, offers a different interpretation. For my discussion see *post.*
3. For Kant's criteria of a republican constitution, see *post.*

The empiricist—according to Kant—is ever forced to equate empirical reality with morality. The political moralist who adapts his maxims to phenomenal appearances imputes his notion of practical wisdom to the divine.[1] The moral politician, on the other hand, for whom the categorical imperative represents an absolute norm, realizes that the lawful organization of government implies a coincidence of the moral attitude in all particular wills. Though the weight of tradition may preclude an immediate modification of institutions, the moral law ever guides his quest, a beacon to follow, an aim to attain. The political moralist knows men, but the moral politician understands man, in the dignity of whose personality resides the only possibility of conceiving a duty, the sole guide to moral action.

Thus politics becomes a task of giving effect to man's transcendental vision of the noumena which underlie all visible workings. The categorical imperative emerges as the norm of all political endeavor, to light the road towards the achievement of a republican constitution and the attainment of eternal peace. The meaning of history results from an inward apprehension that determines the will by its very conception without any regard to its immediate empirical attainability. Peace represents the goal of all human striving, the fulfillment of the purpose of history.

Kant's essay "On Eternal Peace" comprises nine articles for a hypothetical treaty among nations for the assurance of universal peace. The first six—the preliminary articles—are frankly remedial, directed at specific abuses in contemporary diplomacy. Though addressed to technical problems, their obligation derives in each case from the *a priori* conception of the moral law. They are:

1. "No treaty of peace shall be held to be such, which is made with the secret reservation of the material for a future war."
2. "No state having an independent existence whether it be small or great may be acquired by another state through inheritance, exchange, purchase or gift."
3. "Standing armies shall gradually disappear."
4. "No debts shall be contracted in connection with the foreign affairs of the state."
5. "No state shall interfere by force in the constitution and

---

1. Kant, "On Eternal Peace," in Friedrich, *The Philosophy of Kant,* p. 469.

government of another state."

6. "No state at war with another shall permit such acts of warfare
   as must make mutual confidence impossible in time of future
   peace: such as the employment of assassins, of poisoners, the
   violation of articles of surrender, the instigation of treason in
   the state against which it is making war, etc."[1]

The preliminary articles express Kant's conception of the determination of
the will by the categorical imperative on the basis of *a priori* considerations.
The task of achieving peace derives from the transcendental experience of
the moral law, not from any accidental constellation of empirical facts.

If the categorical imperative commands the achievement of eternal
peace, any mental reservation which leaves open the possibility of future
conflicts constitutes a violation of the moral law, for which expediency
offers no excuse. If the moral sanction of the state resides in its conception
of man as an end—expressed in a general will—then no technical reason
exists for treating it as the possession of the ruler. This reduces the state
from a moral person to a thing and violates the categorical imperative.

If the moral law commands the treatment of men as an end, no consideration of utility can legalize standing armies. Professional soldiers become
mere tools, whose very existence moreover creates a constant state of insecurity. No violations of the categorical imperative by other states can serve
as an excuse for war. The very existence of oppression should serve as a
stimulus to others to implement the categorical imperative. To work for
peace represents man's noblest duty, to be violated only in self-defense.

The pervasiveness of the moral law in Kant's philosophy of history now
becomes apparent. Conformity to the categorical imperative contains the
moral sanction of the political world. In this sense, the formulation of diplomatic documents, the maintenance of armies, the utilization of economic
means for foreign policy, the employment of force all reveal violations of a
moral law, of which even the command for eternal peace represents but a
particular instance. Man's experience of freedom in a determined world
issues into ethical activity and furnishes humanity's guide on the journey
through history.

But Kant realized that the application of the categorical imperative to

---

1. Kant, "On Eternal Peace," in Friedrich, *The Philosophy of Kant,* pp. 431–34.

specific abuses could not provide the ultimate foundation of eternal peace. Kant's three definitive articles of "On Eternal Peace" embody his conception of the absolute basis of peace, his recognition that peace implies more than the absence of war, his affirmation of the supremacy of the moral law in the political realm.

Kant argues that a true state of peace results, at least in part, from lawful institutions within nations. If the attainment of peace is a moral law, it can be given effect only by a moral personality. But how can the dictates of the categorical imperative operate in social institutions? Just as the moral law contains the objective principle of all actions, so the republican constitution represents the norm of political institutions. What, however, is a republican constitution? Kant applies three criteria:[1] the principle of the freedom of all members of the society as men; the principle of the dependence of all upon a single common legislation as subjects; the principle of equality for all as citizens.

The republican constitution thus institutionalizes Kant's categorical imperative. The assertion of man as intrinsically valuable expresses the transcendental experience of freedom; the principle of dependence upon common legislation reveals the kingdom of ends, in which each individual is both subject and legislator. This testifies to the moral attitude, to a feeling of responsibility towards the rights of others, to a motivation that derives from a conception of the common good. A political community based on this apprehension of man as an end in itself achieves a synthesis of liberty, expressed in the righteousness of the will, and equality, exemplified by the universal applicability of its laws.[2] Since the republican constitution institutionalizes the categorical imperative, the state becomes a moral person and as such subject to the maxims derived from the transcendental experience of freedom. Therefore, too, Kant's first definitive article states: "The civil constitution in each state should be republican."[3]

With the state conceived as a moral person, the application of the moral law to political events becomes a reality. The categorical imperative now appears as a positive force guiding relations between nations. To be sure, politics never really succeed in freeing themselves from the pervasive reflection of a moral norm, expressed in the lip service paid to the interna-

---

1. Kant, "On Eternal Peace," in Friedrich, *The Philosophy of Kant*, p. 437.
2. This is institutionalized by Rousseau's general will.
3. Kant, "On Eternal Peace," in Friedrich, *op. cit.*, p. 437.

tional law of Grotius, Pufendorf, and Vattel.[1] Peace treaties always claim the sanction of abstract justice, wars are ever defended on moral grounds. Humanity's dim apprehension of morality cannot, however, bear fruit until its maxims have been institutionalized.

The emergence of the republican constitution makes possible the foundation of an eternal peace based on universal principles. Law can now replace the violence of the state of nature, harmony the insecurity of constant strife. The federation of free states contains Kant's vision of the reconciliation of all conflicts. Kant sways between the conception of a union of nations and a federation of states with republican constitutions. Though the vision of all men as ends inclines Kant towards the first alternative, his awareness of political realities makes him accept the latter. He can do so, moreover, without sacrificing the independent validity of his moral maxims, since his first definitive article has already assured the conformity of the state to the categorical imperative. With the state a moral person, the maxims of the moral law become universally applicable. Now peace emerges from discord, reconciliation from conflict. Now a general basis for peace can be created apart from the incidental existence of empirically favorable conditions. In the majesty of the moral law resides the feasibility of its maxims. Eternal peace appears as the emanation of man's moral personality expressed in a republican constitution, organized in a federalism of states. Thus Kant's second definitive article states: "The law of nations should be based upon a federalism of free states."[2]

Kant's conception of man as an end involves the encouragement of contacts among nations, but also implies a denial of the right of conquest. Though humanity is divided into many components, separated by oceans and desert regions, the globe represents a common possession of mankind. Kant argues that men have the right to visit everywhere as long as they don't assert their right by force and as long as they are bound by the principle of hospitality. The law of nations must therefore guarantee the treatment of all foreigners as ends, while preventing the exploitation of the indigenous population. This, again, reveals the pervasiveness of the categorical imperative, which commends peace as humanity's highest task.

The experience of the moral law constitutes man's connection with the

---

1. Kant, "On Eternal Peace," calls them miserable consolers; in Friedrich, *The Philosophy of Kant*, p. 443.
2. Kant, "On Eternal Peace," in Friedrich, *op. cit.*, p. 441.

ultimate reality which he can only feel, never know. Any violation of its maxims anywhere affects the dignity of men in all other parts of the world. Each man is responsible to humanity, for his will gives universal maxims, for good or evil.[1] And so Kant's third definitive article of eternal peace states: "The Cosmopolitan or World Law shall be limited to conditions of universal hospitality."[2]

The essay "On Eternal Peace" continues the symmetrical edifice of Kant's philosophy. The *Critique of Pure Reason* had affirmed the possibility of the experience of freedom, the moral philosophy had given it meaning. In the philosophy of history, the moral law which lifts man above himself stands revealed as the normative principle governing political events. No conflict between theory and practice is here conceivable. Indeed, the categorical imperative represents practice in the objective sense. Humanity's aspirations disclose history's meaning, because only through the experience of freedom does man apprehend the unity which produces all phenomena. The moral law represents the assumptions underlying all purposive activity; approximation to its maxims constitutes the sole test of moral fitness. Peace, for Kant, represents a command of the moral law derived from formal *a priori* considerations independent of any empirical conditions. Peace is man's noblest task, humanity's ultimate purpose.

But in Kant's philosophy of history, the implications pointed out by Schweitzer's become apparent. The erection of a moral philosophy on the base of epistemological idealism is—according to Schweitzer—doomed to failure. Since ethics become meaningful only if they can affect the noumenal reality,[3] a dangerous confusion of the ethical and the natural arises.[4] If the moral law discloses the noumena which govern all appearances, then either everything that occurs is ethical or the moral law has no meaning. Ethics and natural law, the purpose of man and the design of the universe, stand equated.

Though this is by no means a necessary conclusion, the further development of Kant's philosophy of history lends considerable force to Schweitzer's criticism.[5] For peace, which the categorical imperative had commanded as

---

1. For elaboration of this point see *post.*
2. Kant, "On Eternal Peace," in Friedrich, *The Philosophy of Kant,* p. 441.
3. Since phenomena obey natural laws; Schweitzer, *op. cit.,* p. 186 *et seq.*
4. See *post* for discussion of this point.
5. See *ante* for discussion of this point.

humanity's duty, is suddenly revealed as the objective principle of historical events. The moral law realizes itself not through the determination of the will, but as an aspect of a hidden plan of nature. Man's volition can assist in producing the inevitable, but in its absence humanity would still be forced to achieve harmony, "albeit with much inconvenience."[1] Freedom appears as but a mode of causality, peace as the consequence of an immanent inexorability, harmony as an emanation of nature's mechanism. History is not a task but contains a guarantee for the realization of the moral law. This aspect of Kant's philosophy parallels Toynbee's dilemma, the attempt to wrest certainty from the fatedness of life, the endeavor to conjure phenomena to escape the transitoriness of existence.[2]

The Philosophy of History Conceived as a Teleological System

Kant poses three possible modes for the apprehension of historical events: History can be conceived as the unfolding of a plan (either natural or divine, depending on the point of view) to develop humanity from the lowest state of animality to the highest level of human freedom. On the other hand, the succession of political events may reveal no more than the accidental constellation of power relations which may one day achieve a formation which insures stability. Lastly, one can deny any pattern in history, leaving merely a senseless alternation of strife and truce, a constant rise and decline of empires, a hopeless resignation which cannot attain peace.[3] Kant opts for the first alternative. If phenomena required for their cognition the formulation of synthetic *a priori* judgment, if the moral law derived its validity from *a priori* considerations of universality, then history can be conceived only on the basis of an *a priori* principle that reveals its immanence. This principle operates outside the range of human volition and structures the apprehension of events by its own inward necessity.

But how is one to conceive such a philosophy of history? How is one to reconcile man's experience of purposiveness with the meaning of occur-

---

1. Kant, "On Eternal Peace," in Friedrich, *The Philosophy of Kant*, p. 453.
2. See *post* for discussion, the subsequent section on amalgamation of Kant's "Idea for a Universal History" and his "On Eternal Peace." Since the latter sharpens the former's implications, it forms the core of the analysis.
3. For the three alternatives see Kant, "Idea for a Universal History," in Friedrich, *The Philosophy of Kant*, p. 125.

rences? Kant utilizes the argument of his *Critique of Judgment*[1] that a teleological principle must inhere in nature as a condition for the regularity of phenomena. Only thus can the meaning of history emerge out of the otherwise senseless recurrence of seemingly accidental events. Man's freedom appears as an aspect of a pervasive mechanism, purposive activity becomes but the tool of an inexorable directedness. Just as the population statistics of major countries reveal a regularity according to stable natural laws, despite the accidents of individual fortunes, so history considered as a totality may contain a pattern apart from the incidental purposes of human beings. Mankind thus promotes an end unknown to them which moreover "they would care little for if they knew."[2]

But what is this end? What is the *a priori* principle by which historical events become intelligible? Kant maintains that history's purpose is the achievement of peace through law, by states with republican constitutions. This is, however, neither derived from a transcendental experience, nor from the universal obligation of a moral law, but issues from an analysis of the end which the mechanism of nature promotes. Peace becomes a technical task of reconciling empirical conditions with the purpose of existence.[3] The meaning of history is identical with man's aspirations; indeed, humanity's norms constitute but a means for the achievement of an immanent aim.

Kant lays down nine principles for the apprehension of history.[4] Since

---

1. See *post* discussion of this argument.
2. Kant, "Idea for a Universal History," in Friedrich, *The Philosophy of Kant,* p. 117.
3. See Kant, "On Eternal Peace," in Friedrich, *The Philosophy of Kant,* p. 452, and *post.*
4. Kant's nine principles are:
   (1) All natural aptitudes of a creature are destined to unfold themselves completely and purposefully.
   (2) As for man (the only rational creature on earth), these natural aptitudes which are directed toward the use of his reason will develop fully in the species, but not in the individual.
   (3) Nature has willed that man should develop completely by himself everything which goes beyond the mechanical ordering of his animal existence, and that he should not partake of any happiness or perfection except such as he has secured by and for himself through his own reason, independent of instinct.
   (4) The means which nature employs to produce the development of all man's aptitudes is the antagonism in society, since this antagonism becomes in the end the cause of a lawful order of society.
   (5) The greatest problem for the species man, the solution of which nature forces upon him, is the establishment of a civil society which generally administers the law.
   (6) This problem is mankind's most difficult problem and will be the last solved by the species.

history is conceived as subject to a teleology theory which structures its phenomena *a priori*, the natural faculties of all creatures must be destined to unfold completely according to their end. Thus purpose replaces accident, design a senseless mechanism. The goal of men as the only rational creature is the development of his reason. However, the growth in wisdom requires many trials, and much experience, not to be attained in a single life. Consequently man's faculties develop completely in the species, not in the individual.

But existence involves strife, life presents a continuous series of problems. Hardship seems the lot of humanity. Kant argues that the mechanism of nature imposes these difficulties on man in order to force him to create his well-being solely by his own work. Man's real happiness consists of rational self-esteem. Now the eternal violence of history attains new meaning. Man's faculties develop through the antagonism of society and the struggle between nations. The pressure of competition and the insecurity of the state of nature lead to the formation of the civil society, whose invocation of the principle of law testifies to its apprehension, though not immediate attainment, of moral ideals. Man's quarrelsome instincts reveal nature's mechanism for the optimum development of his skills. "Man wants concord, but nature knows better what is good for his kind; nature wants discord. Man wants to live comfortably and pleasurably, but nature intends that he should raise himself out of lethargy and inactive contentment into work and trouble and then he should find means of extricating himself adroitly from these latter."[1]

If society arises in response to the insecurity of constant strife, the organization of the proper constitution must represent mankind's most difficult task. Man can develop his natural faculties to the fullest only under a just civic constitution. Kant considers the reconciliation of freedom with a

(7) The problem of the establishment of a perfect civil constitution is dependent upon a lawful external relation between states and cannot be solved without it.

(8) It is possible to look upon the history of the human species in the large as the execution of a hidden plan of nature—to bring about a constitution which is perfect internally, and for this purpose also externally—because this is the only state in which nature can develop all aptitudes of mankind fully.

(9) A philosophical attempt to treat general world history according to a plan of nature which aims at the perfect civil association of the human species must be considered possible and as itself promoting this purpose of nature. [From "Idea for a Universal History."]

1. Kant, "Idea for a Universal History," in Friedrich, *The Philosophy of Kant*, p. 121.

monopoly of force humanity's central political problem. The tendency to make exceptions in one's own favor ever fights against the assertion of the supremacy of law. Law, again, suffers from the fact that it is a product of man and at the same time conceived as embodying objective principles of justice. The emergence of a just civic constitution will therefore testify to the proper disposition of the will. But this can occur only after many disappointing failures, as the goal of all striving, as the ultimate purpose of history.

The perfect civic constitution, moreover, presupposes lawful relations among states. There is no use in working for domestic peace if war constantly threatens from across the borders. The ceaseless preparation for conflict, the feeling of insecurity engendered by armies, and the ravages of never-ending strife all teach humanity what reason alone would have indicated without all this suffering. Just as the experience of the state of nature among individuals led to the formation of civil society, so the eternal tensions between states reveal nature's mechanism for the attainment of peace. The eventual creation of a just civic constitution, which will forever banish war and begin the era of harmony among mankind, therefore constitutes the purpose of history. The unfolding of events will force the emergence of this constitution, even if moral precepts fail. A philosophy of history based on these assumptions must be possible, according to Kant; a task bequeathed to succeeding generations.

Schweitzer's criticism is thus validated by Kant's "Idea for a Universal History." The meaning of history derived from the categorical imperative is identical with the design of nature. History regarded as a phenomenon discloses the same immanence that the transcendental experience of freedom postulated. The confusion of the ethical and the natural is complete. It makes little difference whether morality claims the sanction of reality or vice versa; in this scheme both are reduced to parallel appearances of the same inexorability. The aspirations of humanity represent but a mode of nature's mechanism.

The sublimity of Kant's moral philosophy derived from his intuition that ethics depended on a direct relation to the Infinite, a transcendental experience that sets its own conditions. The distinction between noumena and phenomena represented the resolve of a soul which wanted to escape the determined inevitability of the physical world and impart its own purposiveness to the causal unfolding of events. The postulates of God, freedom, and immortality testify to a vision which had experienced the noumenal

reality and recognized no obstacles in the empirical world. The nine articles of the essay "On Eternal Peace" reveal the pervasiveness of this moral
experience and its determining effect on all political manifestations. The
true meaning of existence was seen to result from the content ascribed to
the categorical imperative, from the feeling of responsibility towards man
as an end, from the duty to create peace out of discord and reconciliation
out of strife.

What lessons can be derived from the empirical world in such a context?
The *Critique of Pure Reason* had realized that knowledge had to be limited to
achieve belief. The categorical imperative universalized a personal relation to the ultimate reality which underlies all phenomena. But this implied
that the noumena are approachable only by way of a direct experience of
the moral law. The mode of their operation in phenomena cannot be
decided by pure reason, nor really affirmed by the teleological judgment.[1]
The transcendental intuition of freedom does not necessarily reveal the
objective mode of noumenal operation but only its relationship to man. It
lifts man above himself and attaches him to a higher world order by means
of a vision that is essentially incommunicable and certainly unclassifiable
teleologically. The categorical imperative represents its only meaningful
principle when it issues into action.

If Kant were basing his "Idea for a Universal History" and his "On Eternal Peace" on the categorical imperative, a different situation would arise.
He could then assert that the command for peace is an emanation of a
transcendental experience which in its very conception contains its possibility. The implementation of moral maxims would then become a consequence of the determination of the will out of a conception of the moral
law, not a technical problem of manipulating the mechanism of nature.
This, indeed, forms the foundation for the nine articles for "On Eternal
Peace." It cannot be asserted that their obligation depends on empirical
conditions. On the contrary, Kant repeatedly rejects the argument that the
categorical imperative and its application to the problem of peace can take
any account of the accidental constellation of political events.[2] The moral

---

1. See *post* for my brief discussion of *Critique of Judgment.*
2. For example, see this quotation, Kant, "Concerning the Common Saying: This May Be True
in Theory But Does Not Apply to Practice" (Friedrich, *The Philosophy of Kant,* p. 414): "This
maxim about theory and practice which has become common in our wordy and deedless
times causes very great damage if it is applied to moral questions; i.e., moral or legal duty.
For the canon of practical reason is involved in this realm. Here the value of a given practice
depends upon its appropriateness to the theory upon which it is based. All is lost if empirical,

law reveals the objective principle that guides humanity's quest for a meaning of history. It reveals peace as mankind's noblest task, to be achieved through the institutionalization of the categorical imperative in a republican constitution.

The "Idea for a Universal History" derives the sanction for its political maxims from an inexorable development, however. In its view, peace results not from the determination of the will by the moral law, but from the proper evaluation of technical requirements. The vision of universal reconciliation arises as but the revolt of a frustrated soul against the dark uncertainties of constant warfare. Discord may produce harmony, but only through an analysis of its conditions, not from a conception of duty. Experience now produces morality, instead of the categorical imperative supplying norms the approximation to which reveals the moral content of an action. This becomes very apparent in the following quotation from "On Eternal Peace":

"The problem of establishing a state is solvable even for a people of devils, if only they have intelligence, though this may sound harsh. The problem may be stated thus. [Then Kant formulates a hypothetical technical question on the proper balancing of selfish tendencies.] Such a problem *must* be solvable. For it is not the moral perfection of mankind, but merely the mechanism of nature, which this task seeks to know how to use in order to arrange the conflict of unpacific attitudes in a given people in such a way that they impel each other to compulsory laws and thus bring about the state of peace in which such laws are enforced … In short, we can say that nature *wants* irresistibly that law achieve superior force. If one neglects to do this, it will be accomplished anyhow, albeit with much inconvenience."[1] The transcendental experience of morality has disappeared as a guide to action. A mechanism replaces the categorical imperative as a motive force. Freedom becomes but a mode of causality. Volition operates as a tool of an inexorable necessity.

It can be maintained, of course, that Kant formulates this teleology as a

and consequently accidental, conditions of the execution of the law are made the conditions of the law itself. Then a practice which is calculated in relation to the probable result of previous experience is accorded the right of determining the theory itself."

1. Kant, "On Eternal Peace," in Friedrich, *The Philosophy of Kant,* p. 452. In view of Kant's sharp criticism of merely technical solutions in the appendix, one would be inclined to consider this statement as in the vein of gentle irony which permeates "On Eternal Peace." The correspondence of this view to the "Idea for a Universal History" makes this impossible, however.

thought one adds to but does not really find in nature.[1] But this distinction is more apparent than real. The tentativeness of a hypothesis applies only to its conclusions, not to the possibility of solving the problem. Its very existence testifies to a belief in the efficacy of its endeavor. The hypothetical nature of Kant's teleology cannot hide the fact that he considered a conception of specific purposes in the mechanical course of nature both possible and necessary. The tentativeness of the formulation allows a criticism of the specific purpose which Kant finds in history. It cannot affect, however, the basic argument of this discussion, that an ascription of any purpose is neither necessary nor possible, if Kant's original analysis is valid.

If the categorical imperative derives from a transcendental experience of freedom that lifts man above the determined inevitability of phenomena, the mechanical course of nature can have no bearing on its applicability. If the necessary unfolding of events automatically produces the proper disposition of the will, the experience of freedom becomes meaningless and the categorical imperative a mere technical problem. No compromise between these two positions is possible. Either ethical activity can be meaningful out of an apprehension of its principle or it is reduced to a function of nature's mechanism. Though a contemplation of the regularity of phenomena may yield an intuition of a design as the very condition of appearances, purposiveness cannot be equated with specific purposes. One can grant the existence of a higher world order, in which one participates through the experience of freedom, without at the same time defining its conditions.[2]

Again, in order to resolve these difficulties one might draw the inference that the physical world did contain a limiting condition to the universal applicability of the categorical imperative from the following statement in *The Metaphysics of Morals*: "It is our duty to act according to the idea of such an end which reason commands (namely peace) even if there is not the least probability that it can be achieved, provided its impossibility cannot be demonstrated."[3] This represents Friedrich's view, who considers Kant's qualifying clause a fundamental condition of his moral philosophy, an important connecting link between the realm of freedom and the realm of necessity: "No one was more clearly aware ... of the necessity of testing

---

1. Kant, "On Eternal Peace," in Friedrich, *The Philosophy of Kant*, p. 448.
2. See *post* for distinction between purposiveness and purposes.
3. Kant, *The Metaphysics of Morals*, Part I, "Conclusion," p. 6:355.

hypothetical judgment by experience than Kant. No work of Kant's shows this more conclusively than 'Eternal Peace.' In the appendix he insisted (as of course he had often done before) that only what is possible can be morally required, and he recites the dictum of the law *ultra posse nemo obligatur.* This is precisely the reason for showing the possibility that in peacemaking, as in other human affairs, we learn by doing."[1] Thus fact and norm are reconciled, the course of history reveals man's aspirations.

This solution is not completely satisfactory, however. Its validity depends on what Kant meant by a proof for impossibility. Friedrich implies that the applicability of Kant's moral precepts depends on their attainability in the empirical realm. But the whole tendency of Kant's argument denies this. For Kant did not insist on a proof of the feasibility of the moral law. This indeed would make the empirical world the determining principle of the categorical imperative. On the contrary, he affirmed the obligation of the categorical imperative even if there is not the slightest probability of its being achieved. But how can a law be binding in the face of all probability and still not be obligatory if its impossibility is demonstrated?

The apparent contradiction is resolved if we consider that Kant was quite aware of the fact that an absolute proof of impossibility is out of the question. For what methodology could such an effort utilize? If the particular constellation of political circumstances does not suffice to negate the duty to work for eternal peace, if the reconciliation of all conflict is commanded against "all probability" (and probability implies an evaluation of existing relations), then no proof for the impossibility of moral maxims is conceivable. Only an infinite mind, encompassing all possible conditions, could make this demonstration.[2]

But God speaks to man through the categorical imperative.[3] It commands through *a priori* considerations and by its own inward necessity. It

---

1. Friedrich, *Inevitable Peace*, p. 52.

2. Though it may well be that a methodology that disproves impossibility affirms possibility, a psychological difference exists nevertheless. A strict proof of impossibility in the empirical world and particularly in the political realm seems out of the question, since it would involve a grasp of all possible conditions. In the case of logical constructions such as mathematics, in which all conditions are previously defined, the situation is, of course, different. A demonstration of possibility, on the other hand, involves only the evaluation of a particular set of circumstances. This is essentially the procedure of the scientist who affirms first the possibility and then, through an assumption of uniformity, gives it universality. But Kant specifically required a proof of impossibility.

3. This is based on Kant's later writings; see N. Kemp Smith, *op. cit.*, p. 608.

expresses man's experience of that ultimate reality which lies beyond mere phenomenal manifestations. The transcendental import of that moral experience recognizes no limits. Wherever its maxims seem to be in conflict with the empirical world, Kant postulates entities which override all considerations of phenomenal reality. God, freedom, and immortality reveal the strength of an intuition which has perceived a higher world order and will not let itself be denied by the constructions of pure reason.

To be sure, Kant often discusses the question of the "possibility" of his moral maxims. But this feasibility did not depend on evaluation of phenomenal reality. On the contrary, Kant repeatedly asserts that the possibility of the categorical imperative is given in its very conception. For if the experience of the moral law elevates man out of the phenomenal world and shows him a vision of the Infinite, if his experience of freedom reveals a glimpse of the noumena which underlie all visible workings, what obstacle can the physical world possibly provide?[1]

Friedrich draws the inference from Kant's philosophy that we learn by experience. This undoubtedly exhibits the implications of the "Idea for a Universal History" and "On Eternal Peace." But it merely restates the dilemma of how to reconcile man's experience of freedom with an immanent necessity. For what exactly does man learn by experience? It cannot be the formulation of the categorical imperative, for that derives from *a priori* considerations. If he learns the technical implementation of the moral law, then indeed experience is useful, though only as a counsel of prudence and not as a test of the validity of judgments. Historical necessity can never supply a guarantee for the actualizing of a command derived

---

1. Two quotations will illustrate this point. The first is from "Concerning the Common Saying: This May Be True in Theory But Does Not Apply to Practice" (Friedrich, *The Philosophy of Kant*, p. 429).

"... There exists a concept which may be expressed by the words constitutional law ... If this concept has binding force ... [it] has objective practical reality without our considering what good or ill may result; for knowledge of these results is based purely on experience. If this be so then constitutional law is based upon principles *a priori*, since what is right cannot be taught by experience. A theory of constitutional law exists with which practice must agree in order to be valid."

The second quotation is from the *Critique of Practical Reason* (Friedrich, *The Philosophy of Kant*, p. 262): "The second view [the moral experience] raises my value infinitely, as an *intelligence*, through my personality; for in this personality the moral law reveals a life independent of animality and even of the entire world of sense ... This is not restricted to the conditions and limits of this life but radiates into the infinite."

from a transcendental experience. Even granting that the demonstrations for "not impossible" and "possible" are identical, they can never be made to imply "inevitable."[1]

Kant has expressed the nature of the obligation of the moral law, as a guide to the meaning of history, as a norm which validates all striving: "In order to harmonize practical philosophy within itself, it is necessary first to decide the question whether in tasks of practical reason we should start from the material (i.e. substantive) principle, from its end, or from its formal one ... which states: Act in such a way that you could want your maxim to become a general law (whatever its purpose might be). Without a doubt the latter principle must take precedence; for as a principle of right it possesses absolute necessity, whereas the material principle is compelling only on condition that the empirical conditions for its realization exist ... The first principle (which conceives peace as a material end), that of the political moralist, is a mere technical task; the second, which is the principle of the moral politician as an ethical task ... which is now decided not merely as a physical good, but as a condition resulting from the recognition of duty. Much knowledge of nature is required for the solution of the first problem of political prudence, in order to utilize its mechanism for this purpose, and yet it is all rather uncertain as far as the result, eternal peace, is concerned ... By contrast the solution of the second problem of political wisdom readily presents itself, is evident to everyone, confounds all artifice and leads directly to the end ..."[2]

The incommensurability of Kant's critical philosophy and his teleological philosophy of history cannot be overcome by considering the latter a demonstration for the possibility of the moral law. It may be argued, however, that Kant's "Idea for a Universal History" merely reveals another aspect of a methodology which attempts to attain knowledge by means of *a priori* principles. But again the similarity is misleading. The categories represent forms that explain the process of cognition. The categorical imperative derives from a transcendental experience of freedom and rec-

---

1. The fact that this historical necessity is hypothetical does not affect the argument. See *ante*. I am not arguing against a specific purpose but against the possibility of making any such determination in the light of Kant's previous analysis.

2. Kant, "On Eternal Peace," in Friedrich, *The Philosophy of Kant*, p. 465. These quotations are presented at such length because the difference is one of interpretation, which can only be resolved by a reading of the text, not by disproving one interpretation by another one.

onciles a personal experience with universal applicability. The content of both the categories and the categorical imperative depends, however, upon subsequent experience.

But the conception of a definite purpose in the unfolding of events goes beyond these limits. It does not reveal a method for apprehending phenomena, but prescribes their essence. Instead of obtaining its sanction from a direct relationship to noumenal reality, it attempts to claim the sanction of phenomena for its aspirations. Peace or a civic constitution is therefore not analogous as an *a priori* principle to either the categories or the moral law. The categories are truly *a priori* in that they merely provide the structure for subsequent experience. The categorical imperative is beyond dispute as soon as one admits man's transcendental experience of morality. But peace or a civic constitution (which implies lawful external relations) constitutes the instantiation of a general principle, not a necessary mode of historical apprehension. As a specific purpose (since it does not represent a truly *a priori* principle), it can be refuted by any other postulation of hypothetical goals.

What then is this general principle? Kant's *Critique of Judgment* addresses itself to the problem of a teleological conception of phenomenal reality. Kant argues that the regularity exhibited by phenomena implies a design in nature. Just as the appearance of a hexagon on a deserted island could not be explained by an accidental constellation of events, but would involve a principle of purposiveness, so man can postulate a teleology in the unfolding of phenomena. It provides the condition for the regularity of appearances and makes intelligible the consistency of natural laws.[1] But a general principle of purposiveness does not necessarily imply a knowledge of specific purposes. Kant admits this and draws a sharp distinction between a determinative and a reflective purposiveness, between a derivative and a constitutive design.[2] A determinative purposiveness describes the claims of a rationality which attempts to impose its aspirations as a pattern of objective reality. A constitutive design invokes its principles as the objective immanence of phenomenal occurrences. Kant, on the other hand, obtains his teleology from the reflective judgment which is led to this conclusion through an intuition that a mechanistic conception of the universe cannot account for the organic aspects of growth. The design he

---

1. Kant, *Critique of Judgment* (trans. Bernard), p. 28.
2. Bernard, *op. cit.*, p. 259 *et seq.*

postulates is derivative because it conceives the world as a process of becoming only to make meaningful the reality revealed by pure reason.

Kant's *Critique of Judgment* thus completes his metaphysics and his moral philosophy. The noumena for the cognition of which the *Critique of Pure Reason* provided necessary forms, and whose pervasiveness was affirmed by the moral philosophy, now appear as the principle which makes causal knowledge possible. Kant calls attention to the fact that a mechanistic conception of the universe cannot suffice for its understanding and that reason must add a teleology, not indeed known by the methods of the first two *Critiques* but nonetheless certain. Yet this judgment limits itself to ascribing an intrinsic purposiveness, the embodiment of which in specific purposes remains a mystery.[1] Causality explains the incidental appearances, teleology the underlying unity of organic growth.[2]

But the consistency of Kant's philosophy begins to be destroyed by his subsequent introduction of the concept of extrinsic purposiveness.[3] Since man, he argues, is the only creature capable of forming an idea of teleology, he is also the final purpose of the universe. Yet this again mistakes a personal experience for an objective principle of reality. To be sure, man can form a conception of purposes, but Kant himself has derived the recognition of this supersensuous world order from the experience of freedom.

Since experiences are, however, personal and unique, their content can-

---

1. The following quotation illustrates Kant's distinction between purposiveness and purposes, between an intrinsic and an extrinsic teleology. Bernard, *op. cit.*, p. 272.

"We can hence easily see that external purposiveness can be regarded as an external natural purpose only under the condition that the existence of that being, to which it is immediately or distantly advantageous, is in itself a purpose of nature. Since that can never be completely determined by a mere contemplation of nature it follows that relative purposiveness, although it hypothetically gives indications of natural purposes, yet justifies no absolute teleological judgment. Snow in cold countries protects the crops from the frost; it makes human intercourse easier by means of sleighs. [Here follows an enumeration of conditions that make existence in arctic countries possible.] Here is a wonderful concurrence of many references of nature to one purpose ... But then we do not see why, generally, men must live there at all. Therefore to say that vapour falls out of the atmosphere in the form of snow, that the sea has its currents which float down wood that has grown in warmer lands, and that there are in it great sea monsters filled with oil, *because* the idea of advantage for certain poor creatures is fundamental for the cause which collects all these natural products, would be a very venturesome and arbitrary judgment." It is interesting to note that despite this refutation Kant uses almost exactly the same argument in his "On Eternal Peace" (see Friedrich, *The Philosophy of Kant*, p. 449 *et seq.*).

2. Note similarity to Spengler's morphology.

3. Bernard, *op. cit.*, p. 361 *et seq.*

not be claimed as the objective mode of operation of phenomena. The manner in which noumena operate in the physical world must therefore remain undecided.[1] If man's purposes are equated with nature's purposiveness, the ethical and the natural become identical, and freedom emerges as but a mode of causality. Every event is both an effect and an inward experience. As an effect, it is subject to causal analysis and to a teleological judgment which postulates an intrinsic purposiveness. As an experience, it reveals man's personality, and constitutes the means for transcending the necessity of the phenomenal world. The experience of freedom requires man to give his own meaning to his particular existence. If a transcendental vision guides the quest for the purpose of existence, phenomena can offer no further guarantee, the empirical world no permanent obstacles. If man's essence consists of the ability to act purposefully out of conception of duty, then empirical reality furnishes at best a challenge, never a condition. The sublimity of the moral law, the wonder which Kant felt at its operation within him, involves a task for which we cannot wrest an assurance of success out of the unfolding of events. "Anyone who finds history speaking optimistically lends her a language which is not her own."[2] Man's freedom derives from a mystic relationship to the Infinite, from a direct intuition of limits, given effect by the categorical imperative.

The invocation of the mechanism of nature as a sanction for a specific purpose destroys this apprehension. Now the meaning of history results from an evaluation of specific conditions which in the absence of a transcendental guiding principle can be overthrown by any alternative hypothesis. The meaning of existence and the purpose of occurrences cannot be identified in this fashion. Toynbee's philosophy, which carries out the plan laid down by Kant in his ninth principle of the "Idea for a Universal History," testifies to the futility of the attempt.[3]

Thus Kant argues *a priori* only when his teleological judgment derives from a transcendental experience, when the categorical imperative illuminates humanity's journey through the tasks of history. The noumena that produce appearances are perceived through a personal experience, and this accounts for man's essential loneliness in the face of the fatedness of

---

1. This does not say that history works against man's aspirations but simply that we cannot derive our norms by claiming them as history's patterns.
2. Schweitzer, *The Philosophy of Civilization*, p. 41.
3. See *ante*.

existence.[1] But it also makes possible the concept of the dignity of the individual whose will gives universal maxims despite his insignificance as but a speck in a determined system. "On Eternal Peace"[2] testifies to this vision, to the norms which man gives himself as beacons to follow, to the meaning which humanity may impart to the inexorability of events. The categorical imperative makes possible the reconciliation of all conflicts, the eternal peace which accords with man conceived as an end.

Kant had a tremendous intuition of the world as design and phenomena. In an edifice imposing in its consistency and scope, he combined a profound metaphysics with a moral philosophy which reconciled a personal experience with universal applicability. He limited knowledge to achieve belief. The rigorous examination of knowable reality made possible an experience which elevated man out of the determined universe of phenomena and brought him into a direct relation with a supersensuous world order. History reveals a task for the achievement of the eternal peace commanded by the moral law. No conflict can exist between theory and practice, for the possibility of the categorical imperative is given in its very conception. The meaning of history is identical with man's duty.

Kant's attempt to expand the philosophy of history into a guarantee for the attainability of the moral law failed for the same reason as Toynbee's. The realm of Freedom and Necessity cannot be reconciled except by an inward experience. The mechanism of nature offers no obvious assurance for the implementation of freedom. The identification of the ethical with the natural makes the meaning of history the emanation of the disposition of a will only insofar as this volition is conceived as the tool of an organic necessity.

But Kant's philosophy has nevertheless pointed the way towards a resolution of our enigma of the experience of freedom and our knowledge of necessity. The meaning of life appears as the emanation of a transcendental experience to which the mechanism of nature can offer but a challenge. The pervasiveness of this experience provides its own maxims and overcomes necessity by imparting to it a purposive striving after norms.

But two more problems remain. If the categorical imperative universalizes a transcendental experience, just what is the nature of this mystic relationship to the Infinite? If resignation as to the purposes of the universe

---

1. See *ante.*
2. If one disregards "On Eternal Peace."

provides the condition for ethical activity, what connection exists between our norms and facts, between the experience of freedom and the unfolding of events? What is the meaning of history in a cosmology based on a direct intuition of a supersensuous world order the maxims of which are conceived of absolute validity?

The chapter "The Sense of Responsibility" will outline an attempted solution to these problems.

CHAPTER V

THE SENSE OF

RESPONSIBILITY

Introduction

History viewed in retrospect evokes a dual feeling of inevitability coupled with an inward doubt. The inevitability results from a contemplation of the completed actions, from an apprehension of the facts of occurrence, from the unfolding of a chain of events which the mind orders into a causal sequence. We can never really be certain that another development was possible, that an inexorability did not shape all endeavors. The doubt is a token of rebellion against this view, an assertion of the specificity of the individual, a demand by the soul for its freedom. Whatever one's conception about the necessity of events, at the moment of their performance their inevitability could offer no guide to action. Spengler believed that he could force the past to yield him maxims of effective conduct. His analysis failed as a postulate of action, however, because necessity constitutes an attribute of external reality. It describes the past, but man lives the future. The causality which motivates man is an experience of freedom.

Toynbee understood the purposive element, but he demanded a guarantee of its attainability. He sought to wrest from historical events an assurance of permanence, a pledge of physical salvation. But life does not exhibit this certainty. Phenomena always appear inevitable. At the moment of perception, they already form a part of the past. Purposes, on the other hand, describe the immanence of a soul, the visions that man imparts to his determined surroundings, the hopes which condition activity, the dreams which make life possible. The meaning of life is an inward state.

Kant grasped this. He derived his ethics from a transcendental experience, from a vision of an ultimate reality. The categorical imperative testifies to a vision that lifts man above the sensuous reality and attaches him to a higher world order. A mystic relationship to the Infinite provides the foundation for motivated activity, to which the phenomenal world can offer no permanent obstacles. To be sure, Kant's "Idea for a Universal History" tends to demand of the realm of necessity the gifts of the realm of freedom. But this inconsistency is submerged in the transcendental experience of the moral law, which alone suffices to validate all historical striving.

What is the nature of this experience? It does not derive from the phenomenal world, for this knows only necessity. It is not produced by rational reflection, for it provides the condition for the determination of the will by reason. It must constitute a mystic attitude, then, an inward state that feels the cosmic in the universe. There are moments in every person's life when the tensions fall away and the unity of all creation appears as a sudden vision. These are the occasions when time stands still and man partakes of eternity. This is Spinoza's intellectual love of God, the total apprehension of the divine immanence, the resignation that gives peace, the bliss that elevates man above himself. This is why the Greeks considered the good and the beautiful as a unity: the good as a testimony to the divine in action, the beautiful as an intuition of the Ultimate in contemplation.

Man's freedom, then, is the recognition of necessity which enables him to transcend the determined inevitability of his environment. But how can a recognition of necessity imply freedom? If this is true, why not multiply restrictive measures to increase liberty? But these objections mistake the objective necessity of the phenomenal world for the inward necessity of a recognition of limits. The sanction which we give to the necessity felt as a reality transcending our existence, the meaning ascribed to our particular life (which, as any fact, also sets limits), these testify to a personality, to the unique which each man imparts to the inevitable. This is ethical freedom which reveals the reverence of a soul and exhibits a realization that one is man and not God. From the feeling of reverence stems tolerance, the respect for the dignity of the individual, the apprehensions that set boundaries to one's endeavors.

Schweitzer believed that the will-to-live provided the basis for this inward liberation. But he was mistaken. The will-to-live merely wishes to prevail. At best, as in Hobbes,[1] it may derive maxims of prudence for self-preservation. But ethical activity does not derive its maxims from the struggle for survival. It reveals an inward state which conditions the self-

---

1. Not to be disguised by being defined as laws of nature.

assertiveness of the will, by the recognition of a higher reality which contains the sanction of all endeavor.

Life is suffering, birth involves death. Transitoriness is the fate of existence. No civilization has yet been permanent, no longing completely fulfilled. This is necessity, the fatedness of history, the dilemma of mortality. But Spengler's assertion that the appearances of life exhaust its meaning denies the transcendental fact of existence. We know we must die and yet live with a mode of permanence. However determined our actions appear in retrospect, we perform them with an inward conviction of choice. In the face of all the results so totally incommensurable with intentions, of successes that were not willed, failures that seem undeserved, and the necessity of setting limits to one's actions, the feeling of reverence which does not claim its hopes as a pattern of reality becomes the foundation of morality. This is not a necessity of thought but a condition of an experience, not the utilization of nature's mechanism but the means for its transcendence.

This gives us a clue to our second question: What is the relation of history to man's experience of morality? What is the meaning of the transitoriness of historical existence in the face of man's possibility of self-transcendence? If moral action derived its maxims from phenomenal reality, one would expect that history should disclose some increase in mastery over the human problems of existence. If virtue were merely right knowledge of an objective, naturalistic necessity, the past should disclose some progress towards a definition of universally recognized ethics. Above all, if the cause of nature parallels man's aspirations, then all the hopes of the past become but a cruel joke, and history a tale "told by a madman." Then Virgil's vision of the Sibyl becomes meaningful, of the old seeress who sits in her cave and writes her oracles on leaves which the wind scatters, and "men depart without counsel and hate the Sibyl's dwelling."[1]

But man's freedom does not reside in a manipulatory knowledge of external reality. Morality does not derive from an apprehension of objective necessity, to be mastered as a technical problem. If, on the other hand, man's existence constitutes a mystic relationship to the Infinite, it becomes each individual's responsibility to infuse his specificity into the inevitability of phenomena, and an absolute guide to action appears impossible. If morality reveals a transcendental experience, no necessary connection

---

1. Virgil, *Aeneid*, Book III.

exists between phenomenal reality and man's freedom. The significance of ethical conduct depends on this distinction being maintained. Otherwise the ethical and the natural stand equated, and freedom and causality appear as parallel appearances of the same inexorability.[1]

Since an experience is always unique and solitary, its simultaneous appearance in others cannot be postulated. For this reason, history offers no guarantee for the achievement of man's moral norms, nor does it exhibit values in its own right. This does not mean that the unfolding of events necessarily frustrates man. Such an assertion would also make the physical world the source of moral maxims, for the framework of every rebuttal is determined by its object. This is the token of the Puritans, whose obsession with the dangers of materiality absorbed their energies in a negation of carnal pleasure and led to the invocation of predestination as God's sanction to the elect, revealed by temporal success.

The transcendental experience of the moral law, on the other hand, leaves the question of purposes in history undecided. Its freedom is an inward state that has come to the recognition of its limits and with that realization overcomes the inexorability of phenomena by infusing them with its spirituality.[2] Dante expressed this conception on the pilgrim's journey towards inward peace: " 'Master,' I said to him, 'now tell me also: this Fortune, of which thou hintest to me, what is she that has the good things of the world thus within her clutches?'

"And he to me: 'O foolish creatures, how great is this ignorance that falls upon ye! Now I wish thee to receive my judgment of her. He whose wisdom is transcendent over all made the heavens and gave them guides, so that every part shines on every other part, equally distributing the light; in like manner, for worldly goods he ordained a general minister and guide to change betimes the vain possession from people to people and from one kindred to another beyond the hindrance of human wisdom: Hence one people commands, another languishes, obeying her sentence, which is hidden like the serpent in the grass.'

" 'Your knowledge cannot understand her: she provides, judges, and maintains her kingdom as the other Gods do theirs. Her permutations have no truce; necessity makes her be swift; thus he comes oft who doth a change obtain. This is she, who is so much reviled, even by those who

---

1. See *ante* Ch. "History and Man's Experience of Morality."
2. See *post.*

216

ought to praise her, when blaming her wrongfully, and with evil words. But she is in bliss, and hears it not ...' "[1] Phenomenal reality can offer no motive force for moral action. Resignation as to the purposes of the universe provides the foundations of a meaningful ethics.

Freedom and Necessity Reconciled: A Clue from Poetry

Aristotle stated that poetry is truer than history. He meant that man's hopes reveal his essence more clearly than their incidental embodiment in historical fact. Poetry testifies to humanity's longing in the face of the fatedness of existence, to the unique which each man imparts to his determined surrounding. Poetry is truer than history, for it exhibits the spirituality with which man meets the inexorability of events.[2]

The problem of Freedom and Necessity should therefore be reflected in literature, in a perhaps more pure form because the incidents of the phenomenal world are here less pervasive. This is particularly true of epic poetry, which still concerns itself with men, not things, and draws inspiration from greatness, not from a negative lament over social conditions. For this reason, Homer, Virgil, Dante, and Milton may give us a clue to the meaning of freedom, to the longing for self-realization which characterizes all endeavor. And if poetry is truer than history, the state of their soul should illuminate the spirit of their age, thus to explain the growth and decay that history exhibits.[3]

If freedom resides in the recognition of necessity and if morality depends on the sanction ascribed to the inevitable in the environment, then the progression from Homer to Virgil to Dante to Milton reveals an enlargement of the concept of freedom. The blind necessity of the *Iliad* gives way in the *Odyssey* to the vision of life as a possibility which leaves some margin for human striving and the perseverance of whose hero is rewarded by his return to Ithaca. Freedom achieved by submission to an

---

1. Dante, *Inferno*, Canto 7.
2. See *ante* Ch. "History as an Empirical Science."
3. This, to be sure, will be a very inadequate analysis. But I felt that I should indicate the tendencies of my views on the philosophy of history, which must be of necessity tentative and very confined due to limitations of space.

Dante and Milton are problematical examples of epic poetry, but they seem as close to epic poetry as the West, with its sense of guilt, could produce.

objective necessity was too oppressive, however. In Virgil there appears
the groping for a moral sanction, the change in the concept of *arete* from
outward distinction to inward grace. Yet no such certainty was to be found
in the Augustan Empire and Virgil's sadness results, a testimony to his
loneliness in a valueless world. Dante removes all doubts by attributing a
divine sanction to necessity and solves Virgil's sorrow by the bliss of absolute knowledge. In Milton, freedom is completely internalized, necessity
no longer requires dogmatic buttressing. Justification by faith affirms the
intrinsic worth of the individual.

This gradual enlargement of conceptual freedom through the internalization of a moral code, culminating in the supremacy of the individual
conscience, represents only one aspect of humanity's hopes, however.[1] Life
seems to involve death, in history as in individuals. Though ageing in a
culture is not analogous to physical decay, it does bear a similarity to
another problem of existence, the process of disenchantment. Just as the
life of every person exhibits a gradual loss of the wonder at the world, so
history reveals an increase of familiarity with the environment, a tired
groping for a certainty which will obviate all struggles, a quest for a guarantee of man's hopes in nature's mechanism.

In Homer and Dante the mystery of growth is still noticeable. The
enchantment with beauty, the fresh exultation at creativity comes to
expression. Homer and Dante live within nature; the glistening of the sun
on leaves, the beating of the waves on rocks is not yet so familiar as to be
commonplace, nor yet so remote as to offer a vision of a peace which the
turbulence of the soul denies. The world still appears as a possibility
through a reconciliation of the will with a necessity, in Homer blindly
striving, in Dante blissfully certain.

Virgil and Milton, on the other hand, are both full of inward doubts.
They are both Protestant in that their own standard frequently clashes
with the viciousness of history. The mystery of life has been dissipated and
only the struggle remains. The concern with materiality ensues, not to be
denied by Virgil's description of Dis or Milton's evocation of Pandaemonium. To Homer necessity was unapproachable, and Dante's Fortune
served as but the distributor of meaningless possessions,[2] but to Virgil

1. Whatever progress theory is implied in this analysis does not derive, like Toynbee's,
from physical phenomena, nor does it claim permanence as a criterion.
2. See *ante*.

wealth is itself evil, and Milton's Adam falls because carnal pleasures are intrinsically sinful. The romantic longing appears, the attempt to find release in nature from the uncertainties of existence. The vision of the Golden Age, of Rousseau's state of nature, expresses the bittersweet romantic brooding over the fleetingness of a perfection, which it will ever after be mankind's task to re-achieve.

But what is the greater delusion, the Golden Age or the belief in infinite material progress? As the enchantment of even an inwardly remote nature is dissipated and the cold materialistic intellect replaces the sentimentality of the romantic, life emerges as but a technical problem. The frantic search for social solutions, for economic panaceas, testifies to the emptiness of a soul to which necessity is an objective state, not an inward condition, and which ever believes that just a little more knowledge, just one more formula, will solve the increasing bafflement of a materialistic surrounding. And it is forgotten that matter can defeat only those who have no spirituality to impart to it.

Freedom invariably involves the recognition of limits and the acceptance of one's humanity. But the moral content of ethical freedom resides in the sanction ascribed to that necessity, in the inner content of the reconciliation. The meaning given to necessity reveals a gradual process of disenchantment, but does not negate the ultimate conception of morality deriving from a mystic relationship to the Infinite.[1]

Homer envisioned life as the inevitable unfolding of a pre-ordained fate. The threads of Tyche move all creation, men as well as the gods. Zeus in the *Iliad* holds up the scales to learn, not to determine Hector's fate. His attempts to save Sarpedon and Hector represent (as much as the person of Achilles) man's rebellion at the inevitability of existence, with the important difference that Zeus has achieved his inward peace. He knows that there is really no escaping fate, and he abides by its decision.

Achilles, on the other hand, is the very embodiment of man's lament at the shortness of his lot, the very symbol of an assertion of mastery over fate and of an attempt to wrest out of existence a consolation for one's mortality. But to seek to escape objective necessity involves certain tragedy, to fail to set limits to one's actions characterizes the madness that equates man with God.

Man's triumphs do not lie in a physical conquest of objective necessity.

---

1. See *post.*

Achilles transcends necessity only through an inward acceptance that rises above the now unimportant alternative of a short and heroic or a long and commonplace life. Achilles had been the prisoner of a prophecy, but with his recognition of limits he has achieved freedom, and the meaning of his life no longer depends on external conditions.

This explains the structure of the Homeric poems, which ever stress the general over the unique and achieve a blend of character and fate in representative types. It would be meaningless to stress the specific in a world where only the heroic attitude towards a blind necessity can give peace. The nature of the acceptance of a pervasive fate reveals the hero's character. Freedom represents the undefinable, which man imparts to Tyche's inexorability and is expressed by the speech which completes Achilles' recognition that peace is not an external state of things: "This is the lot the gods have spun for miserable men, that they should live in pain; yet themselves are sorrowless."[1]

Only through this resignation into an inexorable fate can Homer's heroes achieve freedom.

This was a harsh assertion, however. As the wonder went out of the Hellenic world and the exultation of war (still noticeable in the *Iliad*) left only its horrors, when man began to feel apart from society—unthinkable in Homer—the question of the sanction of fate emerged as the central problem of the meaning of freedom. Virgil's *Aeneid* testifies to this endeavor. Aeneas represents the moral man; his tremendous sadness reflects the essential incomprehensibility of a blindly operating necessity. He symbolizes an endeavor to transcend a mere postulation of fate and a quest for a moral ideal to validate all striving.

In the process, the objectivity of Homer is lost. Virgil's history reveals the inevitable triumph of good over evil, both drawn in the crassest possible terms. His hero has to determine himself to action out of a sense of duty and not with the absolute inner spontaneity of Homeric characters. A moral code now serves as the standard, not objective necessity, and deviations must be justified either by divine intervention (Dido's suicide) or pathetic tragedies (Pallas' death).

Virgil finds freedom in the determination of the will by duty, the necessity of which expresses a moral sanction. But whose sanction, in what

---

1. *The Iliad,* Book XXIV, p. 317.

scheme of necessity? The Augustan Empire provided no answer. The extensive sadness of Virgil ensues, the testimony to a valueless reality which had no salvation by faith to fall back on. And in this inner uncertainty Virgil's gods become undignified, his longing pervasive and hopeless.

The medieval period found an answer to Virgil's dilemma. Dante gave meaning to freedom as a recognition of necessity by ascribing a divine sanction to necessity. To be sure, there are hints of this in Homer, as well. Zeus in the *Iliad* seems to represent the conscience of mankind—but he is, after all, unable to save either Hector or Sarpedon. Athena in the *Odyssey* tells Penelope that Telemachus will escape the wooers, since he has not sinned against God—but this represents a fleeting hope rather than explicit affirmation of a meaningful divine sanction.

To Dante, on the other hand, life revealed a divine plan. There was no need here for the creation of representative types. The generality of life is symbolized by God as the creator of a meaningful universe and as its manifestation in all specificity. Freedom is the recognition of the divine immanence achieved under the guidance of reason, until the pilgrim's arrival in Paradise witnesses a complete fusion of will, desire, and reason in a blend of transcendental bliss.[1]

This bliss, this wonder at the miracle of creation, at the meaningfulness of fate, makes Dante more comparable to Homer[2] than to Virgil and testifies to a young culture which can still see the mysteries in life. The divine sanction ascribed to necessity makes its recognition the true liberation, and lifts man above the sensuous world. "This man has come in search of liberty," Virgil tells Cato.[3] When the will has come to its inward realization of limits, expressed by the confession at the river Lethe, true freedom is attained and terrestrial bonds fall away. Now Dante rises above the determined necessity of the physical world and ascends through the heavens. Now he meets the saints who have achieved the inward reconciliation expressed by Piccarda Donati, whose symbolic appearance in the moon is both necessary and willed: "In His will is our peace."[4]

Life to Dante presents a process of achieving freedom in a world of transcendental bliss and purposiveness pervaded by the love of and for

---

1. See *ante* Ch. "History as an Empirical Science" ("Metaphysics").
2. Only as far as the wonder is concerned, not the meaningfulness.
3. Dante, *Purgatorio*, Canto 1.
4. See *ante* Ch. "History as an Empirical Science" ("Metaphysics").

God. Virgil's sadness is overcome by ascribing a divine sanction to necessity. Grace, the force that unbinds the will, represents God's gift to mankind, its possibilities symbolized by Beatrice, who guides the pilgrim's journey in the most desperate moments. To be able to will freely and yet in accordance with God's immanence constitutes Dante's solution to the problem of Freedom and Necessity. This leads to an inward reconciliation that denies all materiality as unimportant,[1] to a faith that transcends phenomenal necessity by infusing it with its own spirituality.

Milton, too, gave necessity a divine sanction. But he represents a later period. Once more, disenchantment had made the world familiar. Again the inward doubts emerge and, despite justification by faith, Milton looks to the physical world for a guarantee of his aspirations. Virgil's problem reappears. Freedom again becomes a conceptual quantity, not an experience. To be sure, Milton argues its content at great length. Without doubt, the inward reconciliation of our will with necessity is passionately asserted. But the whole tendency of Milton denies this. Freedom is seen to reside in the evaluation of objective necessity, not in its inward apprehension. Adam's recognition of limits is not Dante's bliss at seeing the mystical procession, but derives from a shrewd analysis of divine power. (He desists from suicide only because he decides that God's infinite power would nevertheless merely multiply his suffering.)[2]

Since an emphasis on man as the measure of all things tends to emphasize man's shortcomings, there occurs a much greater emphasis on God's wrath and man's inherent sinfulness. The concern with materiality becomes pervasive, for it makes little difference whether the physical world is conceived as a norm or as inherently evil. In either case, material conditions are exalted. God and Christ become humanized and discourse in the fashion of Homeric warlords. The bliss of Mary has gone out of life. No hope appears for a struggling humanity. Milton's hero cannot find peace, and contrition becomes a continuous state, not a climax to an inward experience. No Beatrice lights the way through a now joyless existence. Only the world of the Devil remains, connected by a bridge to earth, ever threatening, ever tempting, unconquerable, for man looks for his freedom outside himself.

The priesthood of all believers in Milton is a concept that opens vistas of

1. Not as evil—like Milton and Virgil.
2. Milton, *Paradise Lost*, Book 10.

duties only. Milton's freedom reveals a continuous struggle to achieve true humility by overcoming materialism, with a recognition of necessity transferred to the environment. Grace represents not an ultimate condition of bliss, but merely a right to struggle.

The vision of freedom contained in these poems reveals a recognition of limits, an apprehension of necessity which man transcends by infusing it with his spirituality. But they also reveal a process of ageing in history. While one can discern a major beat of enlargement of conceptual freedom, expressed in the development of Homer's blind necessity to the internalized divine sanction of Milton, there occur subsidiary movements of growth and decline in inwardness, of wonder at the world followed by familiarity, frustration, misery. Virgil and Milton testify to this disenchantment with history and the groping for certainty in a meaningless reality. Life becomes a process of wresting out of phenomena guarantees which the soul can no longer find within itself. Reading them, we wonder—as one does when a valley that in one's youth may have been mysterious appears today merely commonplace—whether all of life is not a chase after the images, the hopes, the completeness that elude us today, but which were ours when we were young.

But also we feel that we live and that existence requires an attitude nonetheless irrevocable for being committed with inward doubt. If our view of the world derives from a mystic relationship to the Infinite, then the state of the civilization in which one lives can have no bearing on the ethical content of conduct. If we must experience freedom before implementing it, then no merely technical solutions for the dilemmas of the soul are at hand.[1]

Does this mean that mysticism offers the only solution to the problems of existence, with reason in the role of a poser of alternatives? Our distinction between objective and inward necessity has already pointed the way towards an answer. Freedom, as the recognition of the fatedness of existence, proceeds in two stages. Reason discloses objective necessity, the inexorability of causal laws, the linkages which enable man to master his environment. They present life as a technical task and instill a manipulatory attitude. In their sphere they may achieve tremendous successes. The physicist has opened vistas of worlds which even the fatuous optimism of the late nineteenth century would scarcely believe. But a knowledge of

---

1. For this reason, political scientists should cease condemning their profession for not living up to their misnomer.

objective necessity has definite limits. It is confined to a naturalistic mechanism in which the scientist does not directly participate.

But action derives from an inward necessity, from the personal in the conception of the environment, from the unique in the apprehension of phenomena.[1] Consequently, objective necessity can never guide conduct, and any activity reveals a personality. Reason can help us understand the world in which we live. Rational analysis can assist us in developing institutions which make an inward experience possible. But nothing can relieve man from his ultimate responsibility, from giving his own meaning to life, from elevating himself above necessity by the sanction he ascribes to the organic immanence of existence.

For this reason, too, Spengler's analysis was inadequate. He well understood the fatedness of historical events, the disenchantment that accompanies a civilization's growth. But he stopped there. He failed to see that, however inexorable the development, its necessity will appear only in retrospect. He did not grasp that inevitability is a poor guide and no inspiration. But man lives with purposes, and in his hopes glimpses a reality beyond mere phenomena.[2] Success and failure are relative attributes, meaningful only in retrospect and never finally decided. But the attitude which accompanied activity testifies to a character, to the intrinsically unique which man imparts to objective necessity.

Spinoza understood these two stages of inward liberation. His ethics are, in the first instance, frankly naturalistic. Everything expresses *conatus*, the tendency to persevere in its own being, as the ultimate criterion of moral fitness. The sage, acting with enlightened egotism, masters life by a recognition of objective necessity. Reason teaches him that to requite hatred with kindness, and violence with gentleness, increases his power over himself, over the effects of the body, and over his environment. Freedom is right knowledge of an external situation; virtue is power.

But beyond this conception of ethics as a technical mastery, Spinoza had a profounder vision. His intellectual love of God reveals a glimpse of a

---

1. For this reason, the manipulatory, statistical correlations of the psychologists are misleading. A correlation of, say, 85 percent seems to imply that it correctly classifies 85 percent of its subjects. In reality it only classifies each individual 85 percent correctly, the deviation from the fictitious norm representing the essence of individuality. Statistics, as a probability function, are always a confession of doubt.

2. Every man becomes a Don Quixote in the hopes of his creativity. The realists who eventually defeat Don Quixote are not realists, but dreamers with materialistic hopes.

transcendental experience which, when conditioned by the categorical imperative, provides the only truly meaningful ethics. Naturalism is seen not to be enough. As man grows in wisdom, a vision of a higher world order opens before him. Intuition based on reason views reality under the aspect of eternity and becomes at one with the infinite mind of God. The more man knows by this kind of knowledge, the more truly can he be said to act and the more does he participate in the divine. This is the intellectual love of God, by which humanity approaches immortality, and which contains the hope of blessedness, mankind's real liberty.[1] Knowledge of an objective necessity has developed into the intuition of an inward acceptance. Freedom for Spinoza ultimately resides in a mystic relationship to the Infinite, which would, however, have been impossible without the guidance of reason, in a resignation that gives peace, in the tranquillity of perfect knowledge.

Though it would be unfair to say that Spinoza's goal was a will-less resignation, he offered no obvious content to ethical conduct.[2] But Kant's categorical imperative has given us a rule of universal applicability based on a rational conception of *a priori* principles. Now the nature of the transcendental experience of the moral law in Kant becomes meaningful. It reveals a personality which has understood objective necessity through the categories but, beyond mere phenomena, feels an ultimate reality which makes possible all experiences. It testifies to an intuition of the unity of all existence and to a sense of responsibility towards others—expressed as tolerance—in the concept of the dignity of the individual. Knowledge of objective necessity gives power, but recognition of inward necessity gives peace.

"Life is painting a picture, not doing a sum," Oliver Wendell Holmes said. "As twenty men of genius looking out of the same window will paint twenty canvases each unlike all the others and every one great, so, one comes to think men may be pardoned for the defect of their qualities, if they have the qualities of their defects … I learned in the regiment and in the class the conclusion, at least, of what I think the best service that we can do for our country and for ourselves: To see as far as one may, and to feel, the great forces behind every detail—for that makes all the difference between philosophy and gossip, between great action and small; the least

---

1. Spinoza, *Ethics.*

2. It must be emphasized, however, that to Spinoza the intellectual love of God and ethical conduct were identical and that for him no rule was necessary.

wavelet of the Atlantic Ocean is mightier than one of Buzzard's Bay—to hammer out as compact and solid a piece of work as one can, to try to make it first-rate and to leave it unadvertised."[1]

Does this mean that all attitudes are equivalent and no absolute standard of morality exists? Is man doomed to struggle without certainty and live without assurance? In a sense that is so. Man cannot achieve a guarantee for his conduct. No technical solutions to the dilemmas of life are at hand. That is the fatedness of existence. But it also poses a challenge, an evocation of the sense of responsibility to give one's own meaning to one's life. Ethics must always reside in an inward state, in a personal recognition of limits. Reason can guide the soul to a knowledge of objective necessity, as Spinoza demonstrated. Rational principles such as Kant's categorical imperative may give effect to a transcendental experience. But ultimate liberation derives from within us, from an experience both personal and essentially incommunicable. Philosophy may describe the nature of ethical conduct, but it cannot enforce its acceptance. The sanction for our actions must constitute a necessity of our souls, not merely of our thought, as Schweitzer implies.

But if morality issues from mystic relationship, how can one reconcile this with a concept of tolerance? If our transcendental experience is in a sense absolute, must we not assert it against all who disagree to the limits of our strength? To be sure, the reconciliation of an ultimate, but personal, vision with universal applicability constitutes the problem of ethics.[2] But moral conduct reveals not merely the will-to-live, but a will which has been conditioned by a reality transcending man. Freedom derives not merely from an inward state but from an experience that has come to the recognition of limits. This acceptance is tolerance, the knowledge that one must set boundaries to one's striving, and which will lead to the positive intuition in the concept of the dignity of the individual.

Tolerance, too, is achieved in two stages: Objective necessity teaches man his fallibility, his physical weakness in the face of the unpredictability of events, his material dependence on the respect and aid of his neighbors.

---

1. Holmes, "Parts of the Unimaginable Whole," Class of '61: Fiftieth Anniversary Reunion address (1911), in *The Mind and Faith of Justice Holmes*, ed. Max Lerner (New York: Little, Brown, 1943), p. 26.
2. For full discussion see *ante* "History and Man's Experience of Morality" ("Moral Philosophy").

This leads to ethical systems such as Hobbes', whose laws of nature represent technical rules of prudence and whose command for peace reveals the impotence of self-assertiveness. Harmony becomes a limiting condition, and tolerance a maxim of self-preservation.

Inward necessity transcends this mere evaluation of empirical relations. Its experience leads to the bliss of Spinoza, or Dante. It goes beyond mere resignation and becomes active in the categorical imperative of Kant. Now tolerance depends not merely on an understanding of fallibility, or on the physical necessity of mutual support, but on a vision of man as an end. The Ultimate (which a religious soul may call divine), which appears as the condition of all phenomena, that elevates man above his surroundings, is recognized as inhering potentially in all men. This leads to the experience of the dignity of man, to the feeling of reverence which overcomes the struggle for survival by an inward apprehension and transcends the necessity of its environment by viewing the world as a possibility and existence as an inward reconciliation.[1]

What is the relation of this to the philosophy of history? History is the past, and the past represents the most inexorable necessity with which we live. We know the past only as a phenomenon. Even our own actions, in retrospect, lose the inner experience that accompanied them. The past sets the framework which our spirituality must transcend. For this reason our two stages of recognition also appear in the philosophy of history. Spengler had powerfully described history's objective necessity. But existence is also an experience, and we live the future. The past is dead and ruled by

---

1. It must be repeated that this cannot be proved. As an attitude, we can only find it in ourselves. I can only describe what it may be without postulating it as necessary. But this concept also implies something else: It means that differences between ideologies or political systems or individuals may be so fundamental as to be unbridgeable. One can quarrel with a system such as Hobbes', which derives from an evaluation of the requisites of survival; one cannot really bridge the gulf between attitudes. The implementation of an experience is a technical problem and therefore arguable, but the experience itself is personal and incommunicable. If a man has no transcendental experience of freedom, for example, an argument about democracy becomes a discussion of the efficiency of economic systems, which is on the plane of objective necessity and therefore debatable. The inward intuition of freedom, on the other hand, would reject totalitarianism even if it were economically more efficient. For this reason, arguments that international conferences with Russia can magically resolve all differences seem fallacious. If conditions are ripe, they may achieve an understanding on the basis of objective necessity, which, as any evaluation, may be overthrown by subsequent analysis. Permanent understanding on the basis of inward reconciliation seems to require more than conferences, since the differences are more than just misunderstandings.

necessity, but freedom governs the future. Toynbee tried to get beyond the mere postulation of inexorability, but if objective necessity cannot serve as a guide to action, it can also not achieve a guarantee of purposiveness. Kant has opened the vistas[1] for a resolution of this dilemma for finding a goal in life beyond the inevitability of occurrences, and a hope beyond the uncertainties of success. Peace and freedom in Kant reveal the state of a soul, a duty perhaps difficult, but also of a great responsibility.

What about the disenchantment that our brief examination of literature indicated? Life involves suffering and transitoriness. No person can choose his age or the condition of his time. The past may rob the present of much joy and most mystery. The generation of Buchenwald and the Siberian labor camps cannot talk with the same optimism as its fathers. The bliss of Dante has been lost in our civilization. But this describes merely a fact of decline and not its necessity. Man's existence is as transcendental a fact as the violence of history. Man's actions testify to his aspirations, which stem from an attitude of the soul, not an evaluation of conditions. To be sure, these may be tired times. But we cannot require immortality as the price for giving meaning to life. The experience of freedom enables us to rise beyond the suffering of the past and the frustrations of history. In this spirituality resides humanity's essence, the unique which each man imparts to the necessity of his life, the self-transcendence which gives peace:

"In the last analysis one can conclude nothing from history, as from tragedy, save that men's efforts after personal self-realization or social responsibility have been defeated at the hands of relentless fact.

"As soon as high consciousness is reached, the enjoyment of existence is entwined with pain, frustration, loss, tragedy. Amid the passing of so much beauty, so much heroism, so much daring, Peace is then the intuition of permanence. It keeps vivid the sensitiveness to the tragedy; and it sees the tragedy as a living agent persuading the world to aim at fineness beyond the faded level of surrounding fact. Each tragedy is the disclosure of an ideal: —What might have been, and was not: What can be. The tragedy was not in vain. This survival power in motive force marks the difference between the tragic evil and the gross evil. The inner feeling belonging to this grasp of the service of tragedy is Peace—the purification of the emotions."[2]

---

1. If one disregards the "Idea for a Universal History"; see *ante.*
2. Whitehead, *Adventures of Ideas*, p. 369.

APPENDIX

THE CONCEPTS OF MEANING

Introduction

The problem of the meaning of history contains the dilemma inherent in all epistemology: Is truth or meaning a property of reality or the consequence of a metaphysical pattern imposed on phenomenal appearance? Kant opted for the latter alternative and attempted to analyze the categories which structured knowledge.[1] Yet the scientific criticism of the nineteenth and twentieth centuries, opening seemingly limitless vistas for the manipulation of nature, led to the assertion that reality constitutes a property of appearances and meaning denotes that quality which harmonizes subjective cognition with objective phenomena.

All systematic knowledge presupposes a logical structure. Is logic, then, of absolute validity, independent of metaphysics, the ultimate standard of philosophical fitness? Can logic offer a clue to the problem of the meaning of history?

An examination of logical systems demonstrates the soundness of Kant's concepts. Logic itself constitutes an emanation of metaphysics, structuring meaning by its epistemological assumptions. Traditional logic continuously faced dilemmas by its insistence on the theory of existential import. When modern logicians sought to escape these difficulties by restricting logic to the mere analysis of the internal structure of the argument, apart from its philosophical foundation, they could do so only by postulating meaning as the consequence of a metaphysical context dependent in part on the subjective constitution of the speaker.

This will be considered under two aspects. The development of the logical primitive, from the assertional school through the logical positivists (sententialists) to the pre-assertional concept, demonstrates the pervasiveness of the metaphysical assumptions as well as the gradual widening of the range of meaning, finally resulting in the postulate of the pure hypothesis, the answer to which depends on metaphysical and epistemological criteria entirely.

---

1. See *ante* Ch. "History and Man's Experience of Morality."

The modern theory of systems rejects both the self-evidence of axioms and the necessary truth of reality, reducing them to technical postulates that aid in the apprehension of the totality of knowledge. Meaning in these terms becomes the metaphysical context that ascribes significance, not an absolute relation that depends on the empirical verifiability of assertions.

The Logical Primitive

Part of the study of logic consists of the search for a "logical primitive," a unit that will best express the foundation of our thought and the object of our inquiry. Yet the choice of this "logical primitive" depends on factors outside of logic itself, on philosophical considerations regarding the origin and validity of our thinking, the possibility of making an assertion that is true, the feasibility of correlating logic with the physical world. The existential import of judgments is the foundation of "propositional logic"; the concept of meaning derived from a relation between two sets of physical objects—symbols and fact—makes possible sententialism (logical positivism). Both propositional and sentential logic contain as a primitive an assertion which forces them into a philosophic justification, apart from the internal structure of the argument, of the possibility and validity of such judgments.

The difficulties raised by these concepts, coupled with the fact that logic, as an examination of our thinking, a determination of our meaning, became too encumbered with metaphysical and epistemological considerations which structured its analysis *a priori*, gave rise to a new school of thought, that of pre-assertional logic.[1] This attempts to free itself from the pretensions of a theory of knowledge, at the same time widening the scope of the possibility of ascribing meaning.

It tries to achieve a formulation that will allow the analysis of the internal structure of the statement, to examine all its implications prior to committing itself to an evaluation. This, however, implies the metaphysical flexibility of meaning and the psychological element inherent in judgments.

---

1. Developed largely by Professor Sheffer.

PROPOSITIONAL LOGIC[1]

The theory of existential import forms the metaphysical basis of propositional logic, expressed in a judgment as a logical primitive. A judgment consists of the act of distinguishing a particular element, the predicate, in the being of a subject, which could not be thought of unless it contained some other than the predicated character. The judgment contains two elements, called terms. The subject term and the predicate term are joined by a copula, always expressed by the word *is*. "Dogs bark" becomes "Dogs are things that bark." This results from the definition of *judgment* as a condition in the "being" of a subject postulated by the theory of existence.

The distinguishing characteristic of a judgment is its truth or falsity.[2] As a point of fact only true judgments matter, for unless a man says what he does not really think, he declares the truth of his assertion. All judgments therefore, besides affirming or denying a predicate of a subject, imply existence. This does not mean implication of the reality of the grammatical subject, but of the existence of the whole matter of fact asserted in it.

The statement "Griffins are fabulous monsters" does not affirm the existence of griffins. It does, however, imply the existence of a mass of fables in which griffins play a considerable role. If these fables did not exist, a judgment about griffins would be an impossibility. Every statement consequently makes a claim about some portion of the total reality. This explains the use of the existential verb "to be," as the copula.

Bradley carries this view to its ultimate conclusion.[3] Reality is not only implied by every judgment, but represents the ultimate subject of every proposition. The distinction between grammatical, logical, and ultimate subject can be illustrated by the proposition "Morphine stimulates the heart." The grammatical subject is "morphine." The logical subject can be obtained only through a series of interrogatories. "What dilates the heart?" makes "dilates the heart" the logical subject. "What do you know about morphine?" results in "morphine" as the logical subject. But neither "morphine" nor "dilates the heart" represents the ultimate subject. Things cannot be understood by themselves or even as a portion of reality. There

---

1. Primarily based on Joseph, *An Introduction to Logic.*
2. Joseph, *An Introduction to Logic,* p. 156.
3. Bradley, *The Principles of Logic,* pp. 42–60.

can exist only one real system to which all judgments refer. A particular
object must have a place in this system as a requisite for its existence. The
Spinozistic view leads Bradley to deny the possibility of predicating a particular element in a subject and thus implying its existence or the existence
of the system to which this subject refers. The division of a judgment into
subject-predicate terms joined by a copula becomes meaningless, and
instead the judgment as a whole predicates ultimate reality. Thus reality is
implied by, not requisite for, meaningful statement.

This raises certain difficulties. If a judgment implies existence, what
about predicate terms implying a quality such as "The house is black"? If
blackness represents an empirical entity, each judgment would have to be
restated according to the speaker's vision. Traditional logicians (Bradley,
Joseph, and Stebbing) find refuge in the Platonic concept of universals,
which makes the concept the only true reality.

Propositional logic is thus founded on concepts entirely metaphysical.
From there it proceeds to classify judgments according to certainty into
categorical, hypothetical, and disjunctive, according to quantity into universal, enumerative, particular, and singular propositions, and according
to quality (or modality) into assertional, problematic, and apodictic (or
necessary) judgments. It becomes apparent, however, that many of these
subdivisions are in turn metaphysical. Whether a judgment is universal or
enumerative depends less on the inherent structure of the proposition than
on the individual's theory of knowledge. Empiricists would deny any universal judgment, Platonists would adhere to the possibility of universality
even in such a statement as[1] "French ministries are short-lived," merely
referring the matter to the concept of "French ministry." The same applies
to apodictic judgments. The necessity or self-evidence of a proposition
constitutes a problem for epistemology, to which logic can supply no better
clue than internal consistency.[2]

The existential import of propositions involves other, philosophical
problems. While judgments about griffins can be defended as implying
existence, such statements as "Griffins exist" can be justified only with
considerable difficulty. Even Joseph is finally forced to the conclusion that
statements about griffins imply their existence or being (in a system of
reality), while the statement "Griffins exist" would imply not only their

1. Joseph, *op. cit.*, p. 178.
2. See *post.*

being but their being griffins. Thus, to ask whether griffins exist is to ask whether anything existing has the nature intended by the term *griffin*. The existent is thus assumed as the subject of the judgment, which comes very close to Bradley's concept of reality as the ultimate subject.

On the other hand, does a statement about square circles postulate their reality? Propositional logicians would argue with Hume that, though one can imagine a square and a circle, a square circle cannot be conceived, and therefore one would make a judgment known to be false. But on the other hand, as existence is postulated as being implied by judgments instead of a requisite for judgment, this constitutes no reply. Russell[1] attempted to resolve this problem by calling such objects as square circles logical constructions that have a mode of being as contrasted with real existence.

The existential theory of propositions expresses the philosophical assumptions conditioning propositional logic. It structures the statement *a priori* and determines the nature of the analysis. The difficulties raised by this theory can in every instance be traced to its metaphysical formulation. It recognizes meaning as a subjective implication, and reality as the emanation of a psychological state (expressed in the conviction of truth). Yet its inner contradictions proved too great, and subsequent logicians attempted to provide a firmer metaphysical basis, without, however, succeeding in developing an objective criterion for meaning.

MODIFIED PROPOSITIONAL LOGIC

L. S. Stebbing[2] sought to resolve the metaphysical difficulties of traditional logic. She denied the necessity of the subject-term-copula-predicate-term relation, emphasizing instead the internal structure of the statement. "Brutus killed Caesar" involves a different relation between its terms than "This paper is white," and any attempt to achieve uniformity can only distort the meaning of the proposition. The existential import theory is completely abandoned by Stebbing.[3] To begin with, a judgment implies no truth-value but expresses merely the subjective relation of the individual to the proposition.[4] Since the copula "is" plays no necessary role, a semantic implication

---

1. Russell, *The Principles of Mathematics*, p. 449.
2. Stebbing, *A Modern Introduction to Logic*, p. 282.
3. Stebbing, *op. cit.*, pp. 158–60.
4. This, too, makes meaning a subjective relation.

from the verb of existence cannot be made. Moreover, the existence theory of propositions results from a false analysis of judgments. From the propositions "Lions are hunted" one infers the existence of lions, and it would seem that from the statement "I am thinking of griffins" one could deduce their existence. This, however, according to Stebbing, mistakingly assumes that similar grammatical form implies identical logical construction. In the first statement, the property of being a lion and being hunted belong to the same object. In the second, the properties of being a griffin and being thought of do not express interrelated attributes, and "being thought of" is not really a property at all. Thus one cannot think of a lion being hunted without a lion's existence, but a griffin can be conceived even without existence.

This doctrine is interesting but presents certain difficulties. It leaves the question of what constitutes a property unanswered. Moreover, by taking two entities the existence and non-existence of which is clear, it makes the argument relatively facile. Supposing a proposition is made about a subject not as obviously non-existent as griffins, and a relation predicated that could constitute a property, does the proposition then imply existence? According to Stebbing, this would have to be answered affirmatively. The best conclusion to be drawn from Stebbing is that propositions do not necessarily imply existence, which suffices to negate Joseph's and Bradley's theory.

Thus Stebbing discards the philosophical assumptions of propositional logic, but only at the cost of making meaning the psychological attribute of the speaker. If a statement merely expresses a subjective attitude, then the metaphysical aspect of the judgment is simply shifted from the analysis to its formulation.[1]

The more important aspect of Stebbing's[2] work is her concept of descriptions derived from Russell, which constitutes a further step in the direction of making meaning the consequence of a metaphysical and psychological context. This shows that phrases such as "a square circle" can be used significantly even if they apply to nothing, and that the analysis of propositions to which such phrases apply is identical whether they describe something or nothing. Two examples will illustrate. The proposition "Scott is the author of *Waverley*" can be analyzed into three assertions:

---

1. This becomes apparent in pre-assertional logic.
2. Stebbing, *op. cit.*, pp. 138–42.

(1) At least one man wrote *Waverley*
(2) Only one man wrote *Waverley.*
(3) That man is Scott.

The proposition will be false if (1) no one had written *Waverley*, (2) if more than one had written *Waverley*, (3) if one man had written *Waverley* but Scott was not the man.

The second statement concerns what in Russell's original view would be called a logical construction: "The man in the moon is yellow."

(1) There is at least one man in the moon.
(2) There is only one man in the moon.
(3) That man is yellow.

This statement would be false if there (1) were no man in the moon, (2) more than one man in the moon, (3) if there were a man in the moon but he were not yellow.

The significance of this conception cannot be overemphasized. To begin with, logic could separate itself from a metaphysic that determined its analysis *a priori* and begin considering the inherent structure of an argument. This system of descriptions seems a forerunner of pre-assertional logic. For after all, none of the segmental propositions can be answered unless put in question form. Thus the first proposition properly would have to be phrased "Is it a fact that one man wrote *Waverley?*"

The liberation of logic from metaphysics was, however, only achieved by widening the range of meaningful statements, by realizing the implications of the psychological element in assertions, by transferring the epistemological element from the analysis to the judgment.

SENTENTIAL LOGIC[1] (LOGICAL POSITIVISM)

Sentential logic completed the disintegration of the concept of existential import. Its logical primitive is the sentence, which merely constitutes a grouping together of symbols or words not differing in their general characteristics from other physical objects. These symbols, strung together in linear arrangement, have a property which transforms them into propositions. By being brought into relations with other physical objects—facts—they acquire meaning.

Meaning derives reality only from the truth-value of the proposition. Since most propositions at the time of their utterance do not have a determined truth-value, however, another predicate of proposition must be invoked. All unverified sentences have a certain opinion as to the truth attached to them, defined as the weight of the proposition. While a truth-value is a property capable of only two values, the positive and the negative, the weight represents a quality in continuous scale ranging from the utmost uncertainty through intermediary degrees to reliability of the highest degree. Such words as *probably* and *likely* correspond to the weight of the proposition in ordinary language.

Reichenbach formulates two postulates of the truth-theory of meaning.

(1) A proposition has meaning if, and only if, it is verified as true or false.
(2) True sentences have the same meaning if they obtain the same determination as true and false by every possible observation.

Reichenbach's restriction of meaning to verifiable truth seems in the first instance a negation of the Kantian position and an assertion of reality as a predicate of objects. Yet the problem of meaning remains. For what does Reichenbach mean by *verifiability*? What meaning can be attached to descriptions of physical qualities? What is the relation of truth-weight to meaning and to truth-value? This finally resolves itself into a consideration of criteria of knowledge, of which three progressively wider standards are recognized: the technical, the physical, and the logical. The last, in the tradition of Hume, admits as true anything that can be conceived without contradiction.

---

1. Based entirely on Reichenbach, *Experience and Prediction.*

This analysis implies that a statement can be both meaningful or not, depending on the criterion. A five-hundred-year-old man in a logical sense represents no inner contradiction but would have to be denied by physical criteria. Moreover, just as in Russell's theory of descriptions, the assertion can only occur subsequent to a query, and the question will limit a range of possible answers. Thus logical positivism, from an attempt to confine meaning by a test of verifiability, is forced by its inner contradictions into the admission of criteria that extend the range of meaningful statements and by implication becomes the precursor of pre-assertional logic, which faces the metaphysical problem only after its range has been determined by the hypothesis.

SUMMARY
The assertional schools of logic agree in basing their logical primitive on a statement.

This leads to an inquiry into the very possibility of knowledge and an ever sharper definition of epistemological considerations. A gap arises between the metaphysical concepts on the one side and the extensive classification of types of judgments, propositions, and sentences on the other, with the middle ground of the inherent meaning of assertions inadequately analyzed.

The difficulty of this position results in an attempt to burst the metaphysical bounds, achieved only by an implicit affirmation of wider criteria of meaning, which are, moreover, made a psychological function of the speaker. Russell contains hints of such an analysis, and Reichenbach admits various levels of criteria. It remained for pre-assertional logic to develop these implications to their ultimate conclusion and thus allow for the variability of metaphysical assumptions as the condition of meaning.

Pre-Assertional Logic

The school of pre-assertional logic develops a different approach to the problem of meaning. Where propositional logic passes judgments about aspects of reality, or establishes the relation between sentences and facts through an elaborate system of metaphysical and probability theory, pre-assertional logic admits the flexibility of the philosophical assumptions of determining meaning. It refuses to consider such questions as the existential import of propositions as falling outside the realm of pure logic.[1] It maintains that, before one can assert something, one has to know what it is that one wishes to assert. This distinguishes the eventual validity of the assertion from the inherent linguistic and logical structure of the statement.

The quest for the logical primitive in pre-assertional logic then resolves itself into the search for a form of expression which best exhibits the internal structure of the statement, and its logical possibilities. Only after having examined the statement in such a form does pre-assertional logic attempt to pass judgment, to assert, or, to use the language of Professor Sheffer, declare truth and falsity, with the express proviso that any declaration involves a psychological element, the speaker's, and a philosophical one, depending on the criteria used. Pre-assertional logic does not have to conform to the subject-term-copula-predicate-term form of the propositionalists, nor confine itself to the philosophical concepts of Reichenbach's sententialism. It examines the internal structure of the argument and looks for a form that best exhibits its possibilities.

What then is the best form of the logical primitive for pre-assertional logic, or what is the primary logical entity one can create? Even propositional logicians, such as Joseph or Stebbing, agree that the judgment represents only an answer to a question the object of which constitutes the logical subject of the proposition. The assertion, then, expresses the affirmation or denial of a hypothesis. It exhibits more clearly the object of our query than the judgment, for it is devoid of the psychological aspect of the act of judging, in which always inheres the possibility of error. The interrogative is the logical primitive of pre-assertional logic.

Yet which form should this interrogative take? Three possibilities exist. Taking the statement "Chicago is large" as an example:

---

1. This implies that logic can only test the internal consistency and must allow for a variability of the metaphysical; see *post*.

(a) *The Abstractional Answer:*
What we affirm or deny is the largeness of Chicago. This contains great linguistic difficulties if a question is raised regarding the answer; for example, "It is true that the largeness of Chicago is true?" *et cetera.*

(b) *The Interrogational Method:*
What we affirm or deny is the question "Is Chicago large?" This, although exhibiting the argument fully, is also linguistically awkward.

(c) *The Ascriptival Method:*
This method states that what we affirm or deny is the pure hypothesis of Chicago being large. This is linguistically simple and prior to assertion or denial.

The logical primitive, then, constitutes a question framed as a pure hypothesis, that allows examination of the argument before "getting off the fence" and deciding truth. Chicago being large becomes the *ascriptive*, the pure hypothesis offered for examination and affirmation or denial.

The act of assertion occurs when the ascriptive has been fully examined. This, however, recognizes that judgments of truth and falsehood are subjective, and dependent on a metaphysical context. Moreover, simple assertions of truth and falsity are ambiguous, since they say nothing about the standard used. Pre-assertional logic attempts to overcome these difficulties by stating its criterion of judgment as well as its most applicable subdivision. Having offered "Chicago being large" for examination, it can reply affirmatively by an empirical criterion within which subgroup geography, perhaps denoted numerically, would be most applicable. Thus:

Chicago being large ... EP.

Thus, logic has come full cycle. The metaphysical assumptions which structured the analysis as well as the formulation of statements in traditional logic proved too cumbersome. By a gradual process of widening the range of meaningful judgments, logic finally developed the declarative, which constitutes a frank recognition that objective criteria for meaning do not exist and that the consensus an endorsement enjoys represents its only approximation to universality. Analysis reveals that the declarative, is composed of three primary elements: the logical, the psychological, and the philosophical. The ascriptive contains the logical portion, capable of analysis in its internal structure. The act of judgment (represented by the dots in the declarative) exhibits the psychological element. The philosophical aspect is revealed in the endorsement, of which the criterion represents the metaphysical, and the assertion of truth or falsity, the epistemological viewpoint.

If the statement (or declarative) derives meaning from these three components, do any criteria for its evaluation exist? No absolute standards of validity are at hand. The declarative can, in turn, be transformed into an ascriptive, and its endorsement subjected to epistemological criticism. (Thus: "Chicago being large" being empirically positive.) But ultimate criteria of meaning or truth can never be faced by pre-assertional logic. The realm of total meaning is not exhausted by empirical verifiability, and proper standards can be obtained for aesthetic or value judgments.

If logic can be defined as the critical analysis of inherent structure[1] apart from the relation to other fields, then the pre-assertional school has offered the best solution. It does not rely on epistemological presuppositions but attempts to analyze the implications of the hypothesis before its final judgment of validity.

Withal, this merely amounts to a recognition of the variable possibilities of meaning. Each hypothesis contains within itself the possible answers; the very formulation of the query is the consequence of a metaphysical context. Meaning is recognized as a function of the structuring of reality, dependent in part on psychological and in part on philosophical concepts.

If the hypothesis delimits the range of answers, what is the effect on systematic knowledge? Are all hypotheses equivalent, their choice accidental, their pertinence purely psychological? The theory of systems addresses itself to these problems.

---

1. Reichenbach, *Experience and Prediction*, p. 5.

A system has been defined[1] as any body of propositions arranged according to a sequence of logical deductions, so that every proposition, after a certain one, is a logical consequence of some, or all, of the preceding propositions. This body of propositions that implies the rest has been defined as the code by Professor Sheffer.

The necessity of the code results from the limitations of the human mind. A being, such as God, whose knowledge is instantaneous would have no recourse to a code. Yet the average person, who cannot grasp the totality of the propositions contained in the system without deduction, requires a body of propositions from which such a deduction can be effected. Few classical sciences, and no empirical science, have in fact been completely systematized, though all system knowledge presupposes a system, its extent usually indicated by the necessity which attends conclusions.

Historically it had been assumed that all systems, such as Euclidean geometry, were based on a set of propositions, self-evidently true, the axioms from which all other propositions, the theorems, followed deductively. Mathematicians have proved in the meantime, however, that the Euclidean axioms cannot be considered universally self-evident. It is possible, for example, to conceive a world[2] entirely enclosed within a large sphere, with the temperature decreasing point by point, reaching zero at the boundary. In such a world, every inhabitant would conceive himself in a universe of infinite extent, for as he approached the boundary, the falling temperature would decrease his size, causing his steps to be smaller and smaller. The geometry of such a world would contain many axioms, the self-evident of which would vary considerably from Euclid's. It can be proved, for example, that the shortest distance between two points in that case would be the arc of a circle, which cuts the bounding sphere orthogonally.[3] This is the basis of non-Euclidean mathematics.

Moreover, from the point of view of modern logic, "self-evidence" cannot be conceived as a predicate of a proposition, but as a dyadic relation between the person making the statement and the proposition.[4] The reality

---

1. Young, *Lectures on Fundamental Concepts of Algebra and Geometry*, p. 2.
2. Poincaré, *Science and Hypothesis*, p. 49.
3. Young, *op. cit.*, p. 17.
4. See *ante*.

of the system does not result in the first instance from its foundation in empirically verifiable fact but from the philosophical assumptions of its postulates.

Professor Royce[1] has classified the various assumptions underlying the use of the term *axiom*. It can be applied either in the sense of inner necessity or self-evidence, subjective necessity; as an unproved hypothesis, from which, however, other propositions can be deduced; as a proposition universally assented to; and lastly as a proposition resulting from an individual's psycho-genetic constitution. The inner necessity theory is discarded because of the impossibility of defining a criterion for certainty. Descartes and Spinoza, for example, despite the fact that their whole philosophy was based on innate ideas, could offer no better criterion than inner conviction. According to Professor Royce, this criterion can only qualify in the sense of "subjective certainty," not self-evidence, and there is no necessary connection between the statement "This is true" and the objective reality of the subject.

The second context in which the term *axiom* has been used, as an unproved hypothesis, will be discussed fully below. In the Aristotelian sense, by which a first principle must inhere in all scientific deductions as a part of a universal first principle, the discovery of a valid system, though its axioms might have been assumed as hypotheses to start with, imparts to those axioms a certain, highly mediated "self-evidence." For practical purposes, however, this self-evidence is equivalent to the assumption of an unproven hypothesis as a starting point.

The third conception of universal assent defining an axiom implies its own contradiction, according to Professor Royce. For one would not invoke universal assent as an argument, except against a person not assenting. One dissent will therefore shake the validity of the axiom, forcing recourse to such limitations on universality as "assent of the wise," "assent of the capable," *et cetera*.

The last meaning of an axiom, imposed by a self-evidence dependent on psycho-genetic factors, is thereby made so vague as to lose all usefulness. To begin with, the subconscious operations of the mind very frequently obscure our real meanings, and thus this is a proper field for the psychiatrist, rather than the philosopher.

This leaves the definition of *axiom*, alluded to before. The axiom is con-

---

1. Hastings, *Encyclopaedia of Religion and Ethics*.

ceived as an unproved proposition, composed of undefined terms and assumed relations, which are required to be intuitively understood, from which to deduce the remaining propositions contained in the system. To be sure, this precludes the existence, or at least the necessary self-evidence, of a universal first principle and a self-contained system of the universe. But on the other hand, it allows the formulation of systems, in the Hegelian sense, in which the axioms and theorems mutually imply each other and in which the axioms of one system can theoretically be the theorems of another, and a high degree of coherence thereby achieved. Thus the theory of systems bases itself on a frank recognition of the structuring effect exerted by metaphysical assumptions and rejects empirical verifiability as its primary criterion for validity.

The arguments of Professor Royce have been developed at such length because they contain the theoretical basis for the modern conception of axioms. Since "self-evidence" has been discarded as a criterion, the last formulation of Professor Royce's is the general usage of an axiom. The axiom, then, contains certain undefined terms and relations and is itself a deductively unproved proposition. The choice of these terms and relations is, however, entirely arbitrary and limited only by their appropriateness to the system, and the proviso of intersignificance. (Thus, the term *point* would preclude the notion of perpendicularity.) The axiom constitutes an emanation of metaphysical assumptions and structures the code by its inner necessity. This means that absolute validity cannot be obtained, the simplicity of the code representing a function of the minimum number of terms required to be intuitively understood.

This raises a question as to the concept of simplicity. Simplicity[1] means logical simplicity. From a logical point of view, every term is equivalent, or determined only by its logical implications, regardless of how many psychological difficulties it presents. Thus a dyadic relation is logically simpler than a triadic relation.

Definitions play an important role in making code-ascriptives or axioms psychologically simpler. Russell offers the following definition of *definitions*.[2] "The definition must be in terms of other expressions already defined. Which are the terms to be previously defined depends to a large extent on the person making the definition."

1. Young, *op. cit.*, p. 163.
2. Quoted in Stebbing, *op. cit.*, p. 441.

It must be noted, as Russell does, that the method of abbreviation does not present a question of fact but of convention and that it imposes only the requirement of adhering to existing conventional meanings. Thus, a definition which conventionally describes a line segment could not, as an abbreviation, utilize the word *circle.*

The difference between definitions and primitive code-ascriptives or axioms is difficult to fix. Indeed, Young calls his set of assumptions "hidden definitions."[1]

If a system comprises initially unproved hypotheses, dependent on metaphysical assumptions expressed in selectivity and theorems connected merely by mutual implication, do any criteria for systematic knowledge exist? Stebbing asserts that the logician, in his quest for axioms, is not concerned with their truth or falsity, but only with testing all their consequences, the real criterion for the validity of the axioms being the validity of the theorems.[2] Yet what is meant by validity? Three properties are usually sought for in a system: consistency, independence, and completeness (or categoricalness).

Independence describes that postulate or code-ascriptive that is not implied by any of the preceding code-ascriptives, nor their conjunct. The proof of independence consists of finding a concrete application which satisfies all axioms except the axiom in question. Independence is useful for distinguishing between theorems and axioms, but has no necessary significance. Moreover, complete independence, despite the above proof, may still be lacking, for a certain amount of implication or overlapping, by which a part of the postulates is implied by the preceding or their conjunct, can frequently not be avoided.

Completeness is the predicate of a code that implies all the remaining ascriptives and theorems belonging to the subject matter. The test for completeness will show that any two concrete applications of the code are simply isomorphic. Completeness is not an absolute necessity. Indeed, sometimes a part-code, to analyze special portions of a system, is even desirable.

Consistency, then, is the one essential property of a code. Its absence prevents any deduction, the construction of any system. Tests for consistency and a general discussion of the notion will be developed in relation to

---

1. Young, *op. cit.*, p. 53.
2. Stebbing, *op. cit.*, p. 164.

the pre-code.[1] Thus, though the hypotheses contain assumed relations and determine the code by their implications, criteria for the evaluation exist, if only in terms of internal consistency. Yet this consistency does not indicate absolute validity. The scope of the axioms can only be revealed by the range of the theorems, and consistency tells us nothing about the adequacy of the metaphysical assumptions.

Generalization of the Notion of a Code[2]

In 1904, Oswald Veblen developed a code for geometry utilizing only the notion of a point and the relation between. In 1911, Veblen conceived another code, adding the notion of congruence to the terms above. In order to make his code psychologically simpler, Veblen divided his second code into several sections based on code-ascriptives dealing with a certain subject matter, such as assumptions of order, of points on a line, *et cetera*.

Huntington in 1913 developed a code based on the notion of spheres and the relation of inclusion. A great complexity of code-ascriptives resulted, and yet Huntington's code is logically simpler than Veblen's due to the dyadic relation of inclusion, compared to the triadic relation of *between*.

Several examples from Veblen's first code will be presented to illustrate the nature of a code-ascriptive and to serve as a connecting link to the discussion of the generalized notion of the code.

> Assumption II. If points *A, B, C* are in the order *ABC*, they
> are not in the order *BCA*. *ABC* thus implies *not between BCA*.

Veblen's assumptions are thus composed of two elements: the geometrical, represented by the terms *point* and *between*, and the logical. The act of logicizing is independent of the notion of *point* and *between*, which arises only out of the actual representation in a concrete system of the logical part, as applied to a predicate and a triadic relation. The generalization of the notion of the code derives from the conception of the code as a single, highly complex, quantified ascriptive. Since the notions of *point* and *between*

---

1. See *post.*

2. This section is based on the articles by Veblen and Huntington in Young, *Monographs on Topics of Modern Mathematics.*

arise only through application to a concrete system, generalization will consist of substituting a quantified ascriptive composed of schemata, and thereby allowing the full examination of the merely logical aspect. This representation is called the pre-code.

What is the meaning of consistency in relation to pre-code, and what criteria does it offer? Two considerations must be discussed. Propositional logic asserts that an attribution of consistency to a judgment is equivalent to its affirmation.[1] The fallacy of this becomes particularly apparent when applied to pre-codes. If a consistent pre-code is instantiated by an empirical code, this code must also be consistent. But consistency does not guarantee physical existence. (An ascriptive about the existence of a five-hundred-year-old man would be consistent, but also EN.)

Though this limits the analysis to internal consistency, it tells nothing about a criterion. Yet an absolute standard for consistency does not exist. To prove consistency, concepts are utilized that are in turn assumed consistent. A test for consistency, with these reservations, would be the deduction of the pre-code as a theorem from a code of logic that is assumed consistent.

A more general test for consistency is the instantiation of the pre-code. Three possibilities of instantiation—logical, mathematical, and empirical—exist. Thus, if the pre-code is instantiated by a code in Euclidean geometry, and we grant that Euclidean geometry is consistent, we have a proof for the consistency of the pre-code. An example of this is furnished by Whitehead's *Principia Mathematica*, which attempts to demonstrate the foundation of mathematics in logic.

In instantiation in an empirical system, the element of simply passing the burden of proof to a higher order of logic or another set of assumptions is compounded by the following epistemological assumptions:

    (1) The empirical world is consistent.
    (2) Therefore this part of the physical world is consistent.
    (3) And our propositions about this part are true.
    (4) Therefore the code regarding this part is true.
    (5) Therefore the logical portion of the pre-code is consistent.

---

1. See *ante.*

Thus the test of the system is internal consistency, which leaves the scope of the metaphysical assumptions unanalyzed. This raises the question of the use of a pre-code. By generalizing the notion of a code, the possibility of instantiation in any number of different sciences is given. The realization that two different sciences have the same logical structure (that is, utilizing the same pre-code) is the preliminary to translating one science into another. This is essentially the procedure followed by Descartes in transforming algebra into geometry.

Conclusions

The theory of systems, then, contains an examination of a certain unity in nature. The unity is no longer given by self-evident propositions, but by studying all the implications and consequences of a conjunct of originally undefined assumptions or code-ascriptives which derive their validity from the appropriate criteria.

Yet this unity allows for a variability of metaphysical assumptions and a multiplicity of valid criteria. Its only necessary postulate is an inner consistency, which in turn recognizes its epistemological limitations. Meaning is recognized as an emanation of a philosophical point of view. This also applies to a philosophy of history. Historical data by itself is neutral. Its significance constitutes a function of the resolve of a soul. This does not imply that all metaphysical constructions are equivalent, that an unlimited choice exists in the selection of hypothesis, or that historical data may be ignored. A hypothesis must always be in terms of some data, and its relevance to this framework constitutes a test for its efficacy. The wider the range of events that a philosophy of history seeks to explain, the more profound its approach.[1] Events by themselves testify only to a fact of occurrence. Phenomenal appearances contain no moral sanction, and can be apprehended only as a category of necessity. Their inner meaning must always remain a metaphysical creation. Progress and freedom, purpose and meaning, are not attributes of reality, but the revelation of an inward experience.

Gibbon thought that he saw in Rome's collapse the triumph of barbarism

---

1. See example of Newton under the apple tree, *ante*, "Introduction."

and religion. Yet an excellent case has been made for dating the period of decline from Alexander's conquests.[1] Toynbee again considers the Peloponnesian War the beginning of Hellenic disintegration.[2]

Similarly, what caused Hitler's downfall? Was it the invasion of Russia, the declaration of war in 1939, the seizure of Prague or the Anschluss? Or perhaps was the fact of collapse immanent in a personality to whom the recognition of limits constituted an admission of defeat? An answer to these questions is not contained merely in empirical data but in its interpretation, which depends on the predisposition of its author. Hume's constant conjunction must ever represent a philosophical resolution.

There cannot consequently exist one universally valid philosophy of history. It portrays the metaphysical resolution of the dilemma of the experiences of freedom and the knowledge of necessity, and represents as much a testimony to the philosophical assumptions of its creators as an absolute standard for the evaluation of the noumena of history. Since the content ascribed to life, moreover, constitutes the emanation of an inner state, the possibility arises for the attainment of a level of meaning transcending the mere phenomenal appearance of power phenomena. Kant's ethical philosophy testifies to this solution, the ultimate reality of which is only accessible by way of an inner experience.

---

1. See *ante* Ch. "History as Intuition."
2. See *ante* Ch. "History as an Empirical Science."

BIBLIOGRAPHY

BASIC TEXTS

Hegel, Georg W. F.

The Philosophy of History (translated by John Sibree, New York: Willey Book Co., 1944).

The Philosophy of Right (translated by Thomas Malcolm Knox, Oxford: Clarendon Press, 1945).

Kant, Immanuel

Critique of Judgment (translated by J. H. Bernard, London: Macmillan Co., 1914).

Critique of Pure Reason (translated by F. Max Müller, New York: Macmillan Co., 1922).

Die Metaphysik der Sitten (*The Metaphysics of Morals*) (Königsberg: Bey Friedrich Nicolovius, 1797).

"Idea for a Universal History with a Cosmopolitan Intent" (translated by Carl J. Friedrich, in *The Philosophy of Kant*, New York: Modern Library, 1949).

Kant's Critique of Practical Reason and Other Works on the Theory of Ethics (translated by Thomas Kingsmill Abbott, London: Longmans, Green and Co., 1909).

"On Eternal Peace" (translated by Carl J. Friedrich, in *The Philosophy of Kant*).

Schweitzer, Albert

The Philosophy of Civilization (translated by C. T. Campion, New York: Macmillan Co., 1949).

Spengler, Oswald	*The Decline of the West* (translated by Charles Francis Atkinson, New York: Knopf 1926–1928), 2 vols.
	The Hour of Decision (translated by Charles Francis Atkinson, New York: Knopf, 1934).
Toynbee, Arnold	*A Study of History* (London: Oxford University Press, 1934–1939), 6 vols.

BIBLIOGRAPHY ON SPENGLER

Dakin, Edwin Franden	*Today and Destiny: Vital Excerpts from The Decline of the West of Oswald Spengler* (New York: Knopf, 1940).
Gisevius, Hans B.	*To the Bitter End* (translated by Richard and Clara Wilson Boston: Houghton Mifflin Co., 1947).
Hale, William Harlan	*Challenge to Defeat: Modern Man in Goethe's World and Spengler's Century* (New York: Harcourt, Brace and Co., 1932).
Messer, August	*Oswald Spengler als Philosoph* (Stuttgart: Strecker und Schröder, 1924).
Meyer, Eduard	*Oswald Spengler's Untergang des Abendlandes* (Berlin: Curtius Verlag, 1925).
Schröter, Manfred	*Metaphysik des Untergangs: KulturKritische Studie über Oswald Spengler* (München: Leibnitz Verlag, 1949).
	Der Streit um Spengler: Kritik seiner Kritiker (München: Beck, 1922).
	(see also "Periodicals," below)

BIBLIOGRAPHY ON TOYNBEE

Geyl, Pieter, and   *The Pattern of the Past: Can We Determine It?*
Pitirim Sorokin   (Boston: Beacon Press, 1949).

                             (see also "Periodicals," below)

BIBLIOGRAPHY ON KANT

Caird, Edward   *The Critical Philosophy of Kant* (New York:
                             Macmillan, 1889), 2 vols.

Cassirer, Ernst   *Rousseau, Kant, and Goethe: Two Essays* (translated
                             by James Gutman, Paul Oskar Kristeller, and
                             John Herman Randall, Jr., Princeton, N.J.:
                             Princeton University Press, 1945).

Friedrich, Carl Joachim   *Inevitable Peace* (Cambridge, Mass.: Harvard
                             University Press, 1948).

Lindsay, Alexander D.   *The Philosophy of Immanuel Kant* (London:
                             Ernest Benn Ltd., 1934).

Smith, Norman Kemp   *A Commentary to Kant's "Critique of Pure Reason"*
                             (London: Macmillan Co., 1918).

BIBLIOGRAPHY ON LOGIC AND
METHODOLOGY OF HISTORY

Bradley, F. H.   *The Principles of Logic* (London: Oxford
                             University Press, 1922).

Joseph, H. W. B.   *An Introduction to Logic* (Oxford: Clarendon
                             Press, 1906).

Mandelbaum, Maurice   *The Problem of Historical Knowledge* (New York: Liveright Publishing Corp., 1938).

Poincaré, Henri   *Science and Hypothesis* (New York: Science Press, 1907).

Reichenbach, Hans   *Experience and Prediction* (Chicago: University of Chicago Press, 1937).

Russell, Bertrand   *Mysticism and Logic* (London: Longmans, Green and Co., 1918).

The Principles of Mathematics (London: George Allen, 1948).

Stebbing, L. Susan   *A Modern Introduction to Logic* (London: Methuen & Co. Ltd., 1933).

Young, John Wesley   *Lectures on Fundamental Concepts of Algebra and Geometry* (New York: MacMillan Co., 1911).

Monographs on Topics of Modern Mathematics (London: Longmans, Green and Co., 1911).

GENERAL BIBLIOGRAPHY ON THE PHILOSOPHY OF HISTORY

Adams, Brooks   *The Law of Civilization and Decay: An Essay on History* (New York: Macmillan and Co., 1895).

Barth, Paul   *Die Philosophie der Geschichte als Sociologie* (Leipzig: Reisland, 1897).

Collingwood, Robin G.   *The Idea of History* (Oxford: Clarendon Press, 1946).

Croce, Benedetto | *On History* (London: George G. Harrap and Co., 1921).

The Philosophy of Giambattista Vico (translated by R. G. Collingwood, London: Howard Latimer Ltd., 1913).

Dilthey, Wilhelm | *Der Aufbau der Geschichtlichen Welt in den Geisteswissenschaften* (Berlin: Königlich-Preußische Akademie der Wissenschaften, 1910).

Jaspers, Karl | *Vom Ursprung und Ziel der Geschichte* (Zürich: Artemis Verlag, 1949).

Loewith, Karl | *Meaning in History: The Theological Implications of the Philosophy of History* (Chicago: University of Chicago Press, 1949).

Niebuhr, Reinhold | *Faith and History: A Comparison of Christian and Modern Views on History* (New York: Scribner, 1949).

Ortega y Gasset, José | *Toward a Philosophy of History* (New York: W. W. Norton Co., 1941).

Petrie, W. M. Flinders | *The Revolutions of Civilization* (New York: Harper and Bros., 1922).

Popper, K. R. | *The Open Society and Its Enemies* (London: George Routledge and Sons Ltd., 1945).

Sorokin, Pitirim A. | *The Crisis of Our Age* (New York: Dutton and Co., 1941).

Social and Cultural Dynamics (New York: American Book Co., 1937–1941), 4 vols.

Weber, Alfred | *Farewell to European History, or The Conquest of Nihilism* (translated by R. F. C. Hull, New Haven, Conn.: Yale University Press, 1948).

GENERAL REFERENCES

Dante Alighieri *The Divine Comedy* (Carlyle-Wicksteed
translation, New York: Modern Library, 1951).

Dostoevsky, Fyodor *The Brothers Karamazov* (translated by
Constance Garnett, New York: Modern
Library, 1950).

The Idiot (translated by Constance Garnett,
New York: Modern Library, 1935).

Elliott, William Yandell *The Pragmatic Revolt in Politics* (New York:
Macmillan, 1928).

Elliott, William Yandell, *Western Political Heritage* (New York: Prentice-
and Neil A. McDonald Hall, 1949).

Friedrich, Carl J. *The New Belief in the Common Man* (Boston:
Little, Brown, 1942).

Politica Methodice Digesta of Johannes Althusius,
Harvard Political Classics Volume II
(Cambridge, Mass.: Harvard University
Press, 1932).

Hastings, James *Encyclopaedia of Religion and Ethics* (Edinburgh:
T & T Clark, and New York: Charles Scribner
Sons, 1908–26), 13 vols.

Homer *The Iliad of Homer* (translated by Andrew Lang
et al., London: Macmillan, 1917).

Hook, Sidney *The Hero in History* (New York: John Day Co.,
1943).

Jaeger, Werner — *Paideia: The Ideals of Greek Culture* (translated by Gilbert Highet, London: Oxford University Press, 1948), 3 vols.

Lindsay, A. D. — *The Modern Democratic State* (New York: Oxford University Press, 1947).

McIlwain, Charles Howard — *The Growth of Political Thought in the West, from the Greeks to the End of the Middle Ages* (New York: Macmillan Co., 1932).

Nietzsche, Friedrich — *Beyond Good and Evil: Prelude to a Philosophy of the Future* (translated by Helen Zimmern, New York: Macmillan, 1907).

Sartre, Jean-Paul — *Existentialism* (New York: Philosophical Library 1947).

Spinoza, Baruch — *The Chief Works of Benedict de Spinoza* (translated by R. H. M. Elwes, London: George Bell and Sons, 1891).

Tolstoy, Leo — *War and Peace* (translated by Constance Garnett, New York: Modern Library, 1931).

Watkins, Frederick — *The Political Tradition of the West: A Study in the Development of Modern Liberalism* (Cambridge, Mass.: Harvard University Press, 1948).

Whitehead, Alfred North — *Adventures of Ideas* (Cambridge: Cambridge University Press, 1933).

Wolfson, Harry Austryn — *The Philosophy of Spinoza, Unfolding the Latent Processes of His Reasoning* (Cambridge, Mass.: Harvard University Press, 1934), 2 vols.

PERIODICALS

Articles on Spengler: " 'The Decline of the West' in Actual Progress," G. K. Bowes. *Hibbert Journal* 33: 179–95, 1934.

"Spenglerian Finance," A. A. H. Sparrow. *English Review* 47: 855–71, April 1936.

"Plato's Conception of the Future as Opposed to Spengler's," H. Hansler. *Monist* 39: 204–24, April 1909.

"Oswald Spengler, Historian and Philosopher," Merle W. Boyer. *Lutheran Church Quarterly* X: 157–70, 1939.

"Spengler and the New Pessimism," Victor S. Yarros. *Open Court* 4, article 4: 253–58, 1933.

"Skepticker und Prophet: Zum Bilde Oswald Spenglers," Fred Carus. *Die neue Rundschau* 47, no. 2: 855–71, April 1933.

"Spengler als Staats und Wirtschaftsphilosoph," Erwin von Beckerath. *Schmollers Jahrbuch für Gesetzgebung* 47: 33–47, 1924.

"Spengler und Nietzsche," R. H. Grützmacher. *Preußische Jahrbucher* 224: 29–52, April 1931.

Articles on Toynbee: "Toynbee's Time-Machine," Waldemar Gurian. *Review of Politics* 4, no. 4: 508–14, October 1942.

"Some Problems Raised by Historical Relativism," B. J. Loewenberg. *Modern History* 21: 17–23, March 1949.

"Study of History Review," H. Kahn. *Journal of Philosophy* 44: 489–99, August 28, 1947.

"The Meaning of Human History," Morris R. Cohen. Review, H. Cairns. *Law and Contemporary Problems* 13, no. 3: 547–49, 1948.

"Toynbee Against History," Charles Trinkaus. *Science and Society* 12, no. 2: 218–39, 1948.

"Relative Archaism: A New Fallacy and Mr. Toynbee," J. W. Dowling. *Journal of Philosophy* 43: 421–35, August 1, 1946.

"Review of A Study of History," Arnold Toynbee. *Journal of the History of Ideas* 9: 93–124, January 1948.

"Religion in Toynbee's History," James H. Nichols. *Journal of Religion* 28; 99–119, April 1948.

"Some Recent Ideas of Progress," Wendell Thomas. *Personalist* 29: 128–36, April 1948.

Toynbee Reviews: A *Study of History*, Arnold J. Toynbee. Review, Harry Elmers Barnes. *American Sociological Review* 12: 480–86, August 1947.

"Toynbee's Nine Books of History Against the Pagans," M. Watnick. *Antioch Review* 7: 587–602, December 1947.

INDEX

membership in, 37
late cultures, 65–66
life span of, 30, 37, 45, 46,
83, 91
meaning and, 37
myth of, 29–30, 38
nature of, 98–108
organic nature of, 45, 75,
116, 119, 151, 160–62
political and artistic
embodiments in, 46
primitive societies
distinguished from, 101,
116, 161
souls of, *see* souls of
cultures
symbolism in, 48
transition from culture to
civilization, 35, 37, 43,
45, 69, 80
uncreative majority in, 91,
95, 116, 120, 131, 157,
160, 161
youth of, 17, 33, 45
see also philosophy of
history
class, 66, 130, 131
colonialism, 132, 133n4
Columbus, Christopher, 51, 80
Communism, 57, 115, 118
community, worship of,
135–36
compensation, law of, 106, 156
completeness, logical, 248
conatus, 61, 175, 224
concentration camps, 228
conqueror type, 132
conscience, 53, 218
consciousness, 32
see also waking-
consciousness
consensus, 14, 61
consequences, 11, 47, 77
technical knowledge and,
119, 122
consistency, logical, 248–51
Constantine, 58
constitutions and
constitutionalism, 67–69,

188, 189, 191–92, 195,
197, 204
constitutional monarchy,
67, 72
U.S. Constitution, 71
contrition, 53
Copernicus, Nicolaus, 47, 99,
114–15, 178–79
copulas, 235–37, 242
cosmic beat, 18, 34, 35, 37, 38,
43, 48, 69, 75
Cosmos, 49, 58, 139
creativity, 73–76, 96, 116–17,
121, 123–24, 129, 136,
161, 218, 224n2
alternation of torpor and,
91
creative minority, 20, 91,
95, 114, 117, 118, 130, 131,
135, 151, 154, 157, 161
destruction of, 138–40
maximum potential of, 106
nemesis of, 91, 126–28,
135, 160, 161
uncreative majority, 91, 95,
116, 120, 131, 157, 160,
161
vis inertiae and, 102, 123
Critique of Judgment (Kant), 173,
195, 204–5
Critique of Practical Reason
(Kant), 173, 181–82,
202n2
Critique of Pure Reason (Kant),
173, 178–80, 184, 185,
193, 198, 205
Cross, 19, 36, 82, 147, 150
Crusades, 60
crystals, 55–56
cultures, *see* civilizations and
cultures
cyclical theories, 11n2, 22,
79n3, 121
Cyclops, 116

Dante Alighieri, 77n, 117, 149,
152, 216–18, 221–22,
227, 228
Beatrice and, 77n,

164–65, 222
Toynbee and, 93n1, 94, 95,
119
Darkness at Noon (Koestler), 84
Darwin, Charles
evolutionary theory of, 29,
41, 79
Spengler and, 31, 79
Dasein, 32
data, 15, 16, 20, 22, 30, 33, 96,
98, 163, 251, 252
moral validity proved by,
97
see also empiricism; facts;
phenomenal reality
David and Goliath, 126
death, 16, 17, 22, 23, 29, 32,
33, 48, 52, 58, 80, 83,
84, 140, 153n1, 163–65,
215, 218
burial of the dead, 49
of cultures, 17, 20, 35, 37,
43, 45, 48, 75, 83, 85
and withdrawal from life,
146
Decline of the West, The
(Spengler), xiv, 31, 79n3
de Gaulle, Charles, 186
definitions, definition of,
247–48
degeneration, Platonic
conception of, 73
de Gobineau, Arthur, 102
democracy, 39, 43, 68, 69, 118,
227n
Descartes, René, and
Cartesianism, 10, 11, 42,
62, 133n1, 174–76, 178,
246, 251
destiny, 17, 19, 29, 32–35, 37,
41, 45, 54, 67, 72–76, 79,
119–20, 162
Causality and Destiny, 17,
30, 33–36, 64, 69, 74, 86
Incident and Destiny, 43,
55, 80–82
Morality and Destiny, 154
two aspects to, 62–63
see also fate, fatedness

Israel, 125, 146
Italy, 118, 162
    Risorgimento in, 121

Janissaries, 111
Japan, 122, 150, 152n
Jesus, *see* Christ
Jews and Judaism, 60, 134, 141,
    145, 157
    Christ and, 95, 97, 125
Job, 59, 103, 104
Joseph, H. W. B., 236, 238,
    242
judgments, 12–15, 235–39,
    241–44, 250
Julian, 132
Justinian, 125, 146

Kant, Immanuel, xiv, xv, xxii,
    4, 9n, 10, 11n2, 15–18, 21,
    22, 49, 55, 81, 84, 97, 119,
    130, 158, 165, 171–208,
    213–14, 228, 233, 240
    categorical imperative of,
    22, 71, 81, 83, 172, 173,
    183–94, 197–204, 206–8,
    213, 225–27
    Critique of Judgment, 173,
    195, 204–5
    Critique of Practical Reason,
    173, 181–82, 202n2
    Critique of Pure Reason, 173,
    178–80, 184, 185, 193,
    198, 205
    "On Eternal Peace"
    ("Perpetual Peace") essay,
    172–73, 189–95, 198–99,
    200, 202, 205, 207
    on freedom, 18, 22n1, 77n,
    79, 178–85, 187, 188, 190,
    193–95, 197, 198, 200,
    202, 204, 206–8, 228
    "Idea for a Universal
    History," 173, 197–99,
    203–4, 206, 214
    in Königsberg, 158
    metaphysical theory of,
    178–81, 188, 200–201,
    205, 207

The Metaphysics of Morals,
    200–201
    moral philosophy of, 79,
    171–73, 177–95, 197–208,
    213, 214, 225, 252
    nine principles for the
    apprehension of history,
    195
    on phenomenal reality,
    10, 21, 41, 79, 130, 172,
    173, 177–80, 183–85, 187,
    197–98, 202, 204–6
    on philosophy of history
    as a teleological system,
    194–208
    problem of freedom
    and necessity in the
    philosophies preceding,
    171–78
    Sartre and, 185–87
    Schweitzer and, 185–87,
    193, 194, 197
    Spengler and, 47, 79
    on transcendental
    experience, 172, 173,
    177–79, 184, 185, 187,
    188, 191, 195, 197, 198,
    200, 203, 204, 206–7,
    208, 213
Kennedy, John F., xiii
Kennedy, Joseph P., Sr., xiii
Khazar Empire, 156
kingdom of ends, 22
King Lear (Shakespeare), 55
knowledge, 10, 16, 43, 49, 94,
    172, 174, 176–81, 185, 233,
    234, 241
    criteria of, 240–41
    limiting, to make room for
    belief, 172, 178, 179, 198,
    207
    systems and, 245
"Know thyself," 23
Koestler, Arthur, *Darkness at
    Noon,* 84
Koran, 59
Kraemer, Fritz Gustav Anton,
    xiv, xxi–xxii
Kuklick, Bruce, xvii

land, 65, 133
language, 61, 113, 114, 142,
    144, 145
    alphabet, 114, 156
Lateran Council (1215), 53
latifundia, 133
Law, Supremacy of, 144
laws, 96, 156, 163, 164,
    171, 173, 185, 186, 195,
    197, 204
leadership, xvii, 35, 68, 74,
    116, 123, 130, 138,
    139, 157, 161
League of Nations, 84
Lenin, Vladimir, 146n4,
    157–58
Leonardo da Vinci, 41
liberalism, 67
liberty, 65, 80
life, 9, 15, 16–18, 22, 23,
    29, 47, 58, 74, 153n1,
    163, 215, 223, 226,
    252
    activity and decay in, 93
    death and, *see* death
    directedness of, 9, 16–17
    magic attitude towards,
    16, 22
    meaning of, 21, 22, 39,
    84–86, 139, 171–73,
    180, 207, 213–15, 224,
    226, 228
    polarities of, 29
    plane of, in disintegration
    of civilizations, 138, 139,
    144, 150, 151
    prayerful attitude towards,
    16
    rejection of, 146
    succession of problems in,
    19, 84, 91, 93, 105, 118,
    158, 196, 197
    task in, 64
    as technical problem, 219
light waves, 113
limits, 23, 29, 32, 34, 51, 54,
    84, 134, 139, 165, 172,
    206, 214–16, 219, 220,
    223, 226

man in, 239
morality and ethics, xvi, 16,
     20, 22, 23, 34, 55, 59, 71,
     77–79, 97, 130, 132, 153,
     163–66, 175–78, 214–19,
     223–26
  absolute standard of, 226
  data and, 96–97
  Destiny and Morality, 154
  empiricism and, 177
  great deed and, 55
  Kant's philosophy of, 79,
     171–73, 177–95, 197–208,
     213, 214, 225, 252
  necessity and, 187
  personality and, 186
  pessimism and, 78
  and philosophy of history,
     22
  and theory versus practice,
     198n2, 207
More, Thomas, 140
Morgenthau, Hans, xvi
mortality, *see* death
motion, movement, 16, 29,
     42, 50
motivations, 11, 33, 36, 74,
     182, 183
  pleasure and, 81n4, 176
Mozart, Wolfgang Amadeus,
     54
music, 41–42, 53, 54
Mycenaean culture, 48–49
mystery cults, 36, 37, 57, 75
mysticism, mystic attitude,
     11–12, 17, 21, 22, 43, 55,
     72, 149, 214, 223
mythology, 92, 103, 104, 112,
     126, 163, 164

Napoleon, 34, 67, 69, 70
Napoleonism, 66, 69–70, 80
nationalism, 39, 118, 174
nations, law of, 192–93
nation-states, 65, 118, 134
natural resources, 50–51
natural science, *see* science
nature, 14, 34, 39, 41, 42, 45,
     48, 79, 135, 140, 174–76,

     178, 179, 182, 184, 185,
     194–200, 204, 206–8,
     215, 218, 233
  animals, 31, 32
  law of, 61, 183
  plants, 31, 36, 44
  state of, 140, 192, 196,
     197, 219
  unity in, 251
  world-as-nature, 33–35, 47,
     74, 76
Nazi Germany, xiii, xvi, xxi,
     82–83, 132, 145, 150,
     152n, 156, 228, 252
necessity, 9–10, 14, 16, 21, 22,
     29, 31, 35, 36, 74, 77,
     80–83, 86, 92, 98, 148,
     152, 159, 182, 184, 203n1,
     206, 213–15
  Chance and Necessity, 138,
     141
  ethics and, 187
  Freedom and Necessity, *see*
     Freedom and Necessity
  and the possible, 81
  Volition and Necessity, 94
  will and, 222
Neolithic Age, 114
Neo-Platonism, 37, 58
Nestorians, 58
Newton, Isaac, 15, 54
Niebuhr, Reinhold, xvi, 153
Nietzsche, Friedrich, 3, 15, 41
night, 32, 163
nobility and aristocracy, 38,
     56, 64, 65, 68, 73, 76, 118
nomads, 109–11
Norse
  invasions of, 64, 107, 115,
     127
  Sicilian, 127
Northrop, F. S. C., 77
noumenal reality, noumena,
     76, 79, 97, 108, 150,
     162, 172, 179, 180, 182,
     184, 185, 187–89, 193,
     197–98, 202, 204, 206,
     207
numina 33, 65

observation, 29
Octavian, 72
Odyssey (Homer), 106n1, 116,
     217, 221
Oedipus, 49
Oracle of Delphi, 23
organisms
  consciousness in, 32
  civilizations and cultures
     as, 45, 75, 116, 119, 151,
     160–62
Orpheus, 148
Osiris, 148
Osmanlis, 110–11, 122
Other World, 149
Ottoman Empire, 106, 111, 122

Paleolithic Age, 114
Palingenesia, 131
Pandaemonium, 218
Pantheism, 175
Pantheon, 60
papacy, 59, 107, 127, 174
Paradise, 94, 119, 149, 221
Parliament, parliamentary
     state, 66, 67, 126, 152n
Pascal, Blaise, 40
past, and retrospection, 9, 16,
     22, 32, 35, 52, 81, 84, 98,
     125, 145, 159, 213, 215,
     224, 227–28
Paul, Saint, 57, 58, 117, 125,
     128, 157, 162n1
peace, 71, 131, 136, 176n2, 227
  Kant on, 172–73, 175,
     187–95, 197–99, 201, 204,
     207, 228
peasantry, 38, 39, 44, 56, 64,
     114, 133
Peasants' Revolt, 134
Peloponnesian War, 252
perception, 10
Pergamos, 42, 54
Pericles, 112n2
permanence, 23
"Perpetual Peace" essay (Kant),
     see Kant, "Eternal Peace"
persona, 49
personality, 31, 77, 86, 93, 120,

ABOUT THE AUTHOR

Henry A. Kissinger served as National Security Advisor and then Secretary of State under Richard Nixon and Gerald Ford and has advised many other American presidents on foreign policy. He received the 1973 Nobel Peace Prize and the Medal of Liberty, among other awards. He is the author of numerous books on foreign policy and diplomacy and is currently the chairman of Kissinger Associates, Inc., an international consulting firm.